HEALER OF
THE NATIONS

Gary North

Other books by Gary North

Marx's Religion of Revolution, 1968
An Introduction to Christian Economics, 1973
Unconditional Surrender, 1981
Successful Investing in an Age of Envy, 1981
The Dominion Covenant: Genesis, 1982
Government by Emergency, 1983
The Last Train Out, 1983
Backward, Christian Soldiers?, 1984
75 Bible Questions Your Instructors
    Pray You Won't Ask, 1984
Coined Freedom: Gold in the Age of
    the Bureaucrats, 1984
Moses and Pharaoh, 1985
Negatrends, 1985
The Sinai Strategy, 1986
Unholy Spirits: Occultism and
    New Age Humanism, 1986
Conspiracy: A Biblical View, 1986
Honest Money, 1986
Fighting Chance, 1986 [with Arthur Robinson]
Dominion and Common Grace, 1987
Inherit the Earth, 1987
Is the World Running Down?, 1987
The Pirate Economy, 1987
Liberating Planet Earth, 1987
    (Spanish) *La Liberación de la Tierra*, 1987
The Scourge: AIDS and the Coming Bankruptcy, 1988
Tools of Dominion, 1988

Books edited by Gary North

Foundations of Christian Scholarship, 1976
Tactics of Christian Resistance, 1983
The Theology of Christian Resistance, 1983
Editor, *Journal of Christian Reconstruction* (1974-1981)

HEALER OF THE NATIONS

Biblical Blueprints for International Relations

Gary North

Dominion Press
Ft. Worth, Texas

Published by Dominion Press
7112 Burns Street, Ft. Worth, Texas 76118

Typesetting by Thoburn Press, Tyler, Texas

Printed in the United States of America

Unless otherwise noted, all Scripture quotations are from the New King James Version of the Bible, copyrighted 1984 by Thomas Nelson, Inc., Nashville, Tennessee.

Library of Congress Catalog Card Number 87-071021

ISBN 0-930462-51-3

This book is dedicated to

Dr. Fred Schwarz

whose one-hour lecture
got me started on all
this over 30 years ago.

TABLE OF CONTENTS

vii

EDITOR'S INTRODUCTION
by Gary North

Yes, I know. This book is too long. It sticks out like a fat, sore thumb on the shelf of Biblical Blueprints books.

When I first decided to include a book on international relations in the Biblical Blueprints Series, I knew that it would be the most difficult book to write in the series. There is virtually no body of material on Christian international relations and foreign policy, and what little that does parade as Christian is simply warmed-over humanism, and intellectually lightweight humanism at that. (Herbert Butterfield's undated and deservedly forgotten book of the early 1950's, *Christianity, Diplomacy and War*, is an example of such non-Christian "Christian" contributions.) Furthermore, there is no agreed-upon humanist conservative view of what foreign policy is expected to achieve, and just how national foreign policy is supposed to fit into the world of international relations. A few still favor the late Senator Robert Taft's isolationist foreign policy; others favor active anti-Communism and military intervention abroad. Most conservatives call for the abolition of U.S. government non-military foreign aid (except possibly to Israel), but what about military aid? No agreement. Some believe that Franklin Roosevelt needlessly lured this nation into war, and did so unconstitutionally against the wishes of Congress and the voters; others (perhaps even the same people) believe that Lt. Col. Oliver North's efforts to thwart Congress and take a stand against international Communism were right on target.

Let us consider a real-world example of this confusion, an example of potentially great legal importance. I call it the strange case of Gerhard Gesell. Judge Gerhard Gesell is scheduled in 1987 to rule on legal arguments brought by 16 conservative Republican Congressmen and one U.S. Senator who oppose the Boland amendment as unconstitutional. This amendment was added to a large appropriations bill that was signed into law by President Reagan. It limits the Executive's ability to support anti-Communist military activities abroad. It is the law that got Col. North into trouble.

Until I informed the plaintiffs of the following information, weeks after they had initiated legal action, these conservative Republicans had not known that four decades earlier, Gerhard Gesell had served as the Democrats' legal counsel during the 1946 Congressional hearings on the Japanese attack on Pearl Harbor. These hearings investigated the question of whether or not President Roosevelt knew in advance that the Japanese attack might come in early December of 1941. The underlying debate between Republicans and Democrats during those hearings was over the constitutionality of the independent foreign policy of the President during the late 1930's. Republicans after the war claimed that Roosevelt's hostile interventionist foreign policy had been deliberately designed to drag the U.S. into World War II, and that he had lured Japan into the attack.[1] Conservative Republican Congressmen opposed Gesell's efforts in 1946 to defend the Executive's independent and interventionist foreign policy prerogatives. In 1987, however, their ideological heirs hope that he will rule in favor of the independence of the Executive's military prerogatives (and therefore foreign policy prerogatives) as Commander-in-

---

1. George Morgenstern, *Pearl Harbor: The Story of the Secret War* (New York: Devin-Adair, 1947); Frederic R. Sanborn, *Design for War: A Study of Secret Power Politics, 1937-1941* (New York: Devin-Adair, 1951); Charles Callan Tansill, *Back Door to War: Roosevelt Foreign Policy, 1933-1941* (Chicago, Illinois: Regnery, 1952). See also Harry Elmer Barnes (ed.), *Perpetual War for Perpetual Peace* (Caldwell, Idaho: Caxton, 1953). Barnes was a political liberal. Another prominent liberal who agreed with Roosevelt's critics was the distinguished historian and political scientist Charles A. Beard, whose reputation among his peers collapsed when he wrote *President Roosevelt and the Coming of the War, 1941: A Study in Appearances and Realities* (New Haven, Connecticut: Yale University Press, 1948).

Chief of the armed forces. The Democrats, of course, have also reversed their position since 1946. Confusion reigns supreme.

Christianity and Foreign Policy

The whole field is wrapped in mystery for most Christians. I knew that the author who wound up with this topic would have to start from scratch.

I assigned the book to the first author in the fall of 1985. His manuscript did not come close to meeting the needs of the series. The second author came a bit closer, but not close enough. The authors' advances were mounting up, and time was running out. So, in mid-May of 1987, I decided that I would have to write the book. I sat down at my computer, and in between my normal required output of three monthly newsletters and my normal 10 hours per week devoted to writing my economic commentary on the Bible, I hammered out this book. It took five weeks. Had I not had Ray Sutton's model of the Biblical covenant in my mind, I doubt that I could have done it.

Foreign policy in the United States is controlled by a tightly knit "old boy" network of dedicated humanists, who quite properly regard their control over foreign policy as the linchpin in their overall control of the United States government.[2] They do not want outsiders criticizing their little monopoly. They have devoted millions of dollars since World War II to finance books, journals, and studies on American foreign policy, all of which conclude that we must be firm with the Communists until we join with them in a one-world humanistic order. We must be visibly tough negotiators while we are capitulating to the vast bulk of their demands. Most important, the West must not try to roll back Communism. As "realists," we must accept the Soviets' operating principle: "What's ours is ours, and what's yours is negotiable." Then we negotiate. And negotiate. And if the Soviets press us too hard, and demand too much, we then criticize South Africa's apartheid.

---

2. Gary North, *Conspiracy: A Biblical View* (Ft. Worth, Texas: Dominion Press, 1986).

Christians today are blissfully unaware of the need for an explicitly Biblical view of international relations, just as they are unaware of the need for an explicitly Biblical view of every other real-world problem. Sleepwalking Christians are the heart of the crisis of Western civilization in our day. They are unwilling or unable to offer explicitly Biblical alternatives to the collapsing humanist order. Until about 1980, they fervently believed that the humanists possessed some legitimate title to the seats of power in this world, and they still believe that common natural law moral and legal principles are sufficient to hold the world system together until Jesus comes back in glory. So they sit on the sidelines of life, waiting for Jesus to bail them out, or *up*, literally. Just as He bailed out Israel when the Assyrians arrived? Just as He bailed out Judah when the Babylonians arrived? Just as He bailed out Latvia, Estonia, and Lithuania when the Soviet troops arrived?

But we're different, of course. We're Americans. No need to worry. And if 1.5 million babies are aborted here each year, it isn't the Christians' fault. Jesus is coming soon. Sit tight. Pray. And don't miss the Superbowl next Sunday.

The Communists, who are our mortal enemies, are self-conscious in their hatred of Christianity and Western society that was built originally by Christian principles. They wish to destroy all traces of Christianity. So do the weak-willed humanists of the West. These humanists are also in agreement with the world-retreating Christians of the West in their unified hostility to any suggestion that Christians should provide the world's intellectual and cultural leadership because Christians alone have access to the Bible through the Holy Spirit. Thus, the Communists do not face any concerted opposition. World satanic empire is expanding without any significant organized opposition from the West. This has been Aleksandr Solzhenitsyn's complaint long before the day that the Soviets expelled him in 1974.

Conclusion

Healer of the Nations is explicitly Christian. It relies on the Bible to define its categories. Because Christians are not used to thinking about international relations in terms of the Bible, they may be shocked by this book. They have allowed humanists to do their thinking for them. They are used to thinking in humanism's political categories, and they do not recognize how deeply humanism has affected their thinking. I realize that this book will be highly controversial in politically conservative Christian circles, precisely because it is explicitly Bible-based. Those Christians who do not like its conclusions should be ready to cite the Bible, chapter and verse, to disprove it. Murmuring is not an appropriate response. I also hope they will quote my words verbatim and in context. Hope springs eternal.

This book has more footnotes than all the other Biblical Blueprints combined. I know that very few Christians have any background in this field, and they need to understand where I am getting my ideas, and what support materials are available. With the exception of possibly two footnotes in this book, all the materials referred to are in my personal library, which I have been collecting for over 25 years, ever since I took my first college course in American foreign policy back in the fall of 1960. That was my first encounter with the Council on Foreign Relations, which had financed the publication of well over half of the seven or eight books we were required to read. Dan Smoot's book, *The Invisible Government*, appeared two years later. Then I understood better what we were facing. We still are facing it, except that the West's military strategy has deteriorated for a quarter of a century.

And then, literally overnight, an electronic ray of hope: Oliver North's televised testimony before a joint Congressional committee in the second and third weeks of June 1987. I am writing this on the final day of his testimony. Worldwide attention has been focused on him. Dan Smoot believes that Col. North's televised testimony has inflicted more damage on the Left than any conservative has inflicted in the last 20 years. I think it goes much deeper than that. It may be the most significant conservative challenge since Whittaker Chambers exposed Alger Hiss in 1946, the event that can accurately be said to have launched the post-war conservative political movement in the United States. But Chambers had little charisma and no television coverage. North had both.

May God use Col. North's testimony to begin a flanking movement around the humanist leadership on both sides of the Iron Curtain. May Oliver North turn out to be more than a two-week celebrity. And may Christians begin to sort out the fundamental principles of international relations, and get them adopted around the world, so that no future patriotic lieutenant colonel will find himself $2 million in debt to lawyers because he did his job well.

Part I
BLUEPRINTS

The purpose of Biblical history is to trace the victory of Jesus Christ. *That victory is not merely spiritual; it is also historical.* Creation, man, and man's body, all move in terms of a glorious destiny for which the whole creation groans and travails as it awaits the fulness of that glorious liberty of the sons of God (Rom. 8:18-23). The victory is historical and eschatological, and it is not the rejection of creation but its fulfilment.

This victory was set forth in the resurrection of Jesus Christ, Who destroyed the power of sin and death and emerged victorious from the grave. As St. Paul emphasized in I Corinthians 15, this victory is the victory of all believers. Christ is the firstfruit, the beginning, the alpha and omega of the life of the saints. Had Christ merely arisen as a spirit from the grave, it would have signified His lordship over the world of spirit but His surrender of matter and history. But by His physical resurrection, by His rising again in the same body with which He was crucified, He set forth His lordship over creation and over history. The world of history will see Christ's triumph and the triumph of His saints, His church, and His kingdom. History will not end in tribulation and disaster: it will see the triumph of the people of God and the manifestation of Christian order from pole to pole before Christ comes again. The doctrine of resurrection is thus a cornerstone of the Biblical dimension of victory. . . .

There is thus a dimension of victory in history, Jesus Christ. The alternative plan of victory is social science, and history as a social science. This means the totalitarian socialist state, the world of *1984*. For the Christian this is rather the dimension of hell, not of victory; for the believer, "this is the victory that overcometh the world, even our faith" (I John 5:4).

R. J. Rushdoony*

------

*Rushdoony, *The Biblical Philosophy of History* (Phillipsburg, NJ: Presbyterian & Reformed, [1969] 1979), pp. 25, 27.

INTRODUCTION

"Therefore I say to you, the kingdom of God will be taken from you and given to a nation bearing the fruits of it" (Matthew 21:43).

This is a book about Christian principles of international relations. It is also a book about the collapse of the humanist West's foreign policies. The institutional problem that we face today is that the Christians are not offering Bible-based alternatives fast enough to stop the disintegration of our humanist-run Western civilization. This is why I decided to publish the Biblical Blueprints Series. Christians do not know what the Bible says about social, economic, and political issues. They are going to have to learn very rapidly if the West is to be salvaged.

As you might imagine, there are not many books on the topic of the Biblical principles of international relations. Foreign policy is a popular topic, but the idea that a nation's foreign policy should be governed by explicitly Biblical principles is regarded by the humanist elite who run every nation's foreign policy as the most "foreign" policy of all. International relations are presumed by everyone in power today to be governed by laws or principles that somehow are common to all nations, regardless of race, color, or creed—especially creed. If there were no common law of nations, most people believe, there could be no international relations; there would only be endless power plays by individual nations. Thus, it is assumed by virtually everyone that so-called *common-ground ethical and legal principles* govern relations between sovereign nations.

This raises another key assumption of modern political humanism: that international relations are international relations among nation-states. This follows from one of modern humanism's most dangerous presuppositions: that the State[1] is the central institution in every area of life. It was also a major presupposition of ancient humanism.[2] It is a demonic belief.

The Church International

I have begun this book by quoting Matthew 21:43. Jesus spoke of a nation that would inherit the kingdom of God. Was He speaking of a particular nation-state? Or was He speaking of the totality of those throughout history who profess faith in Jesus Christ? Was He speaking of a particular nation-state (such as Israel had been) or the Church International? Obviously, it was the latter.

This raises another very important issue: the Biblical definition of the word "nation." I discuss this in Chapter One. Since the Church International is called a nation, relations among the various national and regional churches should serve as the Biblical model for relations among sovereign nation-states. The Church International is *the* nation of nations in New Testament times. It is therefore the appropriate model for international relations.

Any failure of the Church International to resolve its internal differences will necessarily have repercussions in relations among other nations. If churches are in perpetual conflict with each other, unable to find peaceful ways to conduct the affairs of international ecclesiastical institutional order, then we should expect to see analogous disruptions among nation-states. Since nation-states have no other legitimate model for the successful working out of disputes, how can they be expected to achieve lasting peace? It is a case of the blind (or at least the pathetically near-sighted) leading the blind into a ditch. (See Chapter Eleven for details.)

Christians have failed to understand this point. They do not

---

1. I capitalize the word "State" when I am referring to the covenantal institution of civil government; I do not capitalize it when I am referring to a regional political unit called a state.

2. R. J. Rushdoony, *The One and the Many: Studies in the Philosophy of Order and Ultimacy* (Fairfax, Virginia: Thoburn Press, [1971] 1978), chaps. 3-5.

look at the Church International as if it were a model for international relations. They see no connection between the Church model and the State model. The first possesses the God-established monopoly of the sacraments, while the second possesses the God-established monopoly of the sword (violence). But if there is no connection, then why did Jesus speak of the Church International as a nation that inherits the kingdom of God? International relations among churches within this inheriting nation serve as God's designated model for relations among nation-states.

Christians know that a local church is based on a covenantal bond among members. This covenant is based on a public confession that Jesus Christ is Savior and Lord. Some Christians also understand that a denomination is also a church based on a covenant. But they restrict the idea of the covenant to the church and the family: baptism and the marriage vow. They usually stop short of arguing that nation-states are told by God to become forthrightly, openly, *covenantally* Christian, in the way that all individuals are told by God to become forthrightly, openly, *covenantally* Christian. Somehow, for some reason, civil governments are supposed to remain forever covenantally neutral. Old Testament Israel is not an appropriate model in New Testament times, we are told by Christian authorities.[3] The New Testament nation-state model is by definition (whose, it is never said) necessarily secular. The State is therefore always to remain a strictly neutral covenantal institution—a covenant with no god in particular, meaning *a covenant that answers only to the self-proclaimed god of this world, autonomous (self-law) man.*

This is the common faith of modern Christians. This is also the common faith of modern humanists, who over a century ago captured almost every Western nation-state. Even those Christians who argue against the myth of neutrality in general make this exception: the State. *This is the baptized humanist theology of political pluralism through natural law.* This is the politics of hypothetical covenantal neutrality. It is the impotence-producing Christian heresy of our age.

---

3. Meredith G. Kline, *The Structure of Biblical Authority* (rev. ed.; Grand Rapids, Michigan: Eerdmans, 1975), ch. 3.

Healer of the Nations will not be a popular book within most Christian circles, for it pushes the denial of the myth of neutrality into the "prohibited" zone of the nation-state. I have gone to the Bible to see what is required for international relations. I have assumed that the Bible, not John Locke, is the proper Christian standard. I have relied on the Bible, not President George Washington's Farewell Address, as the final court of appeal. What will be shocking to many conservatives is that I have assumed that the Bible is alone authoritative, the final court of appeal, even when it conflicts with the U.S. Constitution. I have begun with this presupposition: the Bible is always the supreme law of every land, the standard by which God judges all nations in history and at the end of time, and this God-established fact should be publicly affirmed, nation by nation, in history, as well as at the end of time.

Because the Bible is the standard across borders and throughout history, in heaven and in earth, it is sovereign. History is the progressive working out of God's decree. God has decreed that there will be a progressive conforming in history of every human institution to the requirements of His Word. God's kingdom will progressively be established visibly in history. Many Christians do not believe this. No humanist believes this. Therefore, there has been a working alliance—philosophically, politically, historically, culturally—between many Christians and all humanists. This book is a direct challenge to this long-term alliance within the field of international relations.

How to Be Healed

If a person came to you and said the following, what would your say in reply?

"My life is in shambles. I drink too much. I just got fired from my job. I am in debt up to my ears. I can't pay my mortgage. We're going to lose our home. My wife is threatening to leave me. My teenage daughter is running around with a hoodlum. I want to get my life back together. What should I do?"

If you are a Bible-believing Christian, you would see this as an opportunity to share the gospel with him. You would tell him that the first thing he needs to do is accept Jesus Christ as his personal sin-bearer before God, the Savior, Lord, and Master of his life. Then you would tell him that he needs to join a Bible-believing church and be baptized. He needs to take the Lord's Supper, preferably each week. He also needs to read the Bible to discover and apply in his life the principles of Christian living.

But what if he replied, "I want to get my life back together, but leave out all this Jesus stuff. That's a lot of nonsense"; what then?

Would you spend a lot of time with him in an attempt to find workable answers to his problems — answers that are acceptable to him in the midst of his crisis — but without ever mentioning his sin, Jesus, repentance, the church, the Bible, or Biblical principles of righteousness? If so, why? Isn't your task to get him to face his real problem, his ethical rebellion against God? Why not remind him of the external judgments of God in his life? Why not tell him of God's plan of salvation — God's *comprehensive* salvation?[4] Why mislead him into thinking that there is some common, universally acceptable humanistic formula for successful, God-honoring living apart from Jesus Christ?

No such formula exists today or ever has existed. It is a myth. Yet, Christians today desperately want to believe in this myth, for they believe that the existence of a formula for neutral civil government enables them legitimately to transfer the power and responsibility for exercising civil judgment to God's covenant-breaking enemies.

Now, it is true that non-Christians can be *partially* restored externally and visibly to a better outward way of life. Alcoholics Anonymous has proven this. The AA program enables full-time drunks to become full-time sober citizens. But mere sobriety does not bring people permanently into favor with God. For the remainder of their lives, AA members introduce themselves pub-

---

4. Gary North, *Is the World Running Down? Crisis in the Christian Worldview* (Tyler, Texas: Institute for Christian Economics, 1987), Appendix C.

licly (covenantally) at their meetings, "I'm an alcoholic." There is no true release from bondage by means of the AA program, though there is valid and desirable day-by-day release. Of course it is better to live next door to a sober honest pagan than a drunk. It is best to live next door to a sober, honest Christian.

In any case, we have yet to find a way to convert a whole society of rebellious, broken, sick people by preaching common humanist principles of restoration without God. Once a formerly Christian society has become universally rebellious, the only way to restore the nation to spiritual health and the peace of God is through a national crisis accompanied by Christian revival.

The crisis is coming. Is revival coming, too?

Heal My Nation

What would you tell the political leader of a nation who came to you with this story?

"My nation is in shambles. Our enemies have five times as many nuclear weapons as we do. My country's people drink too much. Millions of them are on hard drugs. We are headed for a depression. Everyone is in debt up to his ears, especially the government. The nations that owe us money are about to default. Our allies are threatening to leave us. I want to get my nation's life back together. What should I do?"

If you are a Christian, you would tell him the same thing you would tell the individual whose life is in shambles. The first thing he needs to do is accept Jesus Christ as his personal sin-bearer before God, the Savior, Lord, and Master of his life. Then you would tell him that he needs to join a Bible-believing church, get baptized, and take the Lord's Supper on a regular basis. Then he needs to read the Bible to discover and apply in his life the principles of Christian living.

You would tell him that he needs to do this because he is his nation's *representative before God*. He needs to serve as a model. He needs to go before God in the name of his nation the way that Abraham went before God to plead for his nephew Lot's city,

Sodom (Genesis 18), and the way that Moses went before God in the name of Israel (Exodus 32:11-13). This is the number-one assignment that God gives to heads of nations: to represent their nations before God. Most leaders pay no attention to this argument.

Then you would tell him about the other task of the representative leader: to represent God before his people. God told Joshua: "This Book of the Law shall not depart from your mouth, but you shall meditate in it day and night, that you may observe to do according to all that is written in it. For then you will make your way prosperous, and then you will have good success" (Joshua 1:8). The ruler is supposed to tell those under his authority whatever God's law requires. Without obedience to God's law, a nation should expect God's cursings in history (Deuteronomy 28:15-68). It is his job to persuade the people to adopt God's laws nationally, and then enforce them.

But what if he replied, "I want to get my nation's life back together, but leave out all this Jesus stuff. That's a lot of nonsense"; what then?

This is exactly what every leader of every nation in the West is saying: "Leave out all this Jesus stuff!" If we Christians who know Christ, believe in His Bible, and have been chosen by God to preach the healing gospel of Christ to the nations—the disciplining gospel (Matthew 28:18-20)—remain tongue-tied and silent before the nations, what should we expect? The national blessings of God? Or God's cursings on an international scale?

"This Jesus Stuff"

If we are going to discuss Christian principles of international relations, then let us discuss them. Our goal is not to make humanism work better, except as a temporary tactic to buy a little more peace and time until a majority of voters become Christians and then vote for politicians who will support the Christian reconstruction of all aspects of civil government. If Christians are going to attempt to reform today's pagan, humanist imitation of Christian international relations, and if they attempt to do so in terms of a worldview that is acceptable to paganism, then mankind will never achieve a Biblical solution to the crisis in international relations. Christians must think carefully about what the Bible says is required for nations. What is required is *Christianity*. This will come as a shock to many Christians.

Next, Christians must think about how Christian nations are supposed to act toward other nations. To help them discern the fundamental principles of international relations, Christians should think about God's assignment to the ultimate nation in history, the Church International. What is the Church International? How do local congregations fit into it? How is it supposed to relate to nation-states, both Christian and pagan? We need to understand the Church of churches before we attempt to reconstruct international relations, for the Church International is God's model for international relations. The only other available models are Satan's empire or Satan's anarchy.

This is not a book about the Church. It presumes certain ideas about how churches should operate and cooperate with each other, but these details are not spelled out in this book. This book is already the longest in the Biblical Blueprints Series. But this much is assumed: there is a supernatural unity of the Church, Christ's body, which is as ultimate as the distinctives of every local church. There is a cosmic Holy Communion that accompanies local participation in the Lord's Supper. There is Church unity as well as congregational and denominational diversity, for there is a Trinity. This is the model for the nations, once they are covenanted to Christ and to each other.

If the nations refuse to take Christ seriously, then one by one, they will find themselves increasingly pressured to covenant with Satan in his hoped-for world empire. There is no escape from covenants. The question is: Whose covenant will a nation affirm? Christ's or Satan's?

And let Christians never forget: no national decision for Christ's covenant is still a decision. It is a decision to say "no" to Jesus and His kingdom. It is a decision to place the nation under the cursings of God in history.

Washington's Farewell Address

George Washington's Farewell Address is the most famous speech that was never delivered in American history. He wrote the essay, which was dated September 17, 1796, and it was published in the *American Daily Advertiser* on September 19, 1796.[5] Extracts are reprinted in most collections of documents in American history. I am using the full-length version that appears in volume one of *Messages and Papers of the Presidents* (1897).

The address is famous for its phrase, "no entangling alliances." This phrase does not actually appear in the address — another irony about this unspoken speech. What Washington did warn against was permanent alliances. What he meant by permanent alliances was the creation of international treaties that would bind together the United States and other nations to perform certain military actions under specified future circumstances. His countrymen took him seriously. The United States did not enter into a treaty of this sort until the mid-twentieth century.[6]

Washington was careful in his address to reaffirm the new nation's existing commitments (treaties). There was only one: the 1778 treaty with France that had helped make possible the independence of the new nation. This "entangling alliance" with France had been signed in February of 1778, a few months after Great Britain's General John ("Gentleman Johnny") Burgoyne surrendered his forces to General Gates at the battle of Saratoga (in New York) in December of 1777. After his surrender, the French decided that they could risk entering into a permanent alliance with the anti-British rebels of North America.

The treaty placed each of the nations on a most-favored-nation basis commercially. The treaty was to go into effect if France should become embroiled in the existing war against Great Britain. France renounced any designs on Bermuda or

---

5. *Annals of America* (Chicago: Encyclopaedia Britannica, Inc., 1968), III, p. 606.

6. Julius W. Pratt, *A History of United States Foreign Policy* (New York: Prentice-Hall, 1955), p. 43.

upon any of the British parts of North America, as of the Treaty of Paris in 1763. Neither nation was allowed to make a separate peace with Britain. France also guaranteed the liberty, independence and sovereignty of the United States.[7] That was the last time that the U.S. ever signed such a military treaty (international covenant) for well over a century and a half.

Washington's address was primarily a call to respect the national government. It reaffirmed the Constitution as "sacredly obligatory."[8] It attacked any association or faction that would challenge the actions of constitutional authorities. (Factions were the great fear of the founding fathers.)[9] Only in the last few pages of his address did he discuss foreign relations. But it is deservedly famous for this section, comprising about one-sixth of the document.

With Justice for All

He said, "Observe good faith and justice toward all nations. Cultivate peace and harmony with all. Religion and morality enjoin this conduct."[10] There should be no permanent hostility toward any nation. "The nation which indulges toward another an habitual hatred or an habitual fondness is in some degree a slave." Such hostility leads to frequent collisions, suspicions, and wars.

He also warned against passionate attachments to any nation. If we read between the lines, we see France. Jefferson's supporters were great partisans of the French; the Federalists, with a stronghold in New England's Atlantic trade-based commercial community, tended to be aligned with England. With an obvious reference to the Treaty of 1778, he said: "The great rule of conduct for us in regard to foreign nations is, in extending our commercial relations to have with them as little *political* connection as possible. So far as we have already formed engagements let them be fulfilled with perfect good faith. Here let us stop."[11] In 1800, a new

---

7. *Ibid.*, pp. 42-43.

8. *A Compilation of the Messages and Papers of the Presidents*, 20 vols. (New York: Bureau of National Literature, 1897), I, p. 209.

9. See especially Madison's *Federalist* No. 10.

10. *Messages and Papers*, p. 213.

11. *Ibid.*, p. 214.

treaty with France was signed that abrogated the 1778 treaty. The United States made no entangling alliances in the nineteenth century.

Washington understood that European conflicts were not America's. He may have seen that the international wars initiated by the French Revolution would continue to keep Europe in upheaval, which turned out to be the case under Napoleon. The United States should avoid these conflicts, he said. "Hence, therefore, it must be unwise in us to implicate ourselves by artificial ties in the ordinary vicissitudes of her politics. . . ." (Pretty fancy language for a newspaper essay! The loss of literacy since 1796 has been startling. The *Federalist Papers* of 1787 were political tracts published in newspapers; today, few college students can read them with ease.)

The Atlantic Shield

The practical foundation of Washington's recommendation was the geographical isolation of North America. He understood this fact:

> Our detached and distant situation invites and enables us to pursue a different course. If we remain one people, under an efficient government, the period is not far off when we may defy material injury from external annoyance; when we may take such an attitude as will cause the neutrality we may at any time resolve upon to be scrupulously respected; when belligerent nations, under the impossibility of making acquisitions upon us, will not lightly hazard the giving us provocation; when we may choose peace or war, as our interest, guided by justice, shall counsel.
>
> Why forego the advantages of so peculiar a situation? Why quit our own to stand upon foreign ground? Why, by interweaving our destiny with that of any part of Europe, entangle our peace and prosperity in the toils of European ambition, rivalship, interest, humor, or caprice?[12]

---

12. *Ibid.*, pp. 214-15.

He recommended a strictly defensive strategy: "Taking care always to keep ourselves by suitable establishments on a respectable defensive posture, we may safely trust to temporary alliances for extraordinary emergencies." We should not favor any nation in commerce, "neither seeking nor granting exclusive favors or preferences. . . ."[13]

The technical problem we face today is that without a civil defense system of local metal shelters buried ten feet beneath the earth's surface, 25 minutes after launch, the Soviet Union's missiles would kill about 70 percent of everyone in North America. Two weeks later, radiation would bring this total to about 90 percent. (With civil defense shelters, deaths could be reduced to 20 percent.)[14] A defensive strategy is different today. The seas have become a major defensive problem — submarine warfare — not the primary basis of our defense.

Can a nation that relies solely on defense survive the strategic offensive of a satanic empire? George Washington had witnessed only the preliminary phases of this offensive: the French Revolution. It was far away. It is no longer far away. Is defense sufficient? Is Christ's kingdom essentially defensive rather than offensive? Is Christ's "nation," the Church International, primarily defensive? And if it is primarily defensive today, should it be? Is it supposed to be?

And if it is the model for international relations, is it time for Christians to rethink Washington's strategy?

Entangling Alliances

The familiar phrase, "entangling alliances," actually appeared in Jefferson's first inaugural address in 1801, when he listed as one of the principles of American government, "peace, commerce, and honest friendship with all nations, entangling alliances with none. . . ."[15] The confusion in people's minds between Jefferson's

---

13. *Ibid.*, p. 215.

14. Arthur Robinson and Gary North, *Fighting Chance: Ten Feet to Survival* (Ft. Worth, Texas: American Bureau of Economic Research, 1986).

15. *Messages and Papers*, p. 311.

first inaugural address and Washington's Farewell Address stems perhaps from Washington's rejection of permanent alliances that would *entangle* "our peace and prosperity in the toils of European ambition, rivalship, interest, humor, or caprice." In short, he rejected (covenantal) military alliances along the lines of NATO, SEATO, CENTO, and the Anzus Pact. He rejected treaties that would give a blank check to any other nation to pull us into a war. But twentieth-century America has become a nation addicted to writing blank checks, a nation based on IOUs.

Dexter Perkins, a specialist in the history of U.S. foreign policy, has commented that "nothing is more characteristic of American diplomacy than its general aversion to far-reaching contractual commitments."[16] The humanism of the twentieth century has begun to overcome this tradition, to the detriment of America's national sovereignty.

The Growth of Bureaucracy

The first Congress of 1789 created the Department of State. Julius Pratt summarizes the subsequent developments. (Most people will find this story difficult to believe at first.) "Under President Washington the Department of State consisted of the Secretary of State, a chief clerk, three ordinary clerks, and a translator — a total of six persons. For a century or more the Department grew slowly in size and complexity. . . . In 1870 . . . the entire personnel of the Department numbered only 53. This modest number of employees had grown to 202 by 1909. Rapid expansion accompanied both world wars. State Department personnel numbered 963 in 1938, 2,755 in 1943, and 5,905 in 1948 (this figure fell to 5,376 in 1954)."[17] By 1980, the figure had climbed to 23,497.[18] This included over 3,500 Foreign Service Officers, the elite corps of specialists who staff our embassies and consulates.

---

16. Dexter Perkins, *A History of the Monroe Doctrine* (Boston: Little, Brown, 1963), p. 376.

17. Pratt, *History of United States Foreign Policy*, p. 7.

18. *Statistical Abstract of the United States, 1985* (Washington, D.C.: Government Printing Office, 1984), p. 325.

Bryton Barron, a conservative State Department official, resigned on February 1, 1956. He and Dr. Donald Dozer had been involved in editing the Yalta Conference papers and the Tehran Conference papers, respectively. Both claimed that the published documents had been altered significantly from the originals, and many important documents had not been released. Barron wrote a limited-edition book, *Inside the State Department: A Candid Appraisal of the Bureaucracy*, later that year. In its introduction, he made this statement: "This globe-encircling bureaucracy which is the Department of State, with its thousands of employees in Washington and many thousands more all over the world, is fifteen times larger and many times more costly than when I first knew it. Operating behind a curtain of regulations which conceals its workings and protects this bureaucratic empire, the Department is now almost beyond the reach of Congress and the people. Unlike other departments, it does not have to submit an annual report. It cannot be required to show important papers to the Congress."[19]

He had joined the Department in 1929. It had grown 15-fold by 1956. It has grown almost five-fold since 1956. It now has so much autonomy, that only one government agency in Washington can claim greater autonomy, the Federal Reserve System, which in fact is not really a government agency. (In the Washington, D.C. telephone book, only the Board of Governors of the Federal Reserve System is listed under "U.S. Government." The other operations are not. Regional Federal Reserve Banks pay postage; they do not enjoy the free mail "franking" privilege that belongs to U.S. government agencies.) It is these two organizations that are the heart of the invisible government of the United States.

A Century of Bureaucratization

Richard W. Leopold's standard history of U.S. diplomacy has about eight hundred pages of text. Slightly under one hundred

---

19. Bryton Barron, *Inside the State Department: A Candid Appraisal of the Bureaucracy* (New York: A Reflection Book, Comet Press Books, 1956), p. 12.

pages are devoted to U.S. foreign policy prior to 1889. He says in the Preface that the foreign policy experience derived from the years 1889 to 1945 "is much more significant than that gained between 1775 and 1889."[20] His view is representative of twentieth-century political humanism.

What happened in the 1890's to change American foreign policy? Darwinism. Charles Darwin's *Origin of Species* (1859) had blown away men's earlier naive faith in a providential, orderly world — a faith held by Christian philosophers, conservative humanists, and natural law theists. The older faith in a social world operated by magnanimous, harmony-producing forces that lead inevitably to what George Washington, following John Locke and Adam Smith, had called "the natural course of things,"[21] had been shattered. Educated men increasingly turned to a new religion, which in fact is a very ancient religion: faith in the State as the sovereign agent that alone possesses sufficient power to bring peace and harmony to this dog-eat-dog Darwinian world.[22]

During the 1890's, the United States government began to expand into every area of economic life. This centralization came at the expense of private activities and responsibilities. In the field of international relations, no one before this era had perceived a need for the United States government to send official representatives to every nation or to seek alliances, agreements, and arrangements with every nation. People assumed that private interests would be the basis of the vast bulk of international relations. But in the twentieth century, men have lost faith in the power and importance of government-unregulated activities. Nowhere has skepticism regarding private activities been more deeply held than in the area of international relations. In place of international relations in the broadest sense, we have seen the creation of a vast network of inter*governmental* relations.

---

20. Richard W. Leopold, *The Growth of American Foreign Policy: A History* (New York: Knopf, [1962] 1969), p. viii.

21. "Farewell Address," *Messages and Papers*, p. 215.

22. Gary North, *The Dominion Covenant: Genesis* (2nd ed., Tyler, Texas: Institute for Christian Economics, 1987), Appendix A: "From Cosmic Purposelessness to Humanistic Sovereignty."

This is the heart of the crisis of modern international relations. Voters in the West have passively turned over the conduct of foreign policy to professional diplomats, in the sense that Professor Leopold defines diplomacy. "Diplomacy I take to be the art or profession of transacting business among governments."[23] *Business among governments*: humanists have too narrowly defined diplomacy, and we have allowed them to transfer too much authority to diplomats—diplomats who have been hand-picked by humanists according to humanist training and standards.

Foreign relations are broader than mere diplomacy, as Leopold says: "Foreign relations I define as the sum total of all connections—official, private, commercial and cultural—among different countries and different peoples." But step by step, beginning in the late-nineteenth century, government diplomats have taken over the machinery of foreign relations. They have done so as agents of an elite group of bankers, businessmen, scholars, and government officials (see Chapter Eight). This, too, is the heart of the crisis of modern international relations.

Modern men have systematically neglected the chief connection and chief division among men and nations: religion. Religion, not politics or economics, is the crucial issue in international relations. A treaty is always a covenant, and a covenant is either a religious treaty under God or under an imitator of God.

Conclusion

This book is about Christian international relations. It does not ask or attempt to answer the question: "How should mythical neutral civil governments conduct official diplomacy in a way that does not come into conflict with Christian principles?" Instead, it asks and attempts to answer two far more controversial questions: "What does the Bible say that a God-fearing nation should be, and how should such a nation conduct its relations with other nations?"

This book will be dismissed by many Christians as utopian. G. K. Chesterton once defined a utopian as someone who cuts off

---

23. Leopold, *Foreign Policy*, p. viii.

his legs because mankind might someday have wings. I am not in favor of cutting off my legs. I do favor cutting off the U.S. State Department, however. In our present diplomatic situation, nothing really is better than something. As Congressman Lawrence McDonald remarked to me about a year before a Soviet pilot shot down Korean Airlines flight 007 on which he was traveling: "If the failures of the State Department were simply the result of stupidity, the United States would win a diplomatic victory occasionally, just on the basis of randomness. We never do."

It is true that the world I describe as the Biblical standard is presently nowhere visible on earth (Greek: *ou* = no; *topos* = place). But Jesus Christ also is nowhere visible on earth. Is the Church International therefore an institution that proclaims a utopian faith? Humanists think so; Christians disagree. They know that Christ is present covenantally with His people. They eat the Lord's Supper in His presence. They understand a fundamental Biblical principle: *what goes on in heaven is to serve as an ethical model for what should go on in earth.* Christians have been commanded by Jesus Christ to pray: "Thy kingdom come. Thy will be done in earth, as it is in heaven" (Matthew 6:10, King James Version). When Christians stop believing this prayer, they become culturally irrelevant. When Christians stop praying this prayer, they come under the curses of God in history. (Does your church still pray this prayer publicly on a regular basis? If not, it is time for you to find another church, or to start praying and working to change your church.)

If Christians remain unaware of what the Bible says about what this world should be and should do, they will not possess a motivating vision of the Biblically attainable future. Understand, what this book presents is not a program to attain what in principle cannot be attained in history. Instead, it presents God's required blueprint for what must and will be attained by covenantally faithful people in history. Humanists will resent this. World-retreating Christians will also resent this.

To get from here to there will require a world crisis of institutionalized humanism on a scale unmanageable by those who presently hold the seats of secular humanist power, and it will also require a Christian revival on a scale unmanageable by those who presently hold the seats of Christian power. Let us pray that these events occur simultaneously. If they do not, a new dark age lies ahead, for the world crisis of humanism cannot be delayed much longer.

We must never forget that Jesus Christ came to divide people. "Do not think that I came to bring peace on earth. I did not come to bring peace but a sword" (Matthew 10:34). This sword is His dividing Word; it proceeds out of His mouth as Judge of this world (Revelation 19:15). But this sword is also the means of establishing peace among a growing number of people, as the gospel progressively separates men from their sinful patterns of living. So, what we must affirm as Christians is that Jesus Christ divides men ethically in order to heal some of them ethically. This process of healing is comprehensive: physical, psychological, economic, political, and in every other way specified in Deuteronomy 28:1-14. Jesus Christ is the healer of redeemed mankind.

He is also the healer of the nations.

Final Preliminary Remarks

This book, like a majority of the books in the Biblical Blueprints Series, is structured along the five-point model of the Biblical covenant. This model is presented in Ray R. Sutton's book, *That You May Prosper: Dominion By Covenant* (Institute for Christian Economics, 1987). The covenant model is as follows:

1. The absolute transcendence yet universal presence of God
2. The hierarchical authority of man's institutions
3. The law of God as man's tool of dominion
4. The two-fold judgment of God: blessings and cursings
5. The continuity of God's kingdom in history

These five points can and should be used to understand the purposes of international relations. Because Christians have not recognized the universality of this covenant model, they have failed to set forth consistent alternatives to humanist institutional arrangements, which in fact are perverse imitations of God's five-point covenant model.

Because of the almost total lack of any books on Christian international relations, I have decided to depart somewhat from the limits placed on the other books in the Biblical Blueprints Series. This book is considerably longer, and it includes more extensive footnoting. What I present here will be highly controversial in Christian and conservative circles, and I need the extra space and documentation to prove my case. I cannot refer to an existing body of literature that sets forth this case in detail. In this sense, this little book is revolutionary, at least within conservative Protestant circles.

As always, the reader should continue to ask himself these questions as he considers my arguments:

Does the Bible really teach this?
If not, what does the Bible teach?
Does the Bible teach natural law theory?
If Biblical law is not authoritative, by what *other* standard should Christians operate?
If Biblical law is not authoritative, by what *other* standard should the world operate?
Is Jesus a loser in history?
Does Jesus intend that His Church be a loser in history?
Is there ethical and creedal progress in Church history?
Is there progress in world history?

In that day five cities in the land of Egypt will speak the language of Canaan and swear by the LORD of hosts; one will be called the City of Destruction. In that day there will be an altar to the LORD in the midst of the land of Egypt, and a pillar to the LORD at its border. And it will be for a sign and for a witness to the LORD of hosts in the land of Egypt; for they will cry to the LORD because of the oppressors, and He will send them a Savior and a Mighty One, and He will deliver them. Then the LORD will be known to Egypt, and the Egyptians will know the LORD in that day, and will make sacrifice and offering; yes, they will make a vow to the LORD and perform it. And the LORD will strike Egypt, He will strike and heal it; they will return to the LORD, and He will be entreated by them and heal them. In that day there will be a highway from Egypt to Assyria, and the Assyrian will come into Egypt and the Egyptian into Assyria, and the Egyptians will serve with the Assyrians. In that day Israel will be one of three with Egypt and Assyria, even a blessing in the midst of the land, whom the LORD of hosts shall bless, saying, "Blessed is Egypt My people, and Assyria the work of My hands, and Israel My inheritance."

Isaiah 19:18-25

1

GOD CREATED THE NATIONS

And in the days of these kings the God of heaven will set up a kingdom which shall never be destroyed; and the kingdom shall not be left to other people; it shall break in pieces and consume all these kingdoms, and it shall stand forever (Daniel 2:44).

The first point of God's covenant is His transcendence over the world and His presence with the world. He is distinct from the world, yet He is present with everyone throughout history and eternity. The doctrine of the sovereignty of God is fundamental. God created the world and presently sustains the world (providence). He will judge the world at the last day.

Thus, we see the transcendence of God over history. The kingdom of God is supreme; the kingdom of Satan is doomed. The kingdoms of autonomous man will all fall. Like men, men's kingdoms are mortal. They are true kingdoms, for God has raised them up for His purposes. They are also mortal, for God tears them down for His purposes. This was God's warning to Nebuchadnezzar in the dream that Daniel interpreted for the king (Daniel 2). "He removes kings and raises up kings" (Daniel 2:21b). He is transcendent over kings and kingdoms.

Nevertheless, He is also present with all men. They cannot escape the creation's testimony to His presence. "For since the creation of the world His invisible attributes are clearly seen, being understood by the things that are made, even His eternal power and Godhead, so that they are without excuse" (Romans 1:20). He

23

puts the work of the law—though not the law itself—into the heart of every person. "For when Gentiles, who do not have the law, by nature do the things contained in the law, these, although not having the law, are a law unto themselves, who show *the work of the law* written in their hearts, their conscience also bearing witness . . ." (Romans 2:14-15a; emphasis added). God places His claims on every person in history, just as He placed them on Adam.

In the manifestation of His kingdom, we see God's presence with redeemed men. This kingdom, Daniel told the king, would be established as the fifth and final kingdom. It alone shall stand forever. It shall break all the rival kingdoms of men. "And the stone that struck the image became a great mountain and filled the whole earth" (Daniel 2:35b).

There are human kingdoms to which God gives limited, temporary sovereignty in history. There is one great kingdom to which God has given sovereignty throughout New Testament history. That kingdom is the kingdom of His Son, Jesus Christ. All enemy kingdoms to Christ's kingdom will be subdued by Christ. "The LORD said to my Lord, 'Sit at My right hand, till I make Your enemies Your footstool'" (Psalm 110:1).

Before we can consider Biblical international relations, we must consider the question: What is a nation?

The Concept of "Nation"

In both the Old Testament and the New Testament, the words used for nation literally mean something like a swarm, as in a swarm of bees. The Hebrew word is transliterated "goy." In *Strong's Concordance*, the word *goy* is defined as "a foreign *nation;* hence a *Gentile;* also (fig.) a *troop* of animals, or a *flight* of locusts: — Gentile, heathen, nation, people."[1] The word *goy* is sometimes used for Israel as well as for gentile nations, as in God's promise to Abraham: "I will make you a great nation" (Genesis 12:2a). In the

---

1. James Strong, *The Exhaustive Concordance of the Bible* (Iowa Falls, Iowa: Riverside Book and Bible House, n.d.), Hebrew and Chaldee Dictionary, #1471, p. 26.

vast majority of cases in the Old Testament, the English word "nation" is based on the Hebrew word *goy*.

The New Testament Greek word is transliterated *ethnos*. The English word "ethnic" comes from this Greek word. Kittel's *Theological Dictionary of the New Testament* defines *ethnos* as follows: "This word, which is common in Greek from the very first, probably comes from *ethos*, and means 'mass' or 'host' or 'multitude' bound by the same manners, customs or other distinctive features. Applied to men, it gives us the sense of people; but it can also be used of animals in the sense of 'herd' or of insects in the sense of 'swarm.'. . . In most cases *ethnos* is used of men in the sense of a 'people.'" The word "ethnos" is used to describe Israel in many instances. It is not exclusively used to specify gentile nations.[2]

If a nation is a collection of people, in the sense of a swarm of bees, then two questions immediately arise. First, on what basis do individuals *include* others in a collective unit with each other? Second, on what basis do members of one group *exclude* other people? The very word "member" indicates the inability of people to speak of associations and collectives in general without using the organic analogy of the human body, as Paul speaks of the Church as a body in Romans 12 and 1 Corinthians 12. Parts of a body are called "members."

The Biblical concept of "nation" is related closely to the Biblical concept of government. We must begin our search for a Biblical definition of "nation" with a study of the Biblical doctrine of the covenant.

Government Is Covenantal

The covenantal nature of all institutional government — church, State, and family — is surveyed in two books in the Biblical Blueprints Series, Gary DeMar's *Ruler of the Nations* and Ray Sutton's *Who Owns the Family?* The key book is Ray Sutton's study

---

2. Gerhard Kittel (ed.), *Theological Dictionary of the New Testament* (Grand Rapids, Michigan: Eerdmans, 1964), II, p. 369.

of the covenant, *That You May Prosper*.[3]

A government, Biblically speaking, is a monopolistic institution created by God. Membership in it is established by an oath or vow before God, explicit or implicit (for example, registering to vote). The oath places it under the sanctions of God: blessings and cursings. A government is not merely an association, such as a business or a club. Associations cannot legitimately invoke God's curses and blessings by means of a public oath. This is why international alliances are not always covenants; alliances have no shared oaths (see Chapter Nine). If alliances take on the characteristics of international civil governments, but without shared faith in the same God, then they become prohibited alliances, what President Jefferson long ago called "entangling alliances." Civil government always exercises God-given authority as a representative of God (Romans 13:1-7), either explicitly or implicitly. Government is therefore *representative*: it represents God to man, and man to God.

A Biblical covenant has five features:

1. An affirmation of the transcendence yet presence of God
2. A hierarchical system of appeals courts
3. Biblical law
4. A system of sanctions (blessings and cursings)
5. A system of inheritance or continuity

In short, a Biblical covenant is based on a *shared faith in God*. Every imitation covenant also must offer its members a faith of some sort: the pagan equivalent of the Biblical doctrine of the necessity of not being yoked unequally with unbelievers (2 Corinthians 6:14). This necessary unity of confession must be enforced by a sovereign agent who will guarantee the integrity and reliability of the covenant. There are many modern imitation sovereigns: the People, the Party, the Führer, the dialectical forces of history, the mode of production, the march of democracy, and so forth.

---

3. Ray R. Sutton, *That You May Prosper: Dominion By Covenant* (Tyler, Texas: Institute for Christian Economics, 1987).

Each of them is a substitute for the sovereign God of the Bible. They are all false gods.

A nation is a civil government that displays the five points of the covenant, either the Biblical covenant or a pagan counterfeit. Any civil government—local, state (provincial), national, or international—must possess the same five points. What features are unique to all civil governments?

1. Common language (usually)
2. The legal authority to impose taxes
3. Common laws within a shared boundary
4. Common confession (oath): implicit or explicit (e.g., allegiance to a constitution)
5. Citizenship and residency requirements

What features are unique to a nation, as distinct from regional civil governments? A nation possesses all five features of the covenant. The question then rises: What is distinctly an attribute of national sovereignty?

Sovereignty and Tax Immunity

Every civil government has the legal authority to impose taxes. The power to tax is the mark of civil government's sovereignty. It is usually asserted that national civil governments may not be taxed by lower civil governments. As U.S. Supreme Court Chief Justice John Marshall said in the famous *M'Culloch v. Maryland* case in 1819, which struck down as unconstitutional a state tax on a nationally chartered bank, "the power to tax involves the power to destroy. . . . The question is, in truth, a question of supremacy. . . ." The right to impose a tax is a question of supremacy. The higher sovereign agent may not be taxed by the lower sovereign agent.

In Old Testament Israel, the king could lawfully impose permanent taxes as God's authorized civil national representative. This was a mark of his sovereignty. No one could lawfully tax the king. When Jeroboam separated the ten tribes of northern Israel from the two southern tribes of Judah and Benjamin, the dispute was over taxation (1 Kings 12). Jeroboam then created a new worship system based on golden calves, in order to keep his people from going to Jerusalem to worship (1 Kings 12:25-33). His tax rebellion created a new civic nation, which God subsequently judged as a separate covenantal entity: for example, by the Assyrian captivity (2 Kings 17). Israel and Judah possessed a common race, common language, and common verbal confession in God and God's law (though not common ritual), but they were not one nation after Jeroboam's revolt. They did not share in taxes, geography (boundaries), and citizenship requirements.

Tribute as God's Judgment

The distinction in the Bible between tribute imposed by a conquering pagan nation (2 Kings 15:19-20) and taxes imposed by the king (1 Samuel 8) indicates the civic limit of nationhood. Tribute is what is paid temporarily to another nation. It does not mark the creation of a new nation, for there is no common language, borders, confession of faith (oath), or citizenship. An invading nation could impose tribute only in its capacity as a God-authorized scourge, but it was only *temporarily* authorized by God to bring His judgment against His nation in history. As Isaiah prophesied concerning temporarily victorious Assyria over the rebellious northern kingdom of Israel: "Woe to Assyria, the rod of My anger and the staff in whose hand is My indignation. I will send him against an ungodly nation, and against the people of My wrath. I will give him charge, to seize the spoil, to take the prey, and to tread them down like the mire of the streets" (Isaiah 10:5-6). It was God who had scattered the nation of Israel, not Assyria, yet Assyria arrogantly boasted of her own sovereign might:

> By the strength of my hand I have done it, and by my wisdom, for I am prudent. Also I have removed the boundaries of the people, and have robbed their treasuries; so I have put down the inhabitants like a valiant man. My hand has found like a nest the riches of the people, and as one gathers eggs that are left, I have gathered all the earth (Isaiah 10:13-14a).

To this, God responded: "Shall the ax boast itself against him who chops with it? Or shall the saw magnify itself against him who saws with it?" (Isaiah 10:15a). God will devour this arrogant nation (vv. 16-19). Then the remnant of Israel will depend on God rather than on those who defeated them militarily (v. 20); this remnant will return to God spiritually and covenantally (v. 21). It will return to the land of Israel (v. 22). This was unique in the ancient world. Representatives ("remnant") of a defeated, scattered nation-state would survive as a nation without boundaries in a foreign land, governed by a universal God rather than the gods of the conquering city or empire. So, the Biblical concept "nation" does not always require present geographical boundaries, but it requires boundaries as a memory to be revered and as a goal to be achieved. Israel remained a nation during captivity because of the shared faith of the people and their faith in their future restoration to the land. When the captive nation again achieved its boundaries, it again became a nation-state.

The Biblical proof of civil nationhood is 1) the God-authorized legal authority of a coercive political unit ("the sword") directly to tax people, institutions, and economic transactions, implying its legal immunity from involuntary taxation by other governments; 2) the legal right to represent its geographical residents and its citizens in dealings with other nations; 3) the right to specify the laws of the nation; 4) the right to specify qualifications for judges; and 5) the right to specify the terms of succession for civil rulers and citizens. Tribute can be imposed temporarily on a nation by a victorious conqueror, which usually takes place after a war, but a nation retains its national sovereignty by paying the tribute. If it loses all control over its internal and external affairs, and if its citizens come to accept the civil sovereignty of the victorious government, then the nation disappears. An example would be Anglo-Saxon England after the Norman invasion of 1066. Within two centuries, the Saxon nation of England was only a vague and distant memory.

The reason why the Church can never become a nation-state is that it cannot lawfully impose taxation on those outside its membership. It does not possess the sword. The sword is exercised within specified geographical boundaries. The Church has no geographical boundaries. It cannot legitimately impose taxes on all those within a particular geographical area, for it is not a geographically defined institution.

Humanist Nationhood

The modern humanist defines the nation in terms of political power. That geographical and legal entity which possesses supreme political power is defined as the nation. The nation is today incorrectly identified with the State. Conservative sociologist Robert Nisbet writes: "Like the family, or like capitalism, the State is a complex of ideas, symbols, and relationships. Unlike either kinship or capitalism, the State has become, in the contemporary world, the supreme allegiance of men and, in most recent times, the greatest refuge from the insecurities and frustrations of other spheres of life."[4] It is seen by many in the modern world as possessing redemptive power.[5]

In classical Greece, the nation was a closely knit association based on common religious rites, civil government, limited boundaries (the city), a common language, common laws for citizens only, and a common racial heritage. The empire of Alexander the Great shattered this view of the nation in the fourth century, B.C. His empire included many races, laws, and languages. It was not based on shared religious rights, but on power. The Roman Empire was equally diverse, and the only common religious rites were those based on the sovereignty of Rome's power. This is why the early Church was persecuted: it denied Rome's divinity.[6] The breakup of the Roman Empire in Western Europe led to local kingdoms rather than what we call nations: loosely

---

4. Robert A. Nisbet, *The Quest for Community* (New York: Oxford University Press, 1953), p. 99.

5. *Ibid.*, p. 154.

6. R. J. Rushdoony, *The One and the Many: Studies in the Philosophy of Order and Ultimacy* (Fairfax, Virginia: Thoburn Press, [1971] 1978), pp. 138-48. Cf. Ethelbert Stauffer, *Christ and the Caesars* (Philadelphia: Westminster Press, 1955).

knit localities officially under the authority of hereditary kings.

A nation need not have a common language. Switzerland has three major languages: German, French, and Italian. A nation need not have a common religion, but it must possess a common culture based on a shared view of the world. This common world-view is reflected institutionally in the five points of the covenant.

For the first time in recorded history, the twentieth century has seen the demise of kings and queens. As deposed Egyptian King Farouk once said, there are but five kings left on earth: the King of England, and the kings of clubs, hearts, spades, and diamonds. Nevertheless, the modern nation-state, like ancient civil governments, declares original sovereignty by some authority. Whatever is the source of law in society is that society's god.[7] This authority may be the Party, or the Leader, or the People, or the Constitution. This authority (even the Leader) always requires interpreters. The battle for power takes place over title to the authority to speak in the name of the silent authority (point two of the Biblical covenant: the doctrine of representation). Some agent is declared to be the lawful representative of this silent original authority. In the ancient world, priests interpreted the holy revelation; in modern times, lawyers and bureaucrats perform this religious function. In radically totalitarian systems, the supreme authority is said to be infallible, is in essence an *incarnation* of the sovereign authority rather than merely a representative. In this sense, modern totalitarianism is a religious throwback to ancient theocratic dynasties. Instead of calling on the gods to justify the ruler, modern totalitarian parties call upon the name of the People, the *Volk*, or the dialectical forces of history.

Modern humanism has abolished kings, but it cannot abolish national geographical boundaries. National boundaries are a built-in aspect of God's world after the scattering at Babel. Boundaries can change, and languages can disappear or be modified over time, but separate languages and identifiable geographi-

---

7. R. J. Rushdoony, *The Institutes of Biblical Law* (Nutley, New Jersey: Craig Press, 1973), p. 4.

cal boundaries are basic to every map of the world in man's history and future. "And He has made from one blood every nation of men to dwell on all the face of the earth, and has determined their preappointed times and the boundaries of their habitation" (Acts 17:26).

The Nations of Mankind

There are 70 nations listed in Genesis 10. "These were the families of the sons of Noah, according to their generations, in their nations; and from these the nations were divided on the earth after the flood" (Genesis 10:32). The number 70 is repeated frequently in the Bible as the number of the nations. At the feast of the tabernacles in the seventh month, beginning with the fifteenth day, the priests of Israel began a week of sacrifices. For seven days, a descending number of bullocks were sacrificed: 13, 12, 11, 10, 9, 8, and 7, totalling 70 bullocks. Then, on the eighth day, one final bullock was sacrificed (Numbers 29:12-36). These totalled 71 sacrifices for the 70 nations of the world, plus Israel. God's atonement for the whole world was manifested ritually in the Old Testament sacrificial system.

When the Israelites captured the Canaanitic king, Adoni-Bezek, after the death of Joshua, he confessed that he had slain 70 kings (Judges 1:7). This presumably was his way of saying that he had conquered the world—an assertion of his sovereignty.

The point is, the nations of the world existed prior to the scattering at the Tower of Babel in Genesis 11. Mankind was supposed to spread across the face of the earth. This is God's method of subduing the earth to His glory. The one river of the Garden of Eden became four rivers flowing out from the garden (Genesis 2:10), and therefore *down* from the garden, which indicates its status as a mountain location (Genesis 2:10-14). This pointed to man's responsibility of following them to "the four corners of the earth." The garden's originating river revealed mankind's *unity*, while the four rivers flowing outward pointed to mankind's future geographical and cultural *diversity*.

There are many nations, but only one mountain of Zion: "Great is the LORD, and greatly to be praised in the city of our God, in His holy mountain. Beautiful in elevation, the joy of the whole earth, is Mount Zion on the sides of the north, the city of the great King" (Psalm 48:1-2). Symbolized in the Old Testament by the tabernacle, and then the temple in Jerusalem, Zion is God's Church, the spiritual home of the saints. To Zion men must come for salvation. To Zion they *will* come for their salvation:

> Now it shall come to pass in the latter days that the mountain of the LORD's house shall be established on the top of the mountains, and shall be exalted above the hills; and nations shall flow to it. Many people shall come and say, "Come, and let us go up to the mountain of the LORD, to the house of the God of Jacob; He will teach us His ways, and we will walk in His paths." For out of Zion shall go forth the law, and the word of the LORD from Jerusalem. He shall judge between the nations, and shall rebuke many people; they shall beat their swords into plowshares, and their spears into pruning hooks. Nation shall not lift up sword against nation, neither shall they learn war anymore (Isaiah 2:2-4).

The peace that would have prevailed had Adam not sinned has become the Christian standard in history. The international unity that should have prevailed among Noah's heirs was broken by their attempt to build a giant tower as a symbol of man's autonomy from God (Genesis 11). It is not the quest for peace and prosperity under God that is evil; it is man's attempt to gain peace and prosperity *apart from God* that is sinful. As we have seen, Isaiah prophesied that such a world of national diversity under God's law will become a fact in history during the era of full millennial blessings (Isaiah 2). We can debate whether this will be an era in which Jesus reigns physically from Jerusalem, or whether it refers to the millennial blessings that God sends in response to worldwide revival, but there is no way to escape the force of Isaiah's words: there will be an era of peace based on nations' obedience to God's law. "For out of Zion shall go forth the law, and the word of the LORD from Jerusalem."

Establishing a Christian Nation

God establishes nations, kingdoms, and all other units of civil government. Men, as God's delegated sovereigns in history (Genesis 1:26-28), create civil governments as *agents of God*, but not as original creators.

What would be the universal features of a Christian nation? The same five features that we see in every government. The Christian nation would be fully aware of what God requires. It must be stressed from the outset that the creation of such a nation could be accomplished only as a result of *the widespread work of the Holy Spirit*, not through some bureaucratic, top-down, coercively imposed order on a non-Christian majority by a Christian minority. This covenantal transformation of a nation must be the sovereign work of God, with men as delegated agents, not the work of men apart from the outpouring of the Holy Spirit. (Because there has been so much confusion about what the Biblical Blueprints Series is really advocating, I suggest that you reread the last two sentences three times.)

1. A Common View of God

All citizens would acknowledge the sovereignty of the Trinitarian God of the Bible. Only He would be publicly worshipped. Only He would be called upon publicly in times of national crisis. Only He would be given public praise in times of national deliverance. His Word, the Bible, would be acknowledged as the source of the nation's law-order.

2. A Common System of Courts

There must be ways of settling public disputes. A Christian nation would follow the example of Exodus 18 and establish an appeals court system. Men would be free to do as they please unless they violated a specific piece of Bible-based legislation or a specific Biblical injunction that the Bible says must be enforced by the civil government. Government is therefore a bottom-up structure, with the individual operating as a lawful sovereign agent under

God and God's law. The individual, institution, or association ini-
tiates projects; the State only serves as a kind of "night watchman"
to see to it that each person abides by Biblical law in seeking his
various personal goals.

The principle of localism would be affirmed. Local courts
would handle most cases. Only the hard cases would be accepted
by the appeals courts. Local laws would not be overturned unless
they could be proven to be in opposition to a Biblical principle or
in opposition to the agreed-upon covenantal (constitutional)
terms of the next level of civil government. Just as in today's humanist nations, the supreme court can overturn a piece of legislation that violates the national constitution or common law precedent, so a supreme court would overturn a constitutional provision that violates Biblical law. The Bible is sovereign, not some
human compact. However, to keep the supreme court from becoming absolutely sovereign, a combination of other civil authorities could overturn the court. For example, if the United States
were a truly Biblical commonwealth, the combined votes of (say)
three-quarters of all the members of each of the two houses of
Congress, plus the President, would be able to overturn a decision
by the U.S. Supreme Court. There should never be a unitary, absolutely final, earthly court of human appeal.

3. Common Biblical Law

The Bible as the Word of God would be the final standard of
justice. All laws at every level of government would be judged in
terms of the Bible. The national constitution (written or unwrit-
ten) would be officially subordinate to the Bible. The courts would
render judgment in terms of the Bible. A body of legal precedent
would build up over the years, but precedents would always be
subjected to the decisions of juries regarding the proper application of the civil code to circumstances. The Bible would be
declared the supreme law of the land, and it would be taught in
public gatherings on a regular basis (Deuteronomy 31:10-13).

4. Judgment by Citizens

The judges in Exodus 18 were to be men of good character.
There were to have been a lot of judges — far more than an elite

group of legal specialists. One rabbinical estimate (by the medieval commentator Rashi) was that there must have been over 82,000 judges in Israel, or 15 percent of the 600,000 adult males.[8]

The essence of citizenship, Biblically speaking, is the legal authority to render public judgment. Covenanted citizens alone may serve as judges. All other civil rights (legal immunities) belong to every resident. There is to be one law for all people: "One law shall be for the native-born and for the stranger who sojourns among you" (Exodus 12:49).[9] There must be no legal discrimination against non-citizen residents of the nation.

Why should residents be prohibited from serving as judges and jurors? Because a person must be *under* Biblical law covenantally — a personal, voluntary bond among men and under God and God's Bible-revealed law — in order to *administer* Biblical law covenantally.

The preservation of the integrity of the jury system is probably the most important single domestic civil task facing Christians today. If we lose the judicial sovereignty of the jury of our peers in deciding both the justice of the law and the truth or falsity of the testimony, then we have lost the most important remaining institutional bastion against judicial tyranny. It would mean the eclipse of freedom.

5. Continuity

Continuity must be over time and also across borders. Continuity over time would be provided by provisions to amend the Constitution and local legal codes, and also by steady changes in common law precedent, as men's knowledge of God's kingdom principles improves. Each succeeding generation would be trained by Biblical law by parents (Deuteronomy 6:6-7) and by the civil government through public instruction in God's law (Deuteronomy 31:10-13).

Continuity over borders would be provided by permanent

---

8. Michael Walzer, *Exodus and Revolution* (New York: Basic Books, 1985), p. 127.

9. Gary North, *Moses and Pharaoh: Dominion Religion vs. Power Religion* (Tyler, Texas: Institute for Christian Economics, 1985), ch. 14: "The Rule of Law."

treaties. Such treaties are valid only between or among Christian nations. The means of securing the legal basis of such treaties is missionary activity. Christians who are citizens in a Christian nation must send out representatives to preach the gospel to all men. They must send out missionaries to non-Christian societies who will represent various church governments,[10] but who would also represent the particular Christian nation *as a guest in the foreign nation*. He would have to learn to operate in terms of two legal systems—a very difficult skill. His job is the conquest of Satan, but not the subjection of the particular foreign nation to the nation of his earthly citizenship. At most, he would work toward the integration of that nation into a covenanted federation of Christian nations.

We now have some idea of what a Christian nation should be. What does the Bible teach about international relations?

Christians Must Be Consistent

The establishment of a godly foreign policy must be part of a program of comprehensive redemption. It is our responsibility as Christians to seek to reform every area of life. No area of life is outside of God's two-fold judgment: cursing or blessing. No aspect of life is religiously neutral. Thus, for the formerly Christian West to continue to conduct its foreign policy on the assumption of the myth of neutrality is suicidal. The more consistent humanist systems—the empires of history—will always seek to swallow up those less consistent humanist societies that believe that a permanent peace treaty with evil is possible and desirable. God tells us what is in the hearts of empire-builders: *rape*. God will sometimes permit this because of the faithlessness of His people:

> I have likened the daughter of Zion to a lovely and delicate woman. The shepherds with their flocks shall come to her. They shall pitch their tents against her all around. Each one shall pasture in his own place. Prepare for war against her. Arise, and let us go

---

10. Ultimately, this means an International Church government: see Chapter Eleven.

up at noon. Woe to us, for the day goes away, for the shadows of
the evening are lengthening. Arise, and let us go by night, and let
us destroy her palaces. For thus has the LORD of hosts said: "Hew
down trees, and build a mound against Jerusalem. This is the city
to be punished. She is full of oppression in her midst. As a fountain
wells up with water, so she wells up with her wickedness. Violence
and plundering are heard in her. Before Me continually are grief
and wounds. Be instructed, O Jerusalem, lest My soul depart from
you; lest I make you desolate, a land not inhabited" (Jeremiah 6:2-8).

Satan's Soviet Empire

No one has seen more clearly this surrender of the West's less
consistent humanists to Communism's more consistent humanists
than Aleksandr Solzhenitsyn, who was exiled from the Soviet
Union in 1974 because of his anti-Communist books. In his
speech to the graduating class at Harvard University in 1978,
which produced a wave of outraged protests from humanists across
the United States, Solzhenitsyn stated the problem accurately:

> As humanism in its development was becoming more and
> more materialistic, it also increasingly allowed its concepts to be
> used first by socialism and then by communism. So that Karl
> Marx was able to say, in 1844, that "communism is naturalized hu-
> manism.". . . It is no accident that all of communism's rhetorical
> vows resolve [revolve?] around Man (with a capital *M*) and his
> earthly happiness. At first glance it seems an ugly parallel: com-
> mon traits in the thinking and way of life of today's West and
> today's East? But such is the logic of materialistic development.
>
> The interrelationship is such, moreover, that the current of ma-
> terialism which is farthest to the left, and is hence the most consist-
> ent, always proves to be stronger, more attractive, and victorious.
> Humanism which has lost its Christian heritage cannot prevail in
> this competition. Thus during the past centuries and especially in
> recent decades, as the process became more acute, the alignment of
> forces was as follows: Liberalism was inevitably pushed aside by
> radicalism, radicalism had to surrender to socialism, and socialism
> could not stand up to communism. The Communist regime in the
> East could endure and grow due to the enthusiastic support from
> an enormous number of Western intellectuals who (feeling the kin-

ship!) refused to see communism's crimes, and when they no longer could do so, they tried to justify these crimes. The problem persists: In our Eastern countries, communism has suffered a complete ideological defeat; it is zero and less than zero. And yet Western intellectuals still look at it with considerable interest and empathy, and this is precisely what makes it so immensely difficult for the West to withstand the East.[11]

A godly foreign policy must begin with repentance, as Solzhenitsyn elsewhere has written. "Repentance is the first bit of firm ground underfoot, the only one from which we can go forward not to fresh hatreds but to concord. Repentance is the only starting point for spiritual growth. For each and every individual. And every trend of social thought."[12] In this sense, the isolationists have things partially correct, for they say that we must clean up our own societies before trying to clean up everyone else's (see Chapter Four). But they assume that our backyard will never be perfectly clean, and we can therefore forever ignore everyone else's backyard.

If Christians took this perfectionist personal attitude with respect to sharing the gospel with others, or before imperfect churches could send out missionaries, there could be no evangelism. Sanctification is a long-term, lifetime project. It is an inside-out process, for regeneration begins with the individual soul, but eventually sanctification does begin to affect the outside world. Imperfect people are to minister to others.

Imperfect nations are also to minister to others, and I do *not* mean to limit this to national *civil governments*. Nations sometimes must offer protection to other nations. In doing so, they can also gain protection. This has implications for foreign policy and defense policy. For example, the support of specific anti-Communist freedom fighters is often a wise policy; it allows the United States and other Western nations to inflict economic, political,

---

11. *Solzhenitsyn at Harvard* (Washington, D.C.: Ethics and Public Policy Center, 1980), pp. 17-18.

12. Solzhenitsyn, "Repentance and Self-Limitation in the Life of Nations," in Solzhenitsyn, *From Under the Rubble* (Boston: Little, Brown, 1974), pp. 108-9.

and propaganda damage on the Soviet empire at low cost and without a direct military confrontation between the West and the USSR. It challenges the long-term Soviet military policy of encirclement of capitalist nations.

When the latest empire of Satan is on the attack, we must clean up our backyard ethically, but we must also seek to destroy the offensive empire. It does no good to proclaim peace, for there is never peace between nations covenanted to God and nations covenanted to God's enemies. There can only be temporary cease-fire agreements. A war is always in progress. We must not listen to the treaty-signers and the economic deal-doers. We have listened foolishly and hopefully to the corrupt deal-doers and treaty-signers at the highest level of national government because we are ourselves corrupt deal-doers at our own level:

> Because from the least of them even to the greatest of them, everyone is given to covetousness; and from the prophet even to the priest, everyone deals falsely. They have also healed the hurt of My people slightly, Saying, "Peace, peace!" when there is no peace (Jeremiah 6:13-14).

Summary

The first point in the Biblical covenant structure is the transcendence, yet presence, of God. God is transcendent over the affairs of men, including foreign affairs. God is sovereign over history, and His kingdom is a manifestation of this sovereignty. God has promised to subdue all the kingdoms of men to the kingdom of His Son, Jesus Christ. This kingdom cannot be stopped in history.

> Then comes the end, when He delivers the kingdom to God the Father, when He puts an end to all rule and all authority and power. For He must reign till He has put all enemies under His feet. The last enemy that will be destroyed is death (1 Corinthians 15:24-26).

All Biblical domestic political policies and foreign policies must begin with this assumption. Each nation must publicly ally itself with Christ. This is the only way that a nation can become part of Christ's victorious kingdom. Foreign policy in every covenanted nation must reflect this commitment. The goal of Christians in politics should be to extend the visible kingdom of God in the realm of political life, just as it is to be extended in the non-political realms. The goal should be progressively to restrict the influence of non-Biblical law. This is a bottom-up political process that must begin with individual self-government under Biblical law.

Clearly, to establish a godly foreign policy, Christians must first establish Christianity as the religion of their nations. The West needs a revival. So does the East. Any discussion of foreign policy today that presupposes that we live in a world of neutral nations has already given away the case for Christian international relations. The assumption of neutrality leads to the erroneous conclusion that a nation's foreign policy will be constructed either in terms of the principle of humanist internationalism (empire or alliances) or in terms of humanist isolationism. Both approaches to foreign policy are wrong. What we need is Christianity, not the myth of neutrality.

In summary:

1. God is transcendent over all the kingdoms of men.
2. All human kingdoms are temporary.
3. God is present with all men: the *work* of His law in each heart.
4. God is present in a special way with His people: the kingdom of God.
5. A nation is a group of people who are joined together geographically in a civil covenant.
6. The covenant has five parts.
7. A nation begins with a shared faith in God or some other ultimate sovereign agent.
8. A nation has five aspects: shared language, the authority to impose taxes (and escape taxation), common laws within a shared boundary, a common confession (oath), and citizenship requirements.
9. All citizenship requires exclusion.
10. The proper basis of political exclusion is the Biblical covenant.

11. The basis of exercising rule is covenantal: ethics, not bloodlines, initiation, or other means of exclusion.

12. Tax immunity is basic to national sovereignty.

13. Tribute may be paid temporarily to military conquerors, if necessary.

14. Humanists define nationhood in terms of political power.

15. No nation can avoid the question of sovereignty.

16. The modern nation is equated with the State.

17. The State is identified with a sovereign earthly collective: Party, Constitution, People, etc.

18. Nations are a means of subduing the earth to the glory of God.

19. Each nation is to become a place for protecting Zion, the Church of God.

20. God wants people to work toward the establishment of Christian nations.

2

ALL NATIONS UNDER GOD

> He shall have dominion also from sea to sea, and from the River to the ends of the earth. Those who dwell in the wilderness will bow before Him, and His enemies will lick the dust. The kings of Tarshish and of the isles will bring presents. The kings of Sheba and Seba will offer gifts. Yes, all kings shall fall down before Him. All nations shall serve Him (Psalm 72:8-11).

The second point of the Biblical covenant structure is hierarchy. God is sovereign over His creation (point one), and He has established a hierarchical structure of authority to govern His three covenantal institutions: church, State, and family.

We are told, "all kings shall fall down before Him. All nations shall serve Him." This raises the question of the Biblical legitimacy of internationalism. Do they bow as totally independent kings and nations, or do they bow corporately?

We cannot legitimately apply automatically the standards of one covenant to another: church, family, and State. Each is different. We know that in the case of family covenants, when a new family is formed, a covenantal break with parents is legally established (Genesis 2:24). Nevertheless, filial piety is required (Exodus 20:12). Parents are mortal in a way that institutions are not. Different standards apply.

Some Christians (I am *not* one of them) oppose hierarchical church denominations, and would argue that this legal separation is also true concerning churches. What about nations? If there is to be an ascending hierarchy from the local township, county, or city to the state or province and then to the national government, what about a world government? If every form of world civil government is innately evil, then what is the basis of our confidence in the legitimacy of *any* level of civil government beyond local government? Is there something *inherently wicked* about world civil government (or world church government)? If not, then what about hierarchy? May we speak as Christians about the legitimacy of a one-world Christian State,[1] even though we know from the Tower of Babel that a *one-State world* is illegitimate? And if world civil government is covenantally legitimate, what kind of hierarchy should it be?

What is the Biblical concept of covenantal internationalism? To answer this, we must first consider the nature of God.

God Is One and Many

God is a Trinity. He is three Persons, yet also one Person. He is God, yet He is plural. Orthodox Christianity has always confessed this. It is one of the primary marks of Biblical orthodoxy: Trinity, creation, incarnation, redemption, and final judgment. Without this confession of faith, mankind has no legitimate hope.

We know that the whole world testifies to the existence of God (Romans 1:18-22). Sinful men suppress the truth of this revelation of God in nature (including human nature), but it never leaves them. This is one reason why God can legitimately judge all men for their rebellion: they constantly suppress nature's testimony to the existence of God, so "they are without excuse" (Romans 1:20). God confronts man with His own being because all of nature images God, especially mankind, who is made in God's image (Genesis 1:26).

If God is one yet also many, then mankind is one yet also many. We are divided religiously, racially, geographically, culturally, and in many other ways, yet we are all of one blood. Paul preached to the men of Athens that God created the world (Acts 17:24), and He is totally sovereign over all things, in need of noth-

---

1. This assumes, of course, that all the nation-states of the world are covenantally Christian and can therefore legitimately covenant with each other.

ing from man (Acts 17:25). "And He has made from one blood every nation of men to dwell on all the face of the earth, and has determined their preappointed times and the boundaries of their habitation" (Acts 17:26).

If we were not all sons of God, we would not all be responsible before God as rebellious sons. We would not be sons of Adam. We would not need forgiveness. But every person on earth is born in sin, as the covenantal heir of Adam, and therefore all men need redemption. Thus, we are all sons of God by birth — *disinherited* sons. It is foolish to deny the universal Fatherhood of God and the universal brotherhood of man. There is a universal Creator-Father, and He has disinherited His rebellious children. All men really are brothers . . . just like Cain and Abel.

What God does is to adopt rebellious people back into His covenantal family. "But as many as received Him [Jesus Christ], to them He [the Father] gave the right to become children of God, even to those who believe in His name, who were born, not of blood, nor of the will of the flesh, nor of the will of man, but of God" (John 1:12-13). Salvation is by adoption. We are adopted and therefore we have become the *sons of the inheritance*. So, there are two kinds of sons: *disinherited* sons and *adopted* sons. The dividing mark is not blood; the dividing mark is *ethics*. God in His sovereign grace *imputes* (declares judicially)[2] to adopted sons that they now and forevermore possess the righteousness of Jesus' perfect humanity (though never Christ's divinity), which removes forever from these once-disinherited sons God's prior imputation of Adam's sin (Romans 4:8).[3] Christians have become *reconciled* sons of God (Romans 5:10-11).

The Quest for Spiritual Unity

The quest for spiritual unity among all *redeemed* men is not only legitimate; it is required by God. Jesus prayed: "I do not

2. John Murray, *Redemption Accomplished and Applied* (Edinburgh: Banner of Truth, 1961), pp. 123-25.

3. John Murray, *The Imputation of Adam's Sin* (Nutley, New Jersey: Presbyterian & Reformed, [1959] 1977), ch. 4.

pray for these alone, but also for those who will believe in Me
through their word; that they all may be one, as You, Father, are
in Me, and I in You; *that they also may be one in Us*, that the world
may believe that You sent Me. And the glory which You gave Me
I have given them, that *they may be one just as We are one*" (John
17:20-22; emphasis added). We are to do our best to avoid schism
as Christians. The goal is to heal divisions over time, as God's
grace permits (see Chapter Eleven).

Nevertheless, this does not mean that we are to create a one-
State bureaucratic world. That was the vision of those who sought
to construct the Tower of Babel. Christians *are* to work toward the
creation of a one-world Christian *order*. Of course, Christians cannot create it; we only re-create it. We act as God's servants. We reflect in our lives *and in our institutions* what God has already established in principle: an ethically new humanity in Christ and a new
order that reflects this new humanity. Paul writes:

> Therefore, if anyone is in Christ, he is a new creation; old
> things have passed away; behold, all things have become new.
> Now all things are of God, who has reconciled us to Himself
> through Jesus Christ, and has given us the ministry of reconcilia-
> tion, that is, that God was in Christ reconciling the world to Him-
> self, not imputing their trespasses to them, and has committed to
> us the word of reconciliation. Therefore we are ambassadors for
> Christ, as though God were pleading through us: we implore you
> on Christ's behalf, be reconciled to God (2 Corinthians 5:17-20).

Christ's New World Order

This new creation is Christ's New World Order which He created in principle at Calvary. He announced His victory over sin,
death, and Satan at His resurrection. He had inaugurated His
kingdom earlier, when He began to cast out demons: "But if I cast
out demons by the Spirit of God, surely the kingdom of God has
come upon you" (Matthew 12:28). He legally established His
kingdom in history through His death, resurrection, and ascension. He transferred His kingdom from Israel to the Church at
Pentecost, just as He had said He would (Matthew 21:43), when

the Holy Spirit came to the church in Jerusalem. God sealed this legal transfer of the kingdom by the prophesied destruction of the temple in A.D. 70 (Luke 21:20-24).[4]

The kingdom of God is *God's* New World Order. It already is in operation. It encompasses in principle everything in life — full covenantal responsibility. It is in principle (and covenantally in the Lord's Supper) now unified in Spirit, but diversified culturally, racially, geographically, and so forth. The kingdom of God is both one and many, unified and diversified. The full powers and gifts of redeemed mankind are to be progressively manifested in history. Redeemed men are not to seek a unified one-State world, but we are to seek to manifest what Christ has already delivered to His people in principle: an ethically redeemed one-world Christian Order. This is a bottom-up covenantal order, not a top-down bureaucratic empire.

The principle of Christ's kingdom is at war with the principle of Satan's empire. The wheat and the tares compete for the field (the whole world), as we read in Christ's parable of the wheat and tares in Matthew 13. The principle of God's leaven expands to overcome the principle of Satan's leaven. There is a war in progress, a spiritual war that involves every aspect of life, every nook and cranny of the human heart, every square inch of geography that is or can be put under any man's dominion. There is no neutrality. Men struggle to affirm covenantally and manifest in history either the crown rights of King Jesus or the crown rights of King Adam.

Christian Internationalism: Kingdom

The kingdom of God is to be manifested on earth in history. The civil covenant of local government — township, county, city — steadily becomes regional civil government (province, state). The states in turn create agreed-upon covenants to produce national entities.

---

4. David Chilton, *The Days of Vengeance: An Exposition of the Book of Revelation* (Ft. Worth: Dominion Press, 1987).

The question then arises: What about international entities? Why do we refuse to stop covenanting at one border (regional) and not another (national)? Why should we stop covenanting at the county level? Why stop covenanting at the national level? The answer is: we are not supposed to stop until *the religious basis of the covenant* no longer exists because of the problem of rival gods. The issue is theology, not historic geography. The issue is covenant, not blood. The issue is rival confessions of faith, not language barriers. The issue is the kingdom of God vs. the kingdom of Satan.

Because modern humanism's theories of government self-consciously exclude a public religious confession as the basis of civil government, the West has broken with its past. The freedom of the European medieval city was based on a Christian covenantal confession; without this explicitly Christian confession of religious agreement, the medieval city might not have developed.[5]

In the modern world, this covenantal basis of civil jurisdiction has changed drastically. Because citizenship is based on blood (birth), or passing an examination (written or verbal test), or some other non-theological characteristic, the modern world has been threatened by the rise of mass democracy, the politics of "one man, one vote." For instance, mass democracy and the tax-financed welfare State have combined to make immigrants a threat to the citizens of a prosperous nation. Immigration barriers were the product of the so-called Progressive movement in the United States, which flourished from the late 1800's until about 1920. Each new resident is viewed by taxpayers as a potential drain on tax-supported welfare services. Taxpayers want only potential taxpayers to enter the nation. Public goods create a fear of immigrants.[6]

If citizenship were by Christian confession, immigrants would be welcomed as potential converts to the faith, just as visitors to a

---

5. Max Weber, *Economy and Society* (New York: Bedminster Press, [1924] 1968), ch. XVI, Part ii, "The Occidental City."

6. Gary North, "Public Goods and Fear of Foreigners," *The Freeman* (March 1974).

church are welcomed. They could join the civil covenant through covenantal adoption by God. (It is interesting that the U.S. Supreme Court in 1892 actually said that citizenship for immigrants is granted by Congress by means of adoption. Its language was highly religious: naturalization was defined as "the act of adopting a foreigner, and clothing him with the privileges of a native citizen.")[7] Since immigrants could not vote—meaning "vote themselves into our pocketbooks"—until joining the civil covenant, they would not be a threat economically. Because they would work, they would be an asset.

Because citizenship in the United States is automatic through birth inside the national borders (U.S. Constitution, Fourteenth Amendment), immigrants have become an economic and political threat, for their children will become citizens upon reaching adulthood and become eligible to vote. Because of compulsory tax-financed education, their children drain our school budgets. The welfare State, coupled with citizenship by birth, has made immigrants a liability. This situation is radically anti-Biblical and immoral, yet it is the politically inevitable outcome of mass democracy, socialist ideas, and citizenship by birth. A century ago, a liberal was a person who favored open borders—free trade, free immigration—and a minimal State. Today, he favors restricted immigration, high tariffs, and a maximum State. Some liberals in the United States are now considering raising tariffs, abandoning a major belief of nineteenth-century liberalism. Freedom of movement has steadily been sacrificed on the altar of the welfare State.

In ancient Israel, citizenship was by covenant and family, so strangers could live in the cities and share God's blessings on the whole society. With Jesus' complete fulfillment and annulment of the Jubilee Year (Luke 4), which disappeared with Jesus' removal of the kingdom of God from ancient Israel (Matthew 21:43), the family land tenure basis of political citizenship disappeared (Leviticus 25:23-34). Christian civil citizenship must be confessional,

---

7. *Boyd v. Nebraska ex re. Thayer*, 143 U.S. 135, 162 (1892). See *The Constitution of the United States of America: Analysis and Interpretation* (Washington, D.C.: Government Printing Office, 1973), p. 283.

but with open borders. To screen civil citizenship in terms of anything other than Christian confession is to make "undesirable" foreign residents a threat.

There were no passports in the West before 1914. Few Western
nations had rigorous immigration laws. There was also no mass
democracy or socialism. People who would obey the laws and
work hard were seen as a benefit. But mass democracy and the
rise of socialist ideology changed all that. With the progressive income tax came immigration barriers in every nation. The welfare
State is illiberal with regard to work-oriented immigrants. To the
extent that welfare State thinking has become common among
Christians, they too have adopted the closed-border mentality.

Settling International Disputes

Christian nations should seek to settle international disputes
by enforceable law. Here is a real-world example. The Colorado
River flows through the United States into Mexico. Because of
salts that build up in the river because of evaporation from Lake
Mead, which was created by Hoover Dam, and because of fer-
tilizer run-off into the river from the intensely agricultural area
around southern California's Imperial Valley, the water is increasingly polluted as it approaches Mexico. What should be done?
How should this conflict be settled?

A similar problem is acid rain. Pollutants released into the atmosphere by industrial producers in one nation are carried by the
winds into another nation, where it reduces agricultural output.

Another example: political leaders of the northern Mexican
border city of Tijuana say they cannot afford to treat city sewage
adequately before it is dumped into the Pacific Ocean. This
sewage threatens the beaches of the southern California city of
San Diego. San Diego tax revenues now finance most of the cost
of operating the sewage plant of Tijuana. Is this a form of tribute?
Is this the proper answer?

These kinds of issues sometimes require a civil government to
adjudicate them. This means hierarchy. This means covenant.
Major disputes come over pollution: moving fluids (water and air)

that do not honor human boundaries. Another major area of dispute is disputes over boundaries. Each ascending level of civil government must be weaker, dealing with fewer and fewer issues. Localism is Biblical, but so is the appeals court system of Exodus 18. To assume that a nation is the final boundary for every dispute is to create an incentive for war, just as the same assumption brings conflict to provinces, counties, and townships.

To Inherit the Earth

Christ's victory at Calvary in principle reclaimed the ownership of the whole earth from Satan, and it legally transferred this certificate of ownership to God's people.[8] The certificate of ownership is the New Testament itself. The New Testament is a covenant: a legal document. It assigns the inheritance to God's adopted sons (John 1:12). The boundaries of this nation of nations in principle are the whole earth. Though sin will restrict a perfect working out in history of these boundaries, the goal of Christians all over the world should be to work toward this goal: the creation of a formally covenanted confederation of Christian nations under God. God's kingdom must triumph in history over Satan's kingdom. Christ's nation of nations must triumph over Satan's empire of empires.

Christ's work on Calvary is the legal foundation of Christian internationalism. Without it, the world would still belong to Satan. Humanist internationalism and humanist nationalism are both attempts to deny the work of Christ at Calvary. This is why Christians should recognize the legitimacy of a search to create an international confederation of covenanted nations that confesses as a unit that Jesus Christ is both Savior and Lord of nations.[9] This will not be a one-State world, but it will be a nation of covenanted nations. It will be the historical fulfillment of Christ's prophecy to the Pharisees.

---

8. *Inherit the Earth: Biblical Blueprints for Economics* (Ft. Worth, Texas: Dominion Press, 1987), ch. 5.

9. Gary DeMar, *Ruler of the Nations: Biblical Blueprints for Government* (Ft. Worth, Texas: Dominion Press, 1987), pp. 54-58, 93-95.

A nation requires boundaries (point three of the Biblical covenant).[10] How can we explain Christ's prophecy to the Pharisees concerning kingdom and nation? "Therefore I say to you, the kingdom of God will be taken from you and given to a nation bearing the fruits of it" (Matthew 21:43). Israel had been a nation, both ecclesiastical and civil. Then who or what is this new nation? Obviously, it has to be the Church International, not solely in the sense of the monopolistic institution that controls access to the sacraments, but also in the sense of the *ekklesia* — the "called out" gentiles of the nations. It is *a* nation, a collective unit. This cannot possibly mean a single regional church in history, for there have been many Christian regional churches in history. What does it mean?

We know that the Church International in its broadest sense is in the process of claiming its lawful inheritance of God's kingdom. We have also seen that the civil manifestation of a "nation" is a collective assembly with boundaries. How will this kingdom-manifesting process be revealed progressively in the civil realm, for which the institutional church is the only valid model? If the institutional church is to manifest its inherent, God-given position as an international organization, what about Christian civil governments? They too must become a collective noun: a nation of nations.

In principle the Church International exists now. It was established definitively at Pentecost. It develops progressively over time, through the spread of the gospel. When it split apart during the Protestant Reformation, so did European civil government; this led to the creation of European nation-states. Christian civil governments imitate the Church at any point in history. The Church International is to become an institutional reality in history; therefore, so is a civil nation of Christian nations.

When manifested in the future, the international nation of Christian nations will become a legally constituted entity, because all covenants are legal agreements. As a nation, it will possess geographical boundaries. What will be these lawful boundaries?

---

10. Gary North, *Inherit the Earth*, ch. 3.

The whole earth. In principle, the Church International has already inherited God's kingdom; in the future, probably the distant future, it will be co-extensive with the whole earth. So will the Christian civil order that models itself in terms of the covenantal unity of the Church International.

The people who began building the Tower of Babel had "one language" (Genesis 11:1). This should be translated "one *lip.*" This unified lip meant that they had a unified confession of faith, one common religion. What should be the covenantal basis of Christian institutional unity? The same thing: one lip, meaning a common Christian confession—in short, a common Christian *creed.* What will be the source of empowering this institutional unity? The Holy Spirit.

Those who deny the possibility of such unity in the future implicitly are denying the power of the Holy Spirit in history. They also are denying the covenantal unity of Christ's body, the Church. They are denying the power of the creeds, Christian baptism, and the Lord's Supper. Two groups today deny these Bible-revealed truths: anti-Christians and world-retreating Christians (humanists and pietists). Thus, we find that world-retreating Christians agree with power-seeking humanists on this crucial theological doctrine: that the power of God and His Church in history is "utopian"—nowhere in particular and nothing special. This is their common confession ("lip"). They deny that the kingdom of God can ever be manifested in history through the efforts of Holy Spirit-empowered Christians. With respect to the world-transforming power of the gospel of Jesus Christ, these people are in agreement: the power of Christ's gospel is a myth. They never again expect the Church to manifest the unity it displayed in the Church council of Acts 15. They view Church history as a decline from the days of Acts 15, a decline that only the physical return of Christ can reverse.

No Earthly "Divine Right"

In the sixteenth and seventeenth centuries, European kings and their apologists argued for what they called "the divine right of kings." The argument went something like this. "The king holds an office established by God. There is no earthly sovereign over the king. He answers only to God. God holds him accountable, but no other institution of government holds him accountable. The king, and *only* the king, possesses this unique authority directly under God."

In 1688, the Glorious Revolution swept James II from office and established the sovereignty of the British Parliament. Parliament immediately adopted a very similar view of its authority. No human institution could challenge the absolute sovereignty of Parliament. William Blackstone, in his legendary *Commentaries on the Laws of England* (1765), wrote concerning Parliament's sovereignty: "The power and jurisdiction of Parliament is so transcendent and absolute, that it cannot be confined, either for causes or persons, within any bounds. . . . It hath sovereign and uncontrollable authority in the making, confirming, enlarging, restraining, abrogating, repealing, reviving, and expounding of laws, concerning matters of all possible denominations, ecclesiastical or temporal, civil, military, maritime, or criminal: this being the place where that absolute despotic power, which must in all governments reside somewhere, is entrusted by the constitution of these kingdoms. . . . It can, in short, do everything that is not naturally impossible; and therefore some have not scrupled to call its power, by a figure rather too bold, the omnipotence of Parliament. True it is, that what the Parliament doth, no authority upon earth can undo."[11]

The American Revolution began a decade later: a Biblical reaction to such humanistic arrogance. Nevertheless, Parliament did not soon abandon its assertion of total authority, despite its steady loss of actual authority. As late as 1915, the distinguished British legal scholar (and defender of limited government) A. V. Dicey made this statement in the first chapter of his monumental work on Constitutional law: "The principle of Parliamentary sov-

---

11. Cited by A. V. Dicey, *Introduction to the Study of the Law of the Constitution* (8th ed.; Indianapolis, Indiana: Liberty Classics, [1915] 1982), pp. 4-5.

ereignty means neither more nor less than this, namely, that Parliament thus defined has, under the English constitution, the right to make or unmake any law whatever; and, further, that no person or body is recognized by the law of England as having a right to override or set aside the legislation of Parliament."[12]

The sovereignty of the nation is the modern substitute for the divine right of kings and legislatures. It was a doctrine asserted by the French revolutionaries in the "Declaration of the Rights of Man and Citizen" in 1789. Point three declares: "The source of all sovereignty resides essentially in the nation; no group, no individual may exercise authority not emanating from it."[13] Nationalism has since become a major ideology in the modern world. It lodges absolute sovereignty in the nation.

The danger with this is the danger of proclaiming absolute sovereignty for any human institution. When this is done, then men are tempted to overcome its supposedly final judgment through violence. Revolution, terrorism, and military conquest become both the justification and the means of replacing one absolute earthly sovereign with another. The doctrine of "divine right" leads to the doctrine of "might makes right."

The Biblical doctrine is opposed to all theories of divine right. God is absolutely sovereign, and all human sovereignties are delegated by Him. All human sovereignties are under God's law, and God's law is always administered by agencies — not by one single agency, but by *plural agencies*. There must always be a legal and institutional check and balance on every human agency. Furthermore, there *will* always be an institutional check: big bullies eventually encounter bigger bullies or an alliance of defenders. But for the sake of peace, there should be legal checks that invoke lawful, predictable, and legitimate restraints on unwarranted power. Checks and balances are basic to Christian liberty.

This is why the political conservative's rejection of interna-

---

12. *Ibid.*, pp. 3-4.
13. "Declaration of the Rights of Man and Citizen" (27 August 1789), in John Hall Stewart (ed.), *A Documentary History of the French Revolution* (New York: Macmillan, 1951), p. 114.

tional law and international justice is misguided, if this rejection
is based on permanent principle rather than temporary tactics. In
an era such as ours — an era of legal chaos and competing national
religions — nationalism is a legitimate check on the expansion of
humanist empires, but if conservatism's intellectual defense of
national sovereignty is made in terms of an *absolute and permanent*
national sovereignty, then the defender has adopted one more version of the divine rights doctrine: the divine right of autonomous
nations. Only Jesus Christ possesses divine rights, yet He graciously humbled Himself to be judged by a pagan imperial court
for the sake of the world.

All institutions are under God's law. God's laws are to be enforced institutionally. No one can legitimately claim divine rights,
a claim of locating a final, unitary, earthly court of appeal beyond
which there can be no earthly appeal.

International Theocracy

Some critics may complain that I am calling for international
theocracy. They are correct, for this international theocracy is exactly what the Bible requires. More than this: it is what the Bible
says already exists: God (*theos*) rules (*kratos*) internationally. God
now rules the whole universe. He created it; He governs it; He establishes laws for it; He judges it continually, and will judge it
finally; and He sustains it over time.

Every nation is as much under God's sovereign rule as every
individual is. The goal of the gospel is to subdue every soul, every
institution, and every nation under God, through the enabling
power of the Holy Spirit. What is true *definitively* — the absolute
sovereignty of God — is to be manifested *progressively* in history,
because it will be revealed *finally* at the day of judgment. Just as
every redeemed individual is told by God to conform himself to
the image of Christ, as perfect humanity (though not divinity), so
is every human institution, including every nation, to do the
same.

The vast majority of Christians believe that God holds every
person on earth responsible for confessing Christ as his Lord and

savior personally, and that he should then confess Christ as Lord and savior of his marriage, and confess Him as Lord and savior of his church. What is astounding is that Christians today also deny vehemently that anyone should confess Christ as Lord and savior of his nation, especially since Christ commanded the disciples to *disciple* the nations—not simply hearts, minds, souls, families, and local churches, but *nations* (Matthew 28:18-20). These world-retreating Christians implicitly affirm that Satan and his covenanted disciples have the power throughout history (or at least during the so-called "Church Age") to exercise covenantal control of every civil government. Civil government is supposedly non-confessional, meaning non-Christian. Yet many Christians then turn around and affirm confidently that *there is no neutrality*, meaning that every institution is in principle and in fact implicitly or explicitly confessional. They are intellectually schizophrenic.[14]

Christians tell people about the salvation Christ offers to them, and they warn the listener: "No decision is still a decision: the refusal to make a decision *for* Christ is a decision *against* Christ." This argument is correct. Question: Why do Christians refuse to see that this argument also applies to institutions? If a nation does not explicitly confess Christ, it has implicitly confessed Satan. "No confession" is still a confession: a confession for Satan.

Younger schoolchildren in the United States stand before the American flag, place their right hands over their hearts, and confess an oath of loyalty to the nation, the pledge of allegiance to the flag. It was first used at the National School Celebration in 1892, where President Benjamin Harrison officiated. In 1923 and 1924, the American Legion, an association of former military men, expanded its wording. In 1942, Congress officially added it to its formal rules regarding the use of the American flag.[15] It was de-

---

14. Gary North, "The Intellectual Schizophrenia of the New Christian Right," *Christianity and Civilization*, 1 (1982). This journal was published by Geneva Ministries, Tyler, Texas.

15. *The World Book Encyclopedia* (Chicago: World Book, Inc., 1986), Vol. 15, p. 508.

signed for use in humanistic government school classrooms; today, Christian day schools are more likely to require it than the
public schools are. The document is ignored by most college-level
U.S. history textbooks and is not reproduced in most collections
of U.S. historical documents. The children take a daily oath:

> I pledge allegiance to the flag of the United States of America
> and to the Republic for which it stands, one Nation under God, in-
> divisible, with liberty and justice for all.

The phrase "under God" was added in 1954, and is legally op-
tional, though virtually all students repeat it. Jehovah's Witnesses
are unique in refusing to allow their children to take this oath.

Someday, men will implicitly make a similar pledge of
allegiance: "All nations, under Christ, with liberty and justice for
all." The only way to attain liberty and justice is under God's covenant, through Christ's death and resurrection, and by means of
the empowering of the Holy Spirit. If we want liberty and justice
for all mankind, then we must proclaim the necessity of all people
to confess their subordination to God.

Secession

Local church congregations and regional church associations
are allowed by God under tyrannical circumstances to leave the
Church International: here is *the* fundamental doctrine of the
Protestant Reformation. The question then arises: Is the same
God-given right of secession also in principle true for covenanted
nations and covenanted regions that make up a nation? The civil
government bears the sword. If there are continual secessions,
from local counties to nation-states leaving a Christian confederation, how can God's law be enforced in a hierarchical manner?

The case of the tribe of Benjamin is an example of the necessity of the covenanted civil government's legal right to impose
sanctions against regional civil governments that violate Biblical
law. Judges 19-20 describes the events. Men of the city of Gibeah
imitated Sodom, and killed a Levite's concubine. He sent for the
tribes to defend his righteous cause. The tribe of Benjamin de-

fended Gibeah. The other tribes attacked Benjamin, under God's repeated authorization (Judges 20:18, 23, 28), and the war led to the defeat of Benjamin and the destruction of all but 600 men in the tribe.

Nevertheless, this right of law enforcement by the central government is not absolute. In cases of extreme tyranny, God releases the local civil government from its vow of obedience. God's covenants among men are always conditional. Christians seek liberty under God by establishing covenants, but only *conditional* covenants: there must be no continuing major violation of Biblical principle by central authorities. God will deliver righteous regions or nations from central tyranny by raising up local civil magistrates to resist the central civil government. God prohibited Judah's King Rehoboam from attacking the army of Israel after the secession of the ten tribes of Israel under Jeroboam.

> And when Rehoboam came to Jerusalem, he assembled all the house of Judah with the tribe of Benjamin, one hundred and eighty thousand chosen men who were warriors, to fight against the house of Israel, that he might restore the kingdom of Rehoboam the son of Solomon. But the word of God came to Shemaiah the man of God, saying, "Speak to Rehoboam the son of Solomon, king of Judah, to all the house of Judah and Benjamin, and to the rest of the people, saying, 'Thus says the LORD: "You shall not go up nor fight against your brethren the children of Israel. Let every man return to his house, for this thing is from Me."' " Therefore they obeyed the word of the LORD, and turned back, according to the word of the LORD (1 Kings 12:21-24).

Calvin recognized this principle of the right of local resistance by legitimate local magistrates.[16] This was the application to civil covenant of the same principle of officer-led secession that the Reformation announced with respect to the church covenant.

We need a Christian federation upward, just as we need a

---

16. John Calvin, *Institutes of the Christian Religion* (1559), Book IV, Chapter 20. See also Michael Gilstrap, "John Calvin's Theology of Resistance," *Christianity and Civilization*, 2 (1983).

Christian federation downward. Covenant law is binding, and local governments must respect the decisions of the authorized appeals court of the civil government. The central government does have the power of the sword, and it is exercised within geographical boundaries. Local governments, however, do have the legal right to specify their original terms of entering into the covenant. We should not expect Christian nations to enter into covenant with one another without qualifications. It will take centuries of experience to increase mutual trust. Also, local civil governments will retain the lion's share of tax revenues, and also retain local military units. The local militia, not state, national, or international armies, will be the fundamental military unit. In this sense, modern nationalism is both temporary and perverse. We need to return to something closer to medieval feudalism: international in scope, yet primarily local in taxation and authority.

The creation of a bottom-up international Christian confederation will take time, probably centuries. Today, there are few explicitly Christian nations, and the United States is no longer officially one of them, although it still is covenantally bound by the terms of its original Christian confession, and therefore is regarded by God as being in rebellion against the inescapable terms of His covenant. The United States is suffering from national apostasy, as are all of the nations of Europe. Christian internationalism is many decades if not centuries down the road.

I am sketching what the Biblical model for international relations might look like *after a worldwide Christian revival*. A blueprint alone is not the answer to today's immediate problems; a blueprint is not even a house site, let alone a construction crew. Today, Christians should do what we can to resist every attempt of the humanists to build their pagan one-world order. But we also need to know where God says that we ought to be headed. We need to recognize humanism's perverse imitations of Biblically valid arrangements. Just because humanism's imitation is perverse, we should not conclude that the Bible's standard is also perverse. When it comes to fighting the humanists' one-world order, let us never forget: "You can't beat something with nothing."

Yeast expands and raises the loaf. God's Spiritual yeast is supposed to raise the world's cultural standards. "Another parable He spoke to them: 'The kingdom of heaven is like leaven, which a woman took and hid in three measures of meal till it was all leavened' " (Matthew 13:33). The principle of God's holy leaven applies to international relations, just as it applies everywhere else. God's holy leaven is to replace Satan's unholy leaven. We cannot replace something evil with nothing good.

The Appeals Court System

To protect the rights of local civil government, a bottom-up appeals court system must be established. The combined tax burden of all levels of civil government should not equal the tithe of 10 percent of net income. The largest share must be taken by local civil government. Taxes by higher levels should be imposed on the lower governments, but not on citizens directly. By violating this principle of local sovereignty, civil government is centralized, as it was in Samuel's day (1 Samuel 8). He described this process as a curse, but the Israelites did not believe him. Neither does modern man.

Lower levels of civil governments must subject themselves to taxation by higher levels in exactly the same way that citizens consent to being taxed today. They must give up some degree of their sovereignty. We already recognize the legitimacy of this principle with respect to local and regional civil government. Voluntary submission to higher authority is basic to Biblical hierarchy. The citizen submits to local government, and local governments submit to higher ones. That the local governments should have the right to elect members of at least one of the legislative houses, as the U.S. Constitution provided prior to the Seventeenth Amendment (1913), is reasonable: a check on popular sovereignty. It was not random that the Sixteenth Amendment, which authorized the direct taxation of personal income by the national government, was also authorized by the voters in 1913. (Actually, the Sixteenth Amendment was not legally ratified, but the Federal government announced that it was, and this fraud has never been challenged in the courts.)[17]

What is crucial for the preservation of liberty, in both church government and civil government, is the appeals court nature of the hierarchy. The top-down bureaucratic centralization of empire must be avoided, except in wartime. A military chain of command is valid only during wartime, where open hostilities have been declared, and where fixed military objectives are agreed upon by the participants. When peace is declared, central government shrinks, the generals and admirals are forcibly retired, and central taxes are reduced.

A crucial safeguard of liberty is the proper structuring of the tax system. The higher levels of civil government must never be allowed to tax individuals. They must tax only lower levels. The humanists will seek to exploit any other arrangement at the expense of personal liberty. They are self-conscious about this. For example, consider the proposal set forth by Lionel Curtis, a highly influential member of the Round Table Group of Britain, an organization dedicated to establishing a humanistic one-world State with Britain and the English-speaking nations as the central core. This group launched the Council on Foreign Relations in 1919. Curtis wrote a suggestively titled three-volume work, *Civitas Dei* (city of God) in 1934-37, using Augustine's title. A summary of the book appeared in 1938, *The Commonwealth of God*. The theological motivation is clear.

The book recommended the destruction of the League of Nations. In its place, a new league should be formed, but without any power. A parallel effort should be started to create an international commonwealth along the lines of the United States in 1788. Member nations would yield sovereignty to it. The key to understanding the power of this proposed organization was that the central organization would operate directly on individuals, and not indirectly through the member nations. He recognized that a

---

17. Bill Benson and M. J. Beckman, *The Law That Never Was*, 2 vols. (Box 550, South Holland, Illinois: Constitutional Research Associates, 1985, 1987); Burton Limme, *The Constitution's Income Tax Was Not Ratified* (Washington, D.C.: American Liberty Information Society, 1985).

huge propaganda effort would be necessary to achieve this goal. Professor Carroll Quigley comments: "That the chief obstacle to this union was to be found in men's minds was perfectly clear to Curtis. To overcome this obstacle, he put his faith in propaganda, and the chief instruments of that propaganda, he said, must be the churches and the universities."[18] The main book promoting this vision was Clarence Streit's *Union Now* (1939), a former Rhodes Scholar.

My vision is similar, yet radically different. To stifle all plans at creating a humanist world government, we need to starve the beast. We need to limit its sovereignty. The answer to the sovereignty of a central world empire is not a system of autonomous nations that face the onslaught of a concerted Communist empire; the answer is a bottom-up covenanted federation that is openly Christian in its public confession, but which does not allow the higher levels of civil government to tax people directly.

The other safeguard against the tyranny of empire is the right of secession. This principle is not honored in our era of centralized nationalism, but Jeroboam's example is valid. While secession is a disrupting event, to be avoided as much as ecclesiastical schism, unjustified tyrannical taxation is also disrupting, as Rehoboam's legacy indicates. The right of lower magistrates to rebel against higher magistrates is basic to Christian liberty.[19] The top-down bureaucratic hierarchy, except during a formally declared shooting war, is satanic.

Humanist Internationalism

In international relations, the humanists' version of God's universal kingdom is either the creation of an empire or else the creation of some sort of an alliance system that has many of the markings of empire. We sometimes call this internationalism. Humanism's internationalism is based theoretically on the shared

---

18. Carroll Quigley, *The Anglo-American Establishment* (New York: Books in Focus, 1981), p. 283. The manuscript was finished in 1949, but was not published in the author's lifetime.

19. John Calvin, *Institutes of the Christian Religion*, Book IV, Chapter 20.

humanity of fallen mankind, the "family of man," meaning *the family of Cain*. The humanist internationalists[20] take what is a legitimate quest for Christians—the establishment of international peace through adherence to Biblical law internationally—and pervert it. They seek to establish international peace through adherence to humanistic law, either through economic alliances ("deals") or through conquest (empire). It was not an accident that the League of Nations (1920-1946) called its establishing document a Covenant.[21]

A good statement of the humanist position appears in the *Humanist Manifesto II* (1973): "Twelfth: We deplore the division of humankind on nationalistic grounds. We have reached a turning point in human history where the best option is to *transcend the limits of national sovereignty* and to move toward the building of a world community in which all sectors of the human family can participate. Thus we look to the development of a system of world law and a world order based upon transnational federal government. . . . We thus reaffirm a commitment to the building of world community, at the same time recognizing that this commits us to some hard choices."[22]

Nelson Rockefeller, when he was Governor of New York State and still hoping to become the President of the United States, summarized this humanist faith in humanism's one-world order. First, he argued that the United States had been founded "upon our dedicated faith in the brotherhood of all mankind."[23] Then he called Americans to pursue the creation of a world humanist community in the name of the founding fathers—precisely what they had warned against:

---

20. I have in mind here members of the Trilateral Commission.

21. "The Covenant of the League of Nations," reprinted in Inis L. Claude, Jr., *Swords Into Plowshares: The Problems and Progress of International Organization* (2nd ed.; New York: Random House, 1959), Appendix I.

22. *Humanist Manifestos I and II* (Buffalo, New York: Prometheus Books, 1973), p. 21. Emphasis in the original.

23. Nelson A. Rockefeller, *Unity, Freedom & Peace: A Blueprint for Tomorrow* (New York: Random House, 1968), p. 147.

Yet this, in a real sense, could never be enough. No matter how this nation strove to isolate itself in past generations, it could never suppress or deny an impulse toward the world. In one age, this impulse expressed itself through missionaries; in another age, through philanthropy, medical care, deeds of charity; and, most recently, through massive international aid and assistance.

There is a reason why this impulse has asserted itself. Our Founding Fathers, obviously, built a home for one nation. Yet the idea to which they and this nation were committed—the idea of human freedom—was, is and can *only* be universal.

We are bound as a people, in the deepest sense, to live by this commitment with a boldness, a confidence, and a clarity of vision matching those who led us to national life.[24]

He recognized the transition: from Christian internationalism (missions) to humanitarian internationalism (philanthropy) to statist internationalism (government-to-government foreign aid programs) to the humanist one-world State. The problem, of course, is the need for some sort of shared religious principles: "There must be shared values and goals—a comparable comprehension of the nature of man and his place in the universe, specifically with reference to freedom, justice, opportunity, dignity and the rule of law."[25] Question: The rule of *whose* law, God's or self-proclaimed autonomous man's?

The humanists expect a new human consciousness to appear in our era, thus making possible the creation of a new global community. Zbigniew Brzezinski, who served as President Carter's head of the National Security Council, speaks of this development in terms of the New Age slogan, "Toward a Planetary Consciousness." He assured us in 1970 that "it would be wrong to conclude that fragmentation and chaos are the dominant realities of our time. A global human conscience is for the first time beginning to manifest itself. This conscience is a natural extension of the long process of widening man's personal horizons. In the course of time, man's self-identification expanded from his family

---

24. *Ibid.*, pp. 147-48.
25. *Ibid.*, p. 135.

to his village, to his tribe, to his region, to his nation; more recently it spread to his continent. . . ."[26] The creed of unified humanity is to serve as the religious foundation of a humanist one-world order. We must do what we can, he says, to bring Communist nations into this new order.[27] It is the United States' responsibility to work toward this new global community, he says, or else we could get chaos.[28] The key is economics, not faith: "a gradual shaping of a community of the developed nations would be a realistic expression of our emerging global consciousness. . . ."[29]

So there is an emerging world consciousness. Why, then, did the Soviet Union invade Afghanistan in late 1979?

The Tower of Babel

We see in the story of the Tower of Babel another attempt by rebellious mankind to build himself a kingdom without the Creator God of the Bible. This same impulse had been going on since the days of Cain. I am indebted to James Jordan for many of the following insights.

"And it came to pass, as they journeyed from the east [literally, eastward], that they found a plain in the land of Shinar, and they dwelt there" (Genesis 11:2). Just as Cain moved away from God by moving east (Genesis 4:16), so this "eastward" movement indicates movement away from God. This group of people was under the leadership of Nimrod, son of Cush, son of Ham (Genesis 10:6-12). According to these verses, Nimrod founded both Babylon and Nineveh (Assyria), the two great empires that oppressed Israel later in history and that sum up anti-God statism in the Prophets and in the Book of Revelation.

These men knew that their Tower—probably some kind of stepped pyramid, a symbolic "holy mountain" and "holy ladder" to God—would not physically reach into heaven. They were not

---

26. Zbigniew Brzezinski, *Between Two Ages: America's Role in the Technotronic Era* (New York: Viking, 1970), p. 58.
27. *Ibid.*, p. 302.
28. *Ibid.*, pp. 307-8.
29. *Ibid.*, p. 308.

fools. The stairway to heaven was not physical; it was *metaphysical*. It had to do with questions of metaphysics: the underlying nature of the universe. And what the Tower symbolized was that *man is the connection between heaven and earth*. The Tower would serve as a religious center that would enable them, as they thought, to storm the gates of heaven and seize the Tree of Life, from which men were excluded (Genesis 3:24). This is the goal of every form of pagan works-religion, and it was their goal as well. The actual technique they used was magic. (Occultism and magic underlay the Nazi ideal, too.)[30]

We need to notice also that they wanted to make themselves a name. They did not want to be given a name by God, or wear His name. They wanted to make a name for themselves, to glorify themselves. They wanted to define themselves by themselves in terms of themselves. God told Moses that His name is "I am who I am" (Exodus 3:14). The people of the Tower wanted to announce, "We are who we are." They wanted to be God.

Magic proclaims, "As above, so below." Man tries to manipulate the creation and even God. Magic affirms a *continuity of being*. Man and God are both part of the same chain of being.[31] Therefore, mankind seeks unity. As Rushdoony says, if man is god, then this godhead must be unified—unified not just ethically, but metaphysically, at the core of humanity's being.[32] In principle, man and God are one, this humanistic theology teaches.

This unity of God and man is a religious presupposition of most paganism. Historically, we call this *monism*. The underlying reality of man's unity must become a political, historical reality. Without this political unity, mankind is not fully developed, meaning fully evolved. Thus, humanism's internationalism is

---

30. Nicholas Goodrick-Clarke, *The Occult Roots of Nazism: The Ariosophists of Austria and Germany, 1890-1935* (Wellingtonborough, Northamptonshire: Aquarian Press, 1985).

31. Ray R. Sutton, *That You May Prosper: Dominion By Covenant* (Tyler, Texas: Institute for Christian Economics, 1987), pp. 36-39.

32. R. J. Rushdoony, *This Independent Republic: Studies in the Nature and Meaning of American History* (Fairfax, Virginia: Thoburn Press, [1964] 1978), p. 142.

part of a philosophical tradition: the assertion that man's institutions must reflect a unity of being with the true heavenly reality—or, what amounts to the same thing—to deny any heavenly reality over mankind, leaving man to create the true reality on earth.

Such a view is totally opposed to the Biblical view, which asserts that mankind as a species is a creature—totally distinct from God the Creator—and that men are divided ethically and covenantally, a division that extends beyond the grave into eternity. It is covenantal unity—*unity of confession and belief*—that is primary, not political unity or "the oneness of man" as a species.

What was God's response to this new theology? "But the LORD came down to see the city and the tower which the sons of men had built. And the LORD said, 'Indeed the people are one and they all have one language [lip, confession, ideology], and this is what they begin to do; now nothing that they propose to do will be withheld from them. Come, let Us go down there and confuse their language [lip, confession, ideology], that they may not understand one another's speech [lip, confession, ideology]'" (Genesis 11:5-7).

It is surprising to hear God say that because the people are unified, "nothing that they propose to do will be withheld from them." In one sense, we know that God can always stop men from doing anything; but the language used here points to the fact that in terms of the economy God has established in the world, there is strength in unity. God does not want the wicked to rule the world, so He moves to destroy their unity.

It is important to see that it was not a simple unity of language that gave these men power. Rather, they all thought the same way. They had a *common ideology*, a *common religious faith*. Without this anti-God unity, they could not have cooperated. In order to shatter this unity, God did not simply divide their languages. First and foremost, He shattered their ideologies.

What the story of the Tower of Babel tells us is that Biblical religion faced a single rival, anti-God religion. (We are not told that there were faithful covenant people in that rebellious society, but we must presume that there were, for God never allows His church to be completely snuffed out in history, even if only one man and two of his three sons alone remain faithful in the whole world.) At the Tower of Babel, God acted to diversify paganism.

All the heathen religions in the world have the same basic ideas, but each is slightly different from the rest. One group worships Thor and his kin, another Zeus and his family, another Jupiter and his cohorts. One nation goes for Baal, another for Chemosh, another for Molech, and another for Amon-Ra. One group of revolutionary socialists follows Marx-and-Lenin, another follows Marx-and-Mao, another Marx-and-Castro, and another Marx-and-Ho Chi Minh. Still others follow Adolf Hitler. Each pagan nation has its own god, and wars are fought over them.

If it seems strange that God Himself would act to create these different pagan religions, we have to remember that according to Romans 1:18-32, God punishes sin by giving people over to it. Idolatry is destructive to human life, and if men rebel against God, He will give them over to worse and worse forms of idolatry, until either they repent or are destroyed. Man's punishment fits his crime.

God has established Christianity to create a true unity of confession (lip) among all nations and peoples, but this unity will not destroy the diversity of languages. Rather, each nation and language will praise Him in its own tongue (Revelation 7:9). Thus, the scattering of languages at the Tower of Babel was not simply a curse on the covenantally unfaithful. It divided men, which reduced their economic cooperation and productivity (curse), yet it also reduced their political and religious cooperation in creating a one-State world (blessing).[33] Their scattering was the multiplication of pagan religions that showed God's judgment against the Tower-builders. Even here, however, the fact that *God will never permit non-Christians to form a world coalition again* is a blessing to Christians. No matter how hard they try, the pagan dream of a secular "united nations" is doomed to failure.

---

33. Gary North, *The Dominion Covenant: Genesis* (2nd ed.; Tyler, Texas: Institute for Christian Economics, 1987), ch. 10: "Scarcity: Curse and Blessing."

It is true Biblical faith that is destined to triumph in history. We see this new unity of confession definitively manifested at Pentecost, when Jewish residents in the gentile nations were converted to Christ through hearing the common message of salvation in their own languages: ". . . everyone heard them speak in his own language" (Acts 2:6b). Then the gospel went out to every nation—a gospel to heal the nations.

Warring Principles

The principle of empire is always at war with the principle of nationhood. Empires are power States that impose centralized unity over regional, linguistic, and religious civil governments. Those who claim to represent the ultimate sovereign—Party, Leader, or People—seek to expand this sovereign's domain.

The impulse toward unification of the nations has been with mankind at least since the Tower of Babel. Mankind is seen as the true god of history, and men usually want their gods to display unity comparable to their authority. Thus, we find a quest for the total statist order, which ultimately must be an international order. Writes Rushdoony: "The first and basic requirement of a theology is the unity of every godhead. A divided or disunited god, or a schizoid god, is useless to man and to himself. The deity, in order to exercise the control which is required of him, and in order to be an assured source of certainty, must be united; he must be one god. When humanity and a human order takes on the role of a god, the same basic requirement must prevail. The unity of the godhead is a theological necessity. Accordingly, for the religion of humanity, as represented in the United Nations, the unity of mankind, without discrimination or subordination, is a necessity. The central sin becomes, not rebellion against God and His law, but everything that hinders the union and peace of the new god, humanity."[34]

Yet this official lack of discrimination and lack of subordina-

---

34. R. J. Rushdoony, "The United Nations: A Religious Dream," in *Politics of Guilt and Pity* (Fairfax, Virginia: Thoburn Press, [1970] 1978), p. 186.

tion is a myth. There is no escape from covenantal hierarchy. As Rushdoony pointed out in a 1965 essay on the U.N.: "While talking of equality, the U.N. is the most elitist of organizations. The General Assembly has no power but can only recommend action. The Security Council is vested with the actual power, while the Court executes its legal will."[35] Since then, as the power of the U.N. has slowly shifted to the General Assembly, the "superpowers" of the U.S. and U.S.S.R. have steadily abandoned interest in the U.N. As it has become more consistent with its ideology of equality, it has lost power.

Rushdoony argues that all the basic features of the godhead are invested in the modern centralized State: omnipotence (all powerful), omniscience (all-knowing), and transcendence (incomprehensibility by man).[36] Thus, we see the ancient impulse of man in its modern garb: the quest for world government as a manifestation of the sovereignty of man. "The United Nations is the humanistic Mount Olympus and Tower of Babel, a dream of reason whereby man becomes his own god and totally governs the earth and his destiny. The developing omnipotence of the state and of the world order of states can only be undercut as men submit to the total sovereignty of God."[37]

When man attempts to imitate God, he must also establish his covenant. This covenant necessarily involves hierarchy. The doctrine of representation cannot be avoided; it can only be transferred. Men act "in the name of the People," and the more they praise the infallibility of the People, the more the centralized State takes liberty away from individuals and groups within society. The *deification of man* leads to the worship of power and therefore to the *deification of the State* as the highest concentration of human power.

Empire is Satan's primary organizational principle. It is his attempt to control events in history. He is not God. He is therefore

---

35. Rushdoony, "The United Nations," in *The Nature of the American System* (Fairfax, Virginia: Thoburn Press, [1965] 1978), p. 121n.

36. *Politics of Guilt and Pity*, pp. 194-99.

37. *Ibid.*, p. 194.

not all-powerful, all-seeing, and all-knowing. He must rule his followers indirectly, unlike God who is totally sovereign over history. Satan must rule through a top-down chain of command. He needs bureaucracy in order to maintain his personal control, in contrast to Christianity's decentralized, bottom-up appeals court system.[38] Satan's need for bureaucracy manifests itself whenever Satan attempts to develop his alternative to a Biblically valid Christian internationalism that manifests God's kingdom.

These two organizational principles are at war throughout history: Satan's empire and Christ's kingdom. Satan would prefer to centralize power at the top of the hierarchy, while Christ, as absolute Sovereign, can safely allow decentralized power in the hands of individuals. Christ does not fear a "palace revolt"; Satan does. Satan was the first revolutionary, and his empires are always threatened by revolution from below. He will not allow secession in history by his subordinates; Christ does allow it, and did allow it in the garden of Eden. Secession has a price, but it is basic to the preservation of freedom. The disappearance of the doctrine of the legal right of political secession marks the advent of tyranny in our age. That modern man cannot mentally imagine a world that would honor this fundamental political right testifies to the success of the theology of political centralization in modern times.

A Symbol of Unity

Holy Communion is not simply a symbol of unity for the church of Jesus Christ; it is a covenantal reality. It is as real as a prayer to God. Prayers are symbolic representations of man's subordination to God. Prayers are also events that do invoke the response of a real God in history. Thus, when Christians take communion, they testify to the existence of a one-world Christian order, and they also empower themselves to participate in the creation of this one-world Christian order.

The United Nations was designed to fulfill a similar purpose for the humanist internationalists. It has failed in this purpose,

---

38. Ray R. Sutton, *That You May Prosper, op. cit.*, pp. 50-51.

but in the late 1950's, this was not acknowledged by humanist internationalists. The Rockefeller Panel on foreign policy stated in 1959: "The UN stands, finally, as a symbol of the world order that will one day be built. The United States has need of symbols as well as power in its foreign policy."[39]

Christians have their symbols of international unity: the sacraments. They have united Christians from the beginning. Humanists have shifting symbols of their supposed unity. The goal of both groups is the building of a one-world order. The key question is: *Whose?*

Unfortunately, most Christians have neglected the Lord's Supper, and have refused even to think about its implications as a symbol and covenantal means of establishing a one-world Christian order. They do not take Holy Communion very seriously. After all, churches seldom publicly excommunicate people (separate them from Holy Communion). Therefore, they do not take Christian civilization seriously. They reject such an ideal of Christian civilization as utterly utopian. They believe in their hearts that the squabbling denominations that we have seen so far in this history of Christianity are inevitable, and therefore an international Christian community of confederated churches and nations is impossible. (In other words, Christians therefore implicitly recognize that the institutional church serves as the model for Christian international relations.) They also reject the humanist version of internationalism as both utopian and evil. They are correct about the impossibility of the creation of a humanist one-State world; they are incorrect about the impossibility of an international Christian civilization marked by international covenants, both ecclesiastical and civil.

There are a few humanists who recognize that the goal of creating a one-State world is a fantasy. They are called isolationists. They no longer have much influence in humanist intellectual circles.[40]

---

39. *Prospect for America: The Rockefeller Panel Reports* (Garden City, New York: Doubleday, 1961), p. 35.

40. Justus D. Doenecke, *Not to the Swift: The Old Isolationists In the Cold War Era* (Lewisburg, Pennsylvania: Bucknell University Press, 1979).

Humanist Isolationism

Not every God-hater is a defender of empire. Some are defenders of anarchy. There have been far fewer articulate defenders of isolationism in our day than empire-defenders. Nevertheless, we need to recognize this strand of human thought.

The anarchist denies that there can be any kind of legitimate political unity. All civil government is evil. All civil government is tyrannical. Every attempt by civil government to keep men from doing what they want to do is evil.[41] Each man is a god. No one can tell these gods what to do. They do what is right in their own eyes.

In foreign affairs, this anarchist impulse can be seen in what is known as the isolationist movement. No nation is to get involved in the affairs of any other nation. All men are islands, and all nations are islands. Thus, isolationists reject internationalism, both Christian and humanistic, but always in the name of the autonomy of man.

The best example of an isolationist in the Bible is Jonah in his rebellion. God told him to go to Nineveh to preach the gospel. Jonah headed in the opposite direction. He had no intention of giving the people of Nineveh the opportunity to repent. It was none of his business. He would not serve as God's holy ambassador to preach to pagans. He would not go to the people or the king of Nineveh. He would sail away, far from his God-given responsibilities. We know the results of this attitude. Irresponsible covenant people become food for sea monsters.

It could be argued that Jonah was not a representative of the state of Israel. This was true, but he was a representative of God's kingdom. He preached the need for repentance to the king of a rival nation. Paul did the same thing on several occasions. He brought the Word of God to pagan civil magistrates. He was bringing them under the message God sends to all rival kingdoms: repent or be destroyed in history. The gospel speaks to civil governments as well as to individual souls.

---

41. Murray N. Rothbard, *For a New Liberty: The Libertarian Manifesto* (rev. ed.; New York: Collier, 1978).

Consider what Paul was doing. He was going through the Roman Empire preaching the kingdom of God. The Jews were correct in charging the disciples with preaching another King, Jesus. That is exactly what they were doing. And in the end, pagan Rome fell to Christianity. The triumph of Christianity did mark the end of the pagan Roman Empire. Christ triumphed over Caesar in history through His people.[42]

Was Paul an isolationist? Hardly. He was an ambassador of *Christ's international world order.* He warned his listeners of the judgment to come. Christ is King of kings and Lord of lords. This is the message of God's internationalism. This message repels humanist internationalists as much as it repels humanist isolationists. It means that God will destroy their pretensions of autonomy.

What the isolationist does not fully understand is that there is a war on. This war is a war between Christ's kingdom and the kingdom of Satan. Christ's kingdom is revealed in earthly kingdoms, and so is Satan's kingdom. There can be no permanent peace treaty between these two kingdoms. Thus, there can be no permanent peace treaty between the national representatives of the rival kingdoms. There can only be temporary cease-fire agreements concerning certain aspects of the perpetual conflict (Chapter Four). The quest for permanent peace treaties is legitimate, but only between nations that are official, covenanted representatives of Christ's kingdom. The quest for permanent peace on any other basis is an illusion. Such a peace treaty is either a disguised attack on the pagan co-signer or a disguised surrender to the pagan co-signer. There is no third possibility. There is no neutrality in history, and there is no peace until the final judgment.

There can be no perfect peace in history because sin always burdens mankind this side of the final judgment. Nevertheless, there can and will be progressive peace in history as the gospel reduces the rule of sin in history (Isaiah 32; Jeremiah 32), and as God's covenantal blessings pour out on mankind (Deuteronomy 28:1-14). I discuss this in Chapter Five.

---

42. Ethelbert Stauffer, *Christ and the Caesars* (Philadelphia: Westminster Press, 1955).

Humanist nationalism is a kind of halfway house between radical anarchism and radical internationalism. Christians know that the nation is real. Humanistic nationalism asserts that *only* the nation is real. Revolutionary nationalism is the political legacy of Rousseau and the French Revolution.[43] It spread across Europe in response to the French Revolution (1789-1795) and Napoleon (1798-1815).

The Biblical answer to humanist internationalism, humanist isolationism, and humanist nationalism is *Biblical covenantalism*. The covenant is primary. Every institution must be reconstructed in terms of the Biblical covenant. This includes international relations.

Summary

The second point in the Biblical covenant's structure is hierarchy. Hierarchy is an inescapable concept. Humanism's unattainable ideal for internationalism is a top-down centralized bureaucracy. Christianity's internationalism will be a bottom-up decentralized republic.

In contrast to humanism's internationalism is humanism's isolationism. Humanism's isolationism is in principle anarchistic: no civil government at all. Every civil covenant is evil. All distant peoples are outside my responsibility, and I am outside theirs.

But in church communion, all Christians are together in the presence of God in the very throne room of heaven. In principle we are united. Jesus prayed: "I do not pray for these alone, but also for those who will believe in Me through their word; that they all may be one, as You, Father, are in Me, and I in You; *that they also may be one in Us*, that the world may believe that You sent Me. And the glory which You gave Me I have given them, that *they may be one just as We are one*" (John 17:20-22; emphasis added). This unity is eventually to be manifested in the rule of God's law across the face of the earth: primarily self-government under law, but never with a single agency of government as an absolutely final

---

43. James Billington, *Fire in the Minds of Men: Origins of the Revolutionary Faith* (New York: Basic Books, 1980), chaps. 6, 12.

court of appeal. We need plural civil governments under God's law: township, county, city, state, nation, and international order.

The idea of Christian civilization is valid. The idea of any other kind of civilization is invalid. It is God's civilization or man's; there is no middle ground in principle. God definitely desires for redeemed humanity to form a "one-world Christian order"—but never a one-*State* order. This one-world Christian order is not based on might or power, but on the Spirit of God: "This is the word of the LORD to Zerubbabel: 'Not by might nor by power, but by My Spirit,' says the LORD of hosts" (Zechariah 4:6). The Christian idea of a one-world order is not statist, but spiritual. A Christian one-world order can be brought into existence only by the outpouring of the Holy Spirit. Those who deny that such an outpouring will ever come in history therefore reject the idea of a one-world Christian order, or else they predict its creation only after Jesus Christ has physically returned to earth during the millennium, when He sets up a top-down international bureaucracy.

Christopher Dawson gives us a picture of international Christian community when he writes concerning the Middle Ages: "For a thousand years Christian Europe has existed as a true supernatural society—a society that was intensely conscious of its community of culture in spite of the continual wars and internal divisions that made up its history. . . . Today this is no longer so. Europe has lost her unity and the consciousness of the spiritual mission. There is no longer any clear line of division between Christian and non-Christian peoples, and with the disappearance of her Christian consciousness, Europe has begun to doubt her own existence."[44]

What Dawson is getting at is that in a Christian world there are many nations, many cultures, many languages, and many governments—but all share a common bond of faith and cooperation. There is a true unity, but it is not a unity at the level of the

---

44. Christopher Dawson, *The Judgment of the Nations* (New York: Sheed and Ward, 1942), p. 73.

State, but a unity in the church and in the faith. The Middle Ages, in spite of its problems, had such a unity. That unity continued down to the modern era, but with the rise of neo-paganism (secular humanism), that unity is being shattered, for as we have seen, God will not permit pagans to unite.

Nevertheless, pagans desperately want to unite. Some want to unite under a monolithic empire. The means of unity is military conquest. Their Western counterparts want to unite on any basis short of military conquest. Anything is acceptable, short of war. "The international community thus conceived ought to include any state that does not insist on imposing its way of life on others. Any Communist state that is prepared to assume the responsibilities and self-restraints of international life can be an acceptable and constructive member of that group."[45] Murder and repression inside national boundaries must be no barrier to the creation of the humanist New World Order! In short, ethics is irrelevant; mankind's quest for mankind's metaphysical unity through international political covenants is primary. Christianity denies such a position.

In summary:

1. God will visibly exercise dominion in the history of nations.
2. God is a Trinity: one and many.
3. The world reflects this: unity and diversity.
4. Mankind is unified, yet diverse.
5. There is a family of man: disinherited sons.
6. Salvation is by covenantal adoption.
7. There is a legitimate quest for spiritual unity among Christians.
8. We are to work toward a one-world Christian order.
9. Our institutions should reflect Christ's ethically new humanity.
10. Christ has established His New World Order.
11. It involves every aspect of life.
12. It is a decentralized, bottom-up system.
13. Satan's kingdom is a centralized, top-down bureaucracy.

---

45. *Prospect for America*, p. 24.

14. Satan's international organization is empire.

15. Christian internationalism is legitimate.

16. Christian nationhood is by covenant, not blood.

17. So is Christian internationalism.

18. Humanism denies covenantalism based on the Bible and Christian confession.

19. Biblical citizenship is by profession of faith, not birth, for the Jubilee Year was abolished by Christ.

20. International disputes should be settled by Biblical law.

21. Christ transferred His kingdom from the Jews to a new nation.

22. The boundaries of the "new nation" of Matthew 21:43 encompass the whole world.

23. Christians are to inherit the earth.

24. There is no "divine right": all men are under civil governmental authority.

25. No single institution has legitimate final appeal.

26. There should be a Christian international check and balance system.

27. All human institutions are under God's authority, law, and judgment.

28. We need an international theocracy: God (*theos*) rules (*kratos*).

29. God is progressively to be revealed in history as the ruler of this world in every area of life.

30. Someday, men will pledge allegiance to a world kingdom of Christ.

31. The right of national secession must be maintained.

32. The right of regional and local secession must also be maintained.

33. We need a Christian civil federation, from local to international.

34. We need to battle humanism's vision of a one-State order with a Christian vision of a one-world order.

35. The Biblical system is a bottom-up appeals court system.

36. Humanist internationalism is based on the family of fallen man.

37. God destroys all imitations of the Tower of Babel.

38. They are based on magic: man's manipulation of the universe and God.

39. The answer is covenant: shared confession, the "unity of lip."

40. Empires are always at war with the kingdom of God.

41. Most humanists insist on the unity of the godhead: man.

42. Other humanists insist on total national isolation, the "Jonah impulse."

43. Paul was an internationalist.

44. The war goes on: no peace, only temporary cease-fire agreements.

45. The goal of Christian international relations is: "All nations under God."

III. Ethics/Dominion

3

GOD'S WORLD GOVERNMENT
THROUGH BIBLICAL LAW

Then the eleven disciples went away into Galilee, to the mountain which Jesus had appointed for them. And when they saw Him, they worshipped Him; but some doubted. Then Jesus came and spoke to them, saying, "All authority has been given to Me in heaven and on earth. Go therefore and make disciples of all the nations, baptizing them in the name of the Father and of the Son and of the Holy Spirit, teaching them to observe all things that I have commanded you; and lo, I am with you always, even to the end of the age." Amen (Matthew 28:16-20).

The third aspect of the Biblical covenant is law, specifically, Biblical law. Biblical law is the God-given tool of worldwide dominion for Christians.[1] The kingdom-oriented goal of God's people in history is to work toward the worldwide manifestation of the kingdom that exists now in heaven and in principle on earth. This is why Christians are told to pray, "Thy kingdom come. Thy will be done in earth, as it is in heaven" (Matthew 6:10, KJV).

The sign that God's kingdom has come in history is that Christians are obeying His law. As Christians obey God's law ever more faithfully, the kingdom of God in history expands progressively into every area of life. This is the principle of *leaven* (Matthew 13:33). God's leaven replaces Satan's leaven. God's kingdom progressively replaces Satan's kingdom as the dominant factor in world history.

---

1. Gary North, *Tools of Dominion: The Case Laws of Exodus* (Tyler, Texas: Institute for Christian Economics, 1988).

81

The disciples came to a mountain. Like the mountain Garden of Eden, where God gave the law to Adam, and like Mt. Sinai, where God gave the law to Moses, so was this mountain in Galilee: Christ gave them the law. He gave them His Great Commission. Christians are to make disciples of the nations. They are to bring the nations under the discipline of Christ, through the law of God—"teaching them to observe all things that I have commanded you."

Who are Christ's disciples? Those who are *disciplined* by Him. What is their task? To *discipline* the nations. We are under authority; therefore we possess authority. By what means do we discipline the nations? By the preaching of the gospel, which includes God's revealed law. "Now by this we know that we know Him, if we keep His commandments. He who says, 'I know Him,' and does not keep His commandments, is a liar, and the truth is not in him" (1 John 2:3-4).

No law of God means no authority of God; no law of God means no jurisdiction of God; no law of God means no kingdom of God. This is the inescapable Biblical truth that the twentieth-century Church has denied with all its heart, mind, and soul. God has therefore placed His Church under bondage to humanist power-seekers. He may soon choose to place the Church under Marxist empire-builders. That threat is very real, yet the Church, like a sleepwalker, heads toward the precipice.

Even among the disciples who faced a resurrected Christ, "some doubted." Millions of His disciples still doubt. They do not believe that God has assigned such a historical, nation-subduing task to His Church International. Those few who do believe it do not believe the Church International can carry out this task. But Christ did give us the dominion assignment, and He also expects us to carry it out. Christians must discipline the nations. This discipline begins with *self-discipline under God's law*. What we must understand, however, is that *it does not end with self-discipline*. This is what Protestants and traditional conservatives have long ignored.

God's Universal Kingdom

The disciples received Christ's Great Commission: to disciple the nations. They were to become "discipled disciplers." So are all Christians. This reveals the international scope of the gospel. There is no nation, no area of civil sovereignty, that is not to be put under the overall sovereignty of God. This submission to the rule of God must be made visible by public subordination to God's covenants: church, family, and civil. The families of a nation are to become subordinate to God's family covenant; the churches are to become subordinate to God's church covenant; and civil governments (plural) in each national jurisdiction are to become subordinate to God's civil covenant.

It is the *universalism of the Great Commission* that must be recognized by Christians. Certainly the enemies of Christianity have recognized it. God demands that nations submit to Him covenantally—legally, formally, and publicly—because they are *already* under His sovereign jurisdiction as Creator. What is true metaphysically—the underlying reality of the Creator-creature relationship—is to be manifested covenantally in history.

Let us consider this argument in terms of Adam's Fall. Adam was under God covenantally. God assigned to Adam the dominion covenant: to subdue the earth as God's lawful delegated agent on earth (Genesis 1:26-28). He placed Adam under law: do not eat a particular fruit. He threatened sanctions: death for disobedience. He was offered an inheritance: the whole world. But Adam was also subordinate to God metaphysically: as a creature. He did not share God's being. He was a man, not a divine being.

Adam broke the covenant. He placed himself under Satan's sovereignty by asserting his own authority to test the truth of God's threat of death. "I will test God's law to see if I will surely die," he decided. Thus, covenantally, Adam's biological heirs are now under Satan, sharing the devil's fate if they refuse to repent: the lake of fire (Revelation 20:14). But metaphysically, every person is still a creature under God. What *all* men are called to do is to affirm covenantally what is inescapably true by nature: subordination to God. Every human institution is supposed to make this same declaration. This includes the three formal covenant institutions: church, family, and civil government.

This is what is meant by the universalism of God's kingdom. It is universal over geography. It is universal institutionally. It is universal historically. The kingdom of God is as broad as the sovereignty of God. Man's formal, covenantal *acknowledgment* of this kingdom is limited today. It is to grow over time, as more and more people covenantally acknowledge what is inescapably true: their subordination to God as creatures.

Evangelism Through Visible Success

The Old Testament sets forth a fundamental program of world evangelism based on the principle of covenant blessings (point four of the covenant) in response to faithfulness to Biblical law (point three). The Bible recognizes that men who are not totally perverse can distinguish God's visible blessings (Deuteronomy 28:1-14) from God's visible cursings (Deuteronomy 28:15-68). They will be able to recognize a society that is under the covenant, and they will understand that God's visible blessings are worth seeking.

"Surely I have taught you statutes and judgments, just as the LORD my God commanded me, that you should act according to them in the land which you go to possess. Therefore be careful to observe them; for this is your wisdom and your understanding in the sight of the peoples who will hear all these statutes, and say, 'Surely this great nation is a wise and understanding people.' For what great nation is there that has God so near to it, as the LORD our God is to us, for whatever reason we may call upon Him? And what great nation is there that has such statutes and righteous judgments as are in all this law which I set before you this day?" (Deuteronomy 4:5-8).

These statutes were designed for a covenantal nation. The outworking of covenantal faithfulness to these statutes is national prosperity, justice, and international renown. Yet the vast majority of Christians today argue: 1) there is no such thing as a Christian nation; 2) the Old Testament statutes are obsolete; and 3) there are no God-given, God-required standards of national righteousness in New Testament times.

They say this because they have been taught the theology of *antinomianism*, hostility to God's law. They seek to escape from personal responsibility outside the narrow confines of church and family. They have been taught this theology by people who have no commitment to the building up of God-honoring, heaven-reflecting Biblical institutions. They have been taught this in the government schools. They have also been taught this by classroom humanists who have been hired by ostensibly Christian colleges to instruct the next generation. These professors have made their peace with the humanist worldview that governed their graduate school educations, and they are fiercely hostile to Biblical law, Christian civilization, and the unacceptable suggestion that they sold their spiritual birthrights for a mess of academic pottage.[2]

We need to keep asking them (and ourselves): What is the alternative to Biblical law? If the Bible, from Genesis to Revelation, is not our national and international standard, what else is? By what standard? By what *other* standard?

The preferred answer among educated Christians, for almost two thousand years, is natural law.

The Pagan Myth of Natural Law

Satan deludes Christians regarding their task of discipleship by means of a five-step argument. First, New Testament law is far easier and less encompassing than Old Testament law, which was radically different. Second, the law of God does not apply today to the civil government, but only to redeemed individuals, redeemed family governments, and orthodox church governments. God does not judge non-Christian institutions for disobeying His law

---

2. James Davison Hunter, *Evangelicalism: The Coming Generation* (University of Chicago Press, 1987), pp. 165-80.

until the final judgment. Third, because we all know that some sort of law is necessary for social order, the appropriate law-order has been given by God to fit the needs of all men, saved and lost. This law-order is logically discoverable by all men, saved and lost.

There is a fourth argument, seldom stated openly. Since this natural law-order is actually a myth, there can never be agreement concerning true law. Then, they conclude, *all laws are morally relative.* This leads to the fifth unstated argument: *might makes right.* He who has the power establishes the law. This is the reigning faith of the power religion.

In 1938, Mao Tse-tung made a statement which has become his most familiar slogan: "Political power grows out of the barrel of a gun." He did not say it like this. What Mao actually said was far more consistent: "Every Communist must grasp the truth, 'Political power grows out of the barrel of a gun.' Our principle is that the Party commands the gun, and the gun must never be allowed to command the Party. Yet, having guns, we can create Party organizations, as witness the powerful Party organizations which the Eighth Route Army has created in northern China. We can also create cadres, create schools, create culture, create mass movements. Everything in Yenan has been created by having guns. All things grow out of the barrel of a gun."[3]

All things grow out of the barrel of a gun: here in one sentence is the confession of faith of the power religion. It is no accident that a basic strategy of the Chinese Communists when they captured a village was to arrest wealthy residents. They would demand a ransom in the form of rifles. These were extremely scarce in China, and families would have to sell almost everything to buy them. Upon handing over the required number of rifles, the man would be released. If his family had any sign of wealth remaining, he would be arrested again and again, until the family was destitute.[4]

---

3. Mao Tse-tung, "Problems of War and Strategy," (Nov. 6, 1938), in *Selected Works of Mao Tse-tung*, 5 vols. (Peking: Foreign Languages Press, 1965), II, pp. 224-25.

4. Raymond de Jaeger and Irene Corbally Kuhn, *The Enemy Within* (Garden City, New York: Doubleday, 1952), pp. 42-43.

What Christians for almost two millennia have refused to believe is that *there is no such thing as natural law.* Any attempt to create a system of natural law as an alternative to revealed Biblical law inevitably results in the triumph of some religious law-order other than the Biblical law-order. Rushdoony is correct: ". . . in any culture, *the source of law is the god of that society.*"[5] If the source of law is nature, then the god of the system is nature. But nature is fallen. It labors under a curse (Genesis 3:17-18). Nature is not normative, meaning it cannot provide our moral norms. This is argued persuasively by Gary DeMar in his book in the Biblical Blueprints Series, *Ruler of the Nations*, Chapter Three.

The Origin of Natural Law Theory

In the early fourth century before Christ, the Greek city states were disintegrating. Then the Macedonian Empire under Alexander the Great spread across Greece and into Asia Minor in the latter years of the fourth century. This was the third empire predicted by Nebuchadnezzar's dream (Daniel 2:39) and also by Daniel's vision (Daniel 8:5-7). It disintegrated into four separate kingdoms after Alexander's death in 322 B.C., also as predicted in Daniel's vision (8:8).

The religion of classical Greece had rested upon a form of family worship. Access to citizenship was limited to males who were part of the family rites. The religion of each city was a composite of the combined rituals of the families.[6] Citizenship was based exclusively on blood.

This led to a crisis in classical civilization when the Greek city-states fell to Macedonia and then to Rome. The deeper religious question arose: What was the basis of citizenship in an empire?[7]

---

5. R. J. Rushdoony, *Institutes of Biblical Law* (Nutley, New Jersey: Craig Press, 1973), p. 4.

6. Numa Denis Fustel de Coulanges, *The Ancient City: A Classic Study of the Religious and Civil Institutions of Ancient Greece and Rome* (Garden City, New York: Anchor, [1864]), Books II, III.

7. Sheldon Wolin, *Politics and Vision: Continuity and Innovation in Western Political Thought* (Boston: Little, Brown, 1960), pp. 70-71.

The Stoic philosopher Epictetus stated the case for natural law in terms of *man as a divine being*: "When a man has learnt to understand the government of the universe and has realized that there is nothing so great or sovereign or all-inclusive as this frame of things wherein man and God are united . . . why should he not call himself a citizen of the universe and a son of God?"[8]

Here is a doctrine of potentially divine mankind. Natural man is seen as being the heir of God, a citizen of the universe. This theory rests on the pagan idea of the *chain of being*. Men and God are participants together in common being, meaning ultimately that men can become divine. This is Satan's old lure: "You will be like God" (Genesis 3:5b). Yet there are Christian scholars who still cling to natural law theory as the best intellectual defense against modern paganism, never admitting that natural law theory is an invention of ancient pagan imperialism.

Natural law theory was devised by a few Greek scholars who in general had lost faith in politics. They were products of a regional civilization in which politics was the heart of religion. The world of the *polis* was under attack in every sense: spiritually, militarily, and politically. These philosophers did not give specific content to natural law. The idea served as a hypothetical intellectual backdrop, a hoped-for means of uniting all men in a coherent universe—a dream that would have been utterly foreign to Greek political speculation prior to the fourth century, B.C. Before, Greeks had been uninterested in the "barbarian" world, the world outside the city-state. The collapse of that local world forced upon a handful of philosophers the intellectual problem of finding meaning in a world far different from anything earlier Greek philosophers had imagined possible.

The Roman Republic remained indifferent to Greek philosophy, but as it began to expand, taking on the characteristics of the empire, Stoicism began to appeal to Rome's thinkers. Stoicism "appeared to suggest, in the field of relations between states, a sys-

---

8. *Discourses*, I:ix; cited in *ibid.*, p. 80.

tem which could be used to justify Roman expansion."[9] From the beginning, natural law theory was an invention by an elite of pagan Greek intellectuals to comfort themselves in the midst of their collapsing civilization, and it was then used as an intellectual cover for other pagan philosophers who sought universal reasons to justify an expanding Roman Empire. Yet it is this makeshift intellectual system, conceived by pagans in despair, and adopted by tyrants who persecuted the Church (the best example is the Roman emperor-philosopher Marcus Aurelius, under whose tyranny Justin Martyr died) that has captured the minds of Christian philosophers, from the early church until the present.

Today, few people still believe in natural law. Christian scholars are among a handful of philosophers who still accept the idea. The humanists have, for the most part, recognized what Darwin's *Origin of Species* did to natural law. In a world of purposeless change governed by purposeless chance mutations, meaning a world of constant evolution through impersonal natural selection, nature is no longer regarded as a source of man-comforting perpetual moral truths. Man is seen as either the victim of meaningless nature or else the potential master of nature through scientific planning, but there is no room left for the harmonious outworkings of natural moral law in Darwin's dog-eat-dog universe. Christians who still defend the morally empty box of natural law theory have failed to recognize the obvious. They still cling to an idea that originally was a makeshift intellectual proposal offered by a handful of God-hating Greek cultural defeatists which was then taken up by power-seeking Roman apologists for bloody empire. It is time for Christians to abandon natural law theory.

The Law of God and the Heart of Man

But if there is no common natural law, what holds man's social world together? If men of different religions do not agree on phi-

---

9. Gerardo Zampaglione, *The Idea of Peace in Antiquity*, translated by Richard Dunn (Notre Dame: Indiana: University of Notre Dame Press, [1967] 1973), p. 139.

losophical first principles, how is it that such acts as murder and adultery are almost universally condemned? Doesn't this point to the existence of natural law?

No, it points to man as the image of God. God says that He has implanted the *work* of the law—not the law itself—into the heart of every human being.

> . . . for when Gentiles, *who do not have the law*, by nature do the things contained in the law, these, although not having the law, are a law to themselves, who show *the work of* the law written in their hearts, their *conscience also bearing witness*, and between themselves their thoughts accusing or else excusing them (Romans 2:14-15; emphasis added).

The problem is, as men become more and more rebellious against God, their consciences cease to function properly. Paul also wrote:

> Now the Spirit expressly says that in latter times some will depart from the faith, giving heed to deceiving spirits and doctrines of demons, speaking lies in hypocrisy, having their own conscience seared with a hot iron. . . (1 Timothy 4:1-2).

Therefore, the problem is not a lack of logic—"right reason"—but rather a lack of ethics. Man's problem is moral, not philosophical. It is not that rebellious men are stupid; it is that they are in rebellion.

Thus, the work of the law of God can restrain men from gross evil during certain periods of history. But when God withdraws His restraining common grace, men are increasingly evil, and increasingly unwilling to listen to their own consciences. The fact that they have been shown the work of the law becomes more and more irrelevant. Their knowledge serves to condemn them, but not to restrain them.

Even the covenant people of Israel were required to listen as a nation to the reading of God's revealed law once every seven years (Deuteronomy 31:10-13). If natural law is so natural, why would God require the public reading of His law?

In principle, Christians do have the law implanted in their hearts at the point of conversion (Hebrews 8:7-13; 10:16). But this is only a *definitive* implanting of the law of God. Men must respond in faith. They must *progressively* become doers of the Word, and not hearers only:

> But be doers of the word, and not hearers only, deceiving your-selves. For if anyone is a hearer of the word and not a doer, he is like a man observing his natural face in a mirror; for he observes himself, goes away, and immediately forgets what kind of man he was. But he who looks into the perfect law of liberty and continues in it, and is not a forgetful hearer but a doer of the work, this one will be blessed in what he does (James 1:22-25).

Again, the Bible is clear: ethics, not intellect, is the key to righteousness.

Rival Kingdoms, Rival Law-Orders

We know that there are two basic kingdoms: the kingdom of God and the kingdom of Satan. The kingdom of Satan, however, is in principle a divided kingdom. We know this because we know that God's kingdom will eventually triumph, in time and in eter-nity. Why does Satan's kingdom fall? Because it is in principle a divided kingdom.

> Then one was brought to Him who was demon-possessed, blind and mute; and He healed him, so that the blind and mute man both spoke and saw. And all the multitudes were amazed and said, "Could this be the Son of David?" But when the Pharisees heard it they said, "This fellow does not cast out demons except by Beelzebub, the ruler of the demons." But Jesus knew their thoughts, and said to them: "Every kingdom divided against itself is brought to desolation, and every city or house divided against it-self will not stand. And if Satan casts out Satan, he is divided against himself. How then will his kingdom stand? And if I cast out demons by Beelzebub, by whom do your sons cast them out? Therefore they shall be your judges. But if I cast out demons by the Spirit of God, surely the kingdom of God has come upon you" (Matthew 12:22-28).

These rival kingdoms cannot be fused. Jesus warned His lis-teners: "He who is not with Me is against Me, and he who does not gather with Me scatters abroad" (Matthew 12:30). There is no moral neutrality between the rival kingdoms. There can therefore be no long-term covenantal neutrality between them: sovereignty, hierarchy, law, judgment, and continuity.

A lot of Christians affirm that there is no moral neutrality in life, but they do not really believe it. Any attempt to place both kingdoms under a neutral, hypothetically universal, hypothetically permanent "natural law" judicial system is taking Adam's approach: affirming the existence of an independent testing ground that can judge between God's Word and Satan's word. But no such independent judicial testing ground exists. Adam died because he refused to believe this. Why do Christians continue to maintain it?

Let us face reality: *if natural law is a myth, then there is no Biblical alternative to theocracy.* Anyone who says that he is opposed to the myth of neutrality but who simultaneously insists that he is equally opposed to theocracy is intellectually schizophrenic. He cannot long remain in the front lines of the spiritual battlefield. He will have to go do something else with his life, laboring in the shadows where the stark contrast between God's law and Satan's laws is not highlighted by the glare of white-hot conflict. If you are a Christian, either you affirm the myth of neutrality (natural law) or else you affirm theocracy. There is no convenient, uncontroversial halfway house in between.

Since 1980, we have seen several nationally prominent leaders march onto the battlefield carrying two banners: "We must oppose the myth of neutrality" and "We must oppose theocracy." What is noticeable about these leaders is that after a few brief skirmishes with the humanists, they and many of their followers quietly and unobtrusively retreat from the front lines. Intellectual schizophrenia affects a person's ability to lead the troops during a battle.[10]

Covenant Law vs. Natural Law: The Nation

Few if any Christians today believe that the Word of God applies exclusively to a particular nation or race. They say that the

---

10. Gary North, "The Intellectual Schizophrenia of the New Christian Right," *Christianity and Civilization*, No. 1 (1982), pp. 1-40.

Word of God applies to all nations and races. This statement is more true than they imagine. The key word is "applies." Christians are unclear about the Biblical meaning of the word "applies." In what sense does God's Word *apply* to any institution? Specifically, how does it apply to a nation? Answer: it always applies *by covenant*. Through Adam, it applies covenantally throughout history; through Christ, the second Adam, it also applies covenantally throughout history. This is why God will judge men as members of nations (sheep and goats) at the last day (Matthew 25:31-33).

Almost no Christians today believe that the Word of God applies covenantally to any nation or race. They do not believe that a nation or a race can establish a covenantal bond with God through the grace of Christ in history. Supposedly, nations cannot legitimately designate themselves as exclusively *Christian* nations. So, the Bible supposedly applies to all nations in general, but not to any nation in particular. No nation can legitimately claim that the Bible applies to it in a unique way, and most important, no nation can claim that a rival nation is less conformed to the Bible. Modern Christians argue this way because they have rejected the doctrine of the national covenant.

By denying the idea of the national covenant, a person is proclaiming the myth of neutrality, the myth of natural law, the myth of permanent pluralism, the myth of "equal time for Satan." There is no logical escape from this conclusion. If neutrality is a myth, then there is a war on between Christ and Satan, between Christ's kingdom and Satan's empire, between Christ's law and Satan's counterfeit laws.

Most Christians reject the idea of truly Bible-based political action. They do not believe that Christians should work politically to see God's laws replace humanism's laws in civil government. But if Christians as citizens are not required by God to bring their views to bear on politics, and to pass legislation that conforms to God's laws, then the anti-Christians inherit civil government by *default*. Christians who refuse to work to establish a Christian nation are no different from those who refuse to establish Christian schools. (See Robert Thoburn's book in the Biblical Blueprints Series, *The Children Trap: Biblical Blueprints for Education*.) They have publicly and covenantally turned over civil government to Satan through his "neutral" human followers.

It is time for Christians to abandon the myth of natural law. It is time for them to declare instead the covenants of God. It is time for them to proclaim the ethical terms of the covenant, God's revealed law, for God is the Sovereign Creator who governs all of history. It is time to abandon the myth of neutrality.

If neutrality is illegitimate in the heart of each individual, if it is illegitimate in marriage, if it is illegitimate in the church, then why is judicial neutrality legitimate in civil government? If God's law is the standard of judgment on judgment day, why isn't it the standard now, when we serve as apprentice judges? Doesn't God judge individuals, institutions, and nations in history, as well as at the end of history? Isn't Deuteronomy 28 true today, just as it was in Moses' day?

And if we say that God's law is the only valid standard of righteousness for a person, a family, a church, and a nation, then how can we deny that it is valid for all nations? If the gospel proves successful, and the Great Commission is steadily fulfilled, and a majority of people convert to Christ in nation after nation, and then they seek to do God's will in every area of life, won't we see the creation of a worldwide Christian order that will steadily replace the worldwide disorder of Satan's divided kingdom? If not, why not?

World Government Through World Law

There are many volumes of books dealing with the law of nations. These laws are somewhat vague. Because there is no hierarchical court of appeals to enforce the law, there is no system of sanctions to reward those who obey the law or punish those who refuse to obey. Victorious nations can impose "victor's justice" on losers, but this sort of activity can hardly be said to promote righteousness, unless we believe that military governments in the flush of victory are generally righteous.[11] Few people believe this.

The humanists retain faith in the possibility of man-designed, State-enforced world government. Some of the humanists who believe this are Marxists. They have faith in military force, systematic subversion, and terrorism. Others are people who think that various treaties and other international agreements can be hammered out by representatives of major nations. They see international law as the key to establishing world government. They also implicitly understand the structure of the covenant.

In their book, *World Peace Through World Law*, published in 1958 by Harvard University Press, Grenville Clark and Louis Sohn proposed the transformation of the United Nations Organization into a world government. They suggested a six-point program. They insisted: "*First:* It is futile to expect genuine peace until there is put into effect an effective system of *enforceable* world law in the limited field of war prevention" (p. xi). Second, a constitutional prohibition of the use of violence by any nation against another is required. Third, "World judicial tribunals to interpret and apply the world law against international violence must be established and maintained . . ." (p. xii). Fourth, a permanent world police force must be established. Fifth, the complete disarmament of all nations is essential. "*Sixth:* Effective world machinery must be created to mitigate the vast disparities in the economic condition of various regions of the world, the continuance of which tends to instability and conflict" (p. xii).

To restructure this list according to the Biblical covenant model, the authors were suggesting: 1) a constitution, established by the United Nations (source of law); 2) world judicial tribunals (hierarchy); 3) statutes (law); 4) a permanent world police force that can impose sanctions; 5) wealth redistribution to benefit the poor nations at the expense of the richer nations (inheritance/disinheritance). Their fifth point, disarmament, could be placed under point four of the Biblical covenant, sanctions: the transfer

---

11. Gen. Douglas MacArthur's administration of Japan in the post-World War II era is one exception, according to rulers and ruled.

of sanction-imposing power to a new sanctioning agent. It could also be placed under point five of the Biblical covenant: inheritance. If this transfer takes place, each nation's survival is at stake.

We see once again that it is impossible to speak coherently about government apart from the five points of the Biblical covenant.

Biblical World Government

What the Bible calls for is the universal reign of Christ, not just in the hearts of the redeemed, but in every area of life. The crown rights of King Jesus are to be proclaimed fearlessly throughout the earth. We are not talking merely about heaven above or the world after the resurrection. We are talking about visible manifestations of Christ's kingdom in history, before His second coming. We are talking about the "footstool theology" of Psalm 110: "The LORD said to my Lord, 'Sit at My right hand, till I make Your enemies Your footstool.' The LORD shall send the rod of Your strength out of Zion. Rule in the midst of Your enemies!" (Psalm 110:1-2).

The humanists recognize that world government requires world law. The Stoic philosophers of the classical world recognized this, too. The Marxists see it, the radical Muslim sects see it, and modern science has seen it. Christians, in contrast, have failed to see it. They have relied on humanist versions of legal pluralism, what could also be called legal and moral polytheism: many laws, many moralities, many gods. (See Gary DeMar, *Ruler of the Nations*, Chapter Three.)

Christians have understood the universal claims of Jesus on the hearts of men, but they have continued to ignore the universal claims of Christ on the *minds, lives, and public allegiances* of men. They have not restructured their worldview in terms of the idea that God is King of kings and Lord of lords. God has laid down the law to mankind, yet His disciples have paid very little attention to God's law, generation after generation, century after century. They think that they can escape the requirement of the Great Commission to discipline the nations.

This is precisely what Satan wants Christians to think. It makes his defense of his divided, Calvary-wounded kingdom that much easier.

Summary

The third point in the Biblical covenant's structure is ethics, meaning Biblical law. It is the basis of dominion. The Great Commission serves as our marching orders. Christians have been remiss in not affirming the magnitude of the Great Commission. They say that they believe it, but then they limit its greatness. They narrow its impact to the hearts of individuals, to families, and to churches. They deliberately ignore its explicit frame of reference: *nations*. They then say that the Great Commission cannot be fulfilled in history. One Christian author has gone so far as to assert that "In fact, dominion—taking dominion and setting up the kingdom for Christ—is an *impossibility*, even for God. The millennial reign of Christ, far from being the kingdom, is actually the final proof of the incorrigible nature of the human heart, because Christ Himself can't do what these people say they are going to do. . . ."[12]

To avoid the full-scale responsibilities associated with discipling the nations, Christians have adopted several tactics: denying that the Great Commission is all-encompassing; denying that Biblical law is still required by God; affirming the myth of neutrality; affirming the existence of natural law; and using the word "theocracy" as something close to an obscenity. They have sought to build a safe enclosure around Biblical law: the isolated human heart, the isolated family, or the isolated local church. They have denied its applicability in local government, national government, and certainly international government. They affirm the invisible sovereignty of God, which is a threat to no one and nothing until judgment day, and deny the covenantal sovereignty of God, for the covenant involves *public* confession, hierarchy, law, judgment, and inheritance.

---

12. Dave Hunt, *Dominion and the Cross*, Tape Two in *Dominion: The Word and New World Order*, distributed by the *Omega-Letter*, Ontario, Canada, 1987.

In summary:

1. A disciple of Christ is disciplined by Christ.

2. A disciple of Christ is to work in a comprehensive evangelism program to discipline the nations.

3. The standard of God's discipline is His revealed law.

4. No law of God, no authority of God; no law of God, no jurisdiction of God; no law of God, no kingdom of God.

5. Discipleship begins with (but does not end with) self-discipline under God's law.

6. The kingdom is universal.

7. The kingdom is to be made visibly universal.

8. One means of evangelism is through the visible blessings of God.

9. God's laws are designed to impress pagan nations: evangelism through visible success.

10. There is no legitimate alternative to Biblical law.

11. Natural law is a satanic myth.

12. Relativism replaces natural law when it fails.

13. Power replaces relativism: might makes right.

14. The source of law is the god of any society.

15. Natural law theory was first presented by a handful of pagan Greek stoic philosophers.

16. Roman scholars used it to defend the empire.

17. Darwin's *Origin of Species* destroyed the case for natural moral law.

18. The work of Biblical law is written on every man's heart.

19. Rebellious men suppress their knowledge of this law.

20. Conscience alone is not a reliable guide to action.

21. Israel was required to hear the law once every seven years.

22. We are to be doers of the law, not hearers only.

23. Rival kingdoms use rival law-orders.

24. The kingdoms cannot be fused; their laws cannot be fused.

25. Nations are to be brought publicly under God's covenant law for nations.

26. There is no neutrality in national laws.

27. The Bible proclaims universal covenant law.

28. It therefore affirms universal civil government.

29. The universal kingdom of God is to find universal expression covenantally.

4

NATIONS WITH RIVAL COVENANTS
ARE ALWAYS AT WAR

Put on the whole armor of God, that you may be able to stand
against the wiles of the devil. For we do not wrestle against flesh
and blood, but against principalities, against powers, against the
rulers of the darkness of this age, against spiritual hosts of
wickedness in the heavenly places (Ephesians 6:11-12).

The fourth point of the covenant structure is judgment. God
imposes dual sanctions in history: blessings and cursings. Nations
sometimes become God's rods of judgment against other nations,
just as Assyria served as God's rod of affliction against Israel
(Isaiah 10:5).

Paul says that we wrestle against spiritual forces. There is evil
in the world, and for as long as there is evil in the world, covenant-
keepers and covenant-breakers will be in conflict. This conflict is
primarily ethical. It centers around the law of God (point three).
Each side attempts to extend its influence in history: covenant-
keepers by means of covenantal faithfulness to the law of God,
and covenant-breakers by means of power. There is a history-long
struggle between dominion religion and power religion.

Why are there wars? James writes: "Where do wars and fights
come from among you [Christians]? Do they not come from your
desires for pleasure that war in your members" (James 4:1)? If this
is true within the Church International, how much more in the
world? Sin is the cause. We are in a spiritual war of good against
evil. It begins in the life of each person, Paul tells us (Romans 7).
It spreads to the institutions we are part of: family, church, state,

business, etc. And it culminates in wars between nations.

We must never forget where wars come from: sinful hearts. We must also not forget that God takes sides in these wars, as He says repeatedly in the Bible. The Lord of hosts (angelic armies) is on the side of those who remain faithful to His covenant.

War and Peace

Perhaps the most famous Western definition of war was provided by the Prussian scholar, Karl von Clausewitz, who said in his posthumously published book, *On War* (1832), that "War is a mere continuation of policy by other means."[1] What I argue in this book is the other side of this coin: *foreign policy is war conducted by other means.* It is not a war in the sense that Clausewitz meant it: an act of national force to compel our enemy to do our will. God, not man, is the primary agent of compulsion in history, bringing His comprehensive historical decree to pass. King Nebuchadnezzar announced the absolute sovereignty of God in history with far greater assurance than most modern Christians possess today: "All the inhabitants of the earth are reputed as nothing; He does according to His will in the army of heaven and among the inhabitants of the earth. No one can restrain His hand or say to Him, 'What have you done'" (Daniel 4:35)? But this war is nevertheless a real conflict. Christians are God's ambassadors who come in His name with a peace treaty that requires unconditional surrender to the Great King.[2] As ambassadors, they are peaceful warriors. The war between the two supernatural kingdoms never ends in history.

International relations are always governed by questions of war and peace. Nations seek their goals in the international scene. A few nations will always be on the offensive. They seek to impose their will on other nations by imposing sanctions (though not necessarily military sanctions): blessings and cursings. They imitate God in this respect.

---

1. Chapter One, Observation #24, *On War*, edited by Anatol Rapoport (New York: Penguin, [1968] 1982), p. 119.

2. Gary North, *Unconditional Surrender: God's Program for Victory* (3rd ed.; Ft. Worth, Texas: Dominion Press, 1987).

This imitation is legitimate, if done covenantally, meaning as a lawful representative of God. Men are required to think God's thoughts after Him, though as creatures. They are to *image* God. Thus, civil governments must impose sanctions. This is one of the functions of all three covenantal governments: church, civil government, and family. The question is: Do they impose sanctions as hypothetically autonomous (self-law) agents or as delegated sovereigns of God? Another question is this: Under what conditions may they legitimately seek to impose military sanctions on other nations, as Israel imposed sanctions on Canaan? These questions are more appropriate for a Biblical Blueprint on war, but it is clear that national self-defense is legitimate in New Testament times. God establishes certain nations to serve as headquarters for international misssions at certain points in history, and Christians living in these nations may legitimately call for military action to defend these bases from attack.

What is the proper response of nations that are threatened by invasion or other coercive pressures from abroad? When one nation threatens another, or many others, what should the potential victims do? The typical response is to beat plowshares into swords. Victimized nations either prepare for war or else they pretend that the threat to their independence will go away.

We are presently living in the midst of perhaps the major confrontation between Christ and Satan since Calvary. When the former Communist spy Whittaker Chambers defected from the Communist Party in the late 1940's and went before Congress to confess and to identify several networks of Communist spies in the U.S. government, he wrote a letter to his children explaining why he had done what he had done. It is included as the Introduction to his magnificent 800-page testimonial, *Witness* (1952). His words should ring in the ears of every Christian: "For in this century, within the next decades, will be decided for generations whether all mankind is to become Communist, whether the whole world is to become free, or whether, in the struggle, civilization as we know it is to be completely destroyed or completely changed. It is our fate to live upon that turning point in history."[3]

And these words: "There has never been a society or a nation without God. But history is cluttered with the wreckage of nations that became indifferent to God, and died."[4]

The Judgment of God in History

What should be the goal of Christian foreign policy in a world of military pressures? Clearly, the goal is to prepare the way of the Lord internationally. Christian nations are to act and to speak prophetically, just as David did as Israel's delegated agent when he confronted Goliath. They must speak in confidence, knowing that they come in God's name as His designated representatives.

> Then David said to the Philistine, "You come to me with a sword, with a spear, and with a javelin. But I come to you in the name of the LORD of hosts, the God of the armies of Israel, whom you have defied. This day the LORD will deliver you into my hand, and I will strike you and take your head from you. And this day I will give the carcasses of the camp of the Philistines to the birds of the air and the wild beasts of the earth, that all the earth may know that there is a God in Israel. Then all this assembly shall know that the LORD does not save with sword and spear; for the battle is the LORD's, and He will give you into our hands" (1 Samuel 17:45-47).

He made his point clear: the sovereignty of God and not the sovereignty of earthly weapons is the basis of national victory. God is sovereign, not man. The delegated representative institutions of God are sovereign, not the delegated representative institutions of man.

Note, however, that David did not go empty-handed to fight Goliath. He went with staff, sling, and stones. He did not wear Saul's armor, but he was not a proponent of unilateral disarmament.

The goal of foreign policy is to conduct the earthly war of God against enemy nations, but to do so if possible without resorting to armed conflict. The goal is long-term peace through the public

---

3. Whittaker Chambers, *Witness* (New York: Random House, 1952), p. 7.
4. *Ibid.*, p. 17.

covenantal surrender to God of all the nations that are presently enemies of God. Foreign policy is to seek out avenues of long-term peace, but on Christ's terms: *surrender*. Only then can swords safely be beaten into plowshares. The ultimate earthly goal for Christian foreign policy is to live in a world in which swords are beaten into plowshares.

This is not surrender to an individual nation that claims to represent God. It is surrender to a *confederation of nations* that are publicly covenanted together under God's sovereign authority. It is precisely the international covenant that is proof that a single nation is not seeking illegitimate power over its neighbors. Remove this international concept, and it becomes impossible to attain long-term peace among nations, for each will suspect the other of aggrandizement.

The Universal Goal of Peace

There is little doubt that the official goal of every nation's foreign policy is peace. Peace is the universally recognized dream of all mankind. But there is no neutral definition of peace on earth.

The Soviet Union from the beginning has been dedicated to war and struggle with its enemies as a way of life. Lenin did not mince words: life is continual warfare. At the Eighth Party Congress in December of 1920, he said: "The main subject of this talk is to offer proof of two premises: first, that any war is merely the continuation of peace-time politics by other means, and second, that the concessions which we are giving, which we are forced to give, are a continuation of war in another form, using other means."[5] Less than a month earlier, he had announced: "As long as Capitalism and Socialism exist, we cannot live in peace; in the end, one or the other will triumph—a funeral dirge will be sung over the Soviet Republic or over world capitalism."[6]

---

5. V. I. Lenin, "Capitalist Discords and Concessions Policy" (Dec. 21, 1920), in *The Lenin Anthology*, edited by Robert C. Tucker (New York: Norton, 1975), p. 628.

6. Lenin, "Speech to Moscow Party Nuclei Secretaries" (Nov. 26, 1920); cited by Anthony Trawick Bouscaren, *Soviet Foreign Policy: A Pattern of Persistence* (New York: Fordham University Press, 1962), p. 11.

Yet the Soviet Union is forever promoting peace movements, détente, peaceful coexistence, and similar public goals. There have been four of these periods of détente, and all have failed to improve relations between the United States and the USSR. These periods were: 1945-48, ending with the Berlin blockade; 1954-56, ending with the Soviet invasion of Hungary; 1959-61, ending with the Berlin wall; 1972-79, ending with the Soviet invasion of Afghanistan.[7] The Communists preach peace, but it is the peace of unconditional surrender to Communism, or the peace of the grave for their opponents. They have adopted a counter-peace offensive against what was once the Christian West.

The God of Christianity is equally emphatic: *all men will bow the knee to Jesus Christ.*

> Therefore God also has highly exalted Him and given Him the name which is above every name, that at the name of Jesus every knee should bow, of those in heaven, and of those on earth, and of those under the earth, and that every tongue should confess that Jesus Christ is Lord, to the glory of God the Father (Philippians 2:9-11).

Christians should proclaim this and take comfort from it. But the vast majority of Christians see this either as a post-final judgment event or as an event of the millennium, in which Christ rules the whole world from his physical headquarters in Jerusalem. They do not believe that there will be progressive fulfillment of this international kneeling in history (the "Church Age"). Yet Christians also know that Satan seeks to get them to bow the knee before his earthly representatives. They see the Christian strategy as strictly defensive in history. This is not what God says, however:

> "Look to Me, and be saved, all you ends of the earth! For I am God, and there is no other. I have sworn by Myself; the word has gone out of My mouth in righteousness, and shall not return, that

---

7. Constance C. Menges, "Détente's Dark History," *Wall Street Journal* (Jan. 9, 1987).

to Me every knee shall bow, every tongue shall take an oath. He shall say, 'Surely in the LORD I have righteousness and strength. To Him men shall come, and all shall be ashamed who are incensed against Him'" (Isaiah 45:22-24).

Until all knees are bowed before Christ, the war will go on.

Peaceful Warriors

Warfare in the Bible is covenantal. So is peace. Redeemed men are at peace with God through the covenant. He has sworn an oath in His own name that He will honor His covenant. "I have sworn by Myself; the word has gone out of My mouth in righteousness." Redeemed men therefore rely on a totally sovereign God as their absolutely sovereign ruler. He has promised to bring victory to His people—victory over indwelling sin, public victory at the end of time, and public victory as God's lawful *representatives* even in the midst of the earthly war. Isaiah promises in his great passage on millennial peace:

> Then justice will dwell in the wilderness, and righteousness remain in the fruitful field. The work of righteousness will be peace, and the effect of righteousness, quietness and assurance forever. My people will dwell in a peaceful habitation, in secure dwellings, and in quiet resting places (Isaiah 32:16-18).

Peace is said specifically to be the work of righteousness. God promises His covenantal sanction of blessing to covenanted nations that are faithful to the terms of the covenant, His revealed law. Peace can be achieved only alongside the extension of righteousness in history. It is a gift to the faithful.

Thus, Christians can and must claim peace as their goal, but only on God's terms. It must be the product of covenantal faithfulness throughout the world. If armies are not to cross borders, there must be a covenantal peace offensive. This peace offensive is the preaching of the gospel. It must not be the false promised peace of perpetual coexistence with evil. It is the *limited but growing peace* that God grants to victors in the spiritual wars of life.

A War Between First Principles

Humanists begin with the idea that man is sovereign over creation, including man (which really means that an elite group of men is sovereign over everyone else). Christians begin with the idea of the sovereign authority of God, the Creator. There can be no reconciliation between these two religious ideas. Humanism cannot recognize the sovereignty of God and remain humanism. Christianity cannot recognize the primary sovereignty of man and still remain Christianity. A theological war is in progress. It has been going on since the garden of Eden (Genesis 3:5), and it will be going on until the final judgment (Revelation 20:14-15).

If the nations of the free world are to survive the conflict that we are now in, our people and our leaders must recognize that this spiritual war does exist, and that it is being fought in history. It is not some imaginary battle. It is also not purely physical. It is *covenantal*. It is being fought in the midst of time, yet the stakes in this battle are eternal.

Unfortunately, the West's political leaders seem unwilling to admit that we are even in a war. The French commentator Jean François Revel says, "Even conservatives seldom risk naming the threat of totalitarianism as the greatest menace of our time, for fear of seeming fanatical. Democracy, on the defensive against an all-out totalitarian offensive, dares not admit it is fighting. Yet never has such an admission been more warranted."[8] In France, he says, there has been a remarkable reversal of the situation after World War II. After the war, French politicians warned against the Soviet Union, while the "eggheads" and intellectuals sang the praises of Communist tyrannies. Since 1975, the intellectuals have begun to warn against the Communist menace, while the politicians ignore it or cover it up.[9]

This is the moral affliction that Gilbert Murray says cut down Greek civilization: *the failure of nerve*. The West's leaders are afraid.

---

8. Jean-François Revel, *How Democracies Perish* (Garden City, New York: Doubleday, 1984), p. 27.

9. *Ibid.*, p. 45.

They therefore lie: to themselves and to those whom they represent. Solzhenitsyn has described this process: "Many present and former U.S. diplomats have also used their office and authority to help enshroud Soviet communism in a dangerous, explosive cloud of vaporous arguments and illusions. Much of this legacy stems from such diplomats of the Roosevelt school as Averill Harriman, who to this day [1980] assures gullible Americans that the Kremlin rulers are peace-loving men who just happen to be moved by heartfelt compassion for the wartime suffering of their Soviet people. (One need only recall the plight of the Crimean Tatars, who are still barred from returning to the Crimea for the sole reason that this would encroach upon Brezhnev's hunting estates.)"[10]

The Sovereignty of God

God is high above all men and events. He controls men and events. "The king's heart is in the hand of the LORD, like the rivers of water; He turns it wherever He wishes" (Proverbs 21:1). "Woe to him who strives with his Maker!" (Isaiah 45:9a). God is *transcendent*. Yet He is also *present* with us. It is He who gives the victory. "Some trust in chariots, and some in horses; but we will remember the name of the LORD our God. They have bowed down and fallen; but we have risen and stand upright" (Psalm 20:7-8).

We are in what appears to be the final stages of a conflict between a civilization that was once built on faith in God and another that was self-consciously built on atheism. There should be no doubt as to which civilization will win, if one of them trusts in the strong arm of God. Our problem comes from the West's departure from this older faith. Our Communist opponents have made a religion of chariots. They have bet everything on the power of military hardware and the effectiveness of subversion. The Bible says that such tactics cannot win the long-run battle. Sadly for us, such tactics can and do win short-term battles when they are not challenged by strategies and tactics built on faith in God.

---

10. Aleksandr Solzhenitsyn, "Misconceptions About Russia Are a Threat to America," *Foreign Affairs* (Spring 1980), p. 806.

The Lure of "Convergence"

To undermine a society, its opponents must first undermine men's faith in the existing moral and philosophical foundations of that society. The faith which created Western civilization was faith in the God of the Bible. This God calls His followers to wage a lifetime war against sin and against all public and institutional manifestations of sin. The Bible teaches that a great separation will take place at the end of time, with covenant-keepers receiving everlasting blessings, and covenant-breakers receiving everlasting cursing (Revelation 20:14-15). This doctrine of eternal division outrages liberal humanists. It denies their fundamental creed: the unity of man.

The Unification of Man

We are monotheists in the West. The god of our civilization must therefore be a unified god. For over a thousand years, the West, being Christian (with local Jewish subdivisions), historically affirmed the unity of mankind as a creature. All men are created in the image of God, who is Himself unified. Nevertheless, Christianity and Judaism have also simultaneously proclaimed that mankind is *divided ethically.* There are good men and bad men, saved and lost, saints and sinners, covenant-keepers and covenant-breakers. Thus, the goal of the unification of mankind is necessarily limited. Men will never be unified ethically. There will always be a cultural struggle in history between good and evil. The point is, then, to construct institutions that will preserve the peace— civil, ecclesiastical, educational, economic, etc.—but which will also suppress the outward manifestations of evil. Warning: I said outward evil, not inward evil. The State is not to seek to get inside the minds of men. Such a goal is innately satanic. It means that man is again playing God.

In the West, we have until quite recently recognized that God saves men, rather than the State. Laws must suppress outward evil, but they must never be designed to save men ethically. The State is not God. The State is not supposed to make men good; it is only supposed to restrain men from public evil acts. The State has not been granted the power to replace God as Savior. Thus, Western civilization has historically rejected the doctrine of salvation by law, especially statist law. Whenever and wherever the doctrine of salvation by civil law has been preached, then and there we have found a conspiracy against Western civilization. This is what we find today, all over the world.

The motivation of covenant-breakers is simple: to be like God (Genesis 3:5). The covenant-breakers of the West, being Western, have also adopted the notion of *the unity of the godhead.* But who is this god? It is man himself. To achieve (evolve to) this position of divinity, men therefore need to be unified—not just unified through voluntary cooperation (such as in a free market exchange), but *unified ethically and politically.*

It would be futile to attempt to list all the statements by humanist scholars that proclaim the need for the unification of man. A representative example is an interview with Carl Sagan, the popular astronomer (I am tempted to write "pop astronomer") whose multimillion dollar Public Broadcasting System show in 1980, "Cosmos," was a 12-week propaganda blast for evolution, and whose scientifically preposterous "nuclear winter" scenario is a favorite theme in the nuclear freeze, Western disarmament movement.[11] (The "nuclear winter" thesis says that an atomic war will kick up so much dust into the atmosphere that the sun's rays will be insufficient to grow much food, and a new ice age could result. This scientifically preposterous myth was financed by a $200,000 expenditure by the Kendall Foundation back in the spring of 1983. It was a classic public relations job, and is admitted as such by those who pulled it off.[12] A major volcano eruption like Krakatoa's in 1883 would spew more dust into the air than a nuclear war would.)[13] Sagan writes: "I'd say that our strengths are

---

11. That the "nuclear winter" scenario is without scientific value, see the report by Dr. Petr Beckman, "The Nuclear Winter," *Access to Energy* (Jan. 1984). P.O. Box 2298, Boulder, Colorado 80306.

12. "How Nuclear Winter Got on Page One," *The Newsletter of the National Association of Science Writers* (April 1984). P.O. Box 294, Greenlawn, New York 11740.

13. *Access to Energy* (Jan. 1984), p. 2.

a kind of intelligence and adaptability. In the last few thousand years, we've made astonishing cultural and technical advances. In other areas, we've not made so much progress. For example, we are still bound by sectarian and national rivalries."

Recognize that "intelligence and adaptability" are code words for evolution, meaning man-directed social, political, and economic evolution. "Sectarian and national rivalries" are code words for religious differences and nationalism. But Sagan is optimistic. He sees a new world a' comin'. Some people might even call it the humanist New World Order. "It's clear that sometime relatively soon in terms of the lifetime of the human species people will identify with the entire planet and the species, provided we don't destroy ourselves first. That's the race I see us engaged in — a contest between unifying the planet and destroying ourselves."[14]

Back in the 1950's, the slogan was: "Peace in the world, or the world in pieces." It is the same religious pitch: the unification of mankind ethically and politically (the humanist one-world order) is necessary if mankind is to survive as a species. Men must be pursuaded to affirm very similar moral, political, and economic goals. Divisive creeds and opinions need to be educated out of people, preferably by means of compulsory, tax-financed schools. Diversity of opinion concerning these humanistic goals must not be tolerated, for they are the basis of "sectarian and national rivalries." Mankind must not be allowed to reveal differences of opinion on fundamentals. Mankind's unified godhead is at stake.

Now, there are three ways to achieve this unity: persuasion ("conversion"), manipulation, and execution. The first approach takes forever, or at least it seems to take forever in the opinion of humanists. It also eats up lots of resources. It takes teams of "missionaries." People just never seem to agree on these humanistic first principles. They bicker. They battle. They refuse to be persuaded. Mankind reveals its lack of agreement on religion and ethics. This, you understand, must not be tolerated.

If you cannot persuade men to cooperate, either by force of

---

14. *U.S. News and World Report* (Oct. 21, 1985), p. 66.

reason, or an appeal to self-interest, or a moral appeal, then you have only two choices remaining: manipulation or execution. Either you confuse the bickering factions by means of an endless process of shifting international alliances, thereby gaining their cooperation under a unified (but necessarily secret) elite of planners, or else one faction must eliminate all rivals by force: you kill your opponents or make them slaves. There is no third alternative, given the false doctrine of the ethical unity of man. Man is in principle ethically unified, this theology proclaims; therefore, any visible deviations from this hypothetical unity must be suppressed, one way or another.

Détente

The West's political and economic leaders are humanists. They have adopted the soft-core humanism of Western liberalism. They are not dedicated to fighting an all-encompassing war against evil. They are dedicated to pursuing universal peace through endless peace treaties. They want to achieve in history what God says is opposed to His plan in history: a stalemate between good and evil, between covenant-keeping nations and covenant-breaking nations.[15]

The Soviets know better, being hard-core humanists. They use their opponents' naive view of history to their advantage. They promise endless treaties, in order to lure their enemies into complacency. From the day they signed the Treaty of Brest-Litovsk in early 1918 after they had surrendered to Germany, Lenin knew exactly what he was doing. He began to break the treaty, imitating Adam's decision in the garden. Broken treaties are the heart of man's rebellion. "Yes, of course, we are violating the treaty; we have violated it thirty or forty times. Only children can fail to understand that in an epoch like the present, when a long, painful period of emancipation is setting in, which has only

---

15. Gary North, *Backward, Christian Soldiers? A Manual for Christian Reconstruction* (Tyler, Texas: Institute for Christian Economics, 1984), ch. 11: "The Stalemate Mentality."

just created and raised the Soviet power three stages of its development—only children can fail to understand that in this case
there must be a long, circumspect struggle."[16]

Yet, we still hear academicians and politicians speaking end-
lessly of the coming convergence of the two systems. They all echo
Armand Hammer, multi-billionaire self-styled capitalist, whose
father, Julius, was one of the founders of the American Communist Party in 1919. Already a millionaire by age 23, Armand won a
trading license with the USSR in 1921, which he freely admits in
his autobiography.[17] What he judiciously fails to mention is that
the firm that had made him a millionaire gained much of its
wealth through its trading in pharmaceuticals with the USSR
from 1918 onward.[18] He makes it appear that he just happened to
get a chance meeting with Lenin in 1921; in fact, Soviet sources
place the Hammers' first meeting with Lenin in 1907, when his
father met him at the International Socialist Congress.[19] Armand
seems to have forgotten Joseph Finder's observation: "Throughout the spring and summer of 1920, Hammer's company made a
full-scale effort to purchase supplies from the other concerns and
ship hundreds of cases of codeine, camphor, gauze, morphine,
and quinine to Moscow."[20]

Hammer claims that his trade with the USSR declined after
Stalin's rise to power in 1930, although this is denied by his dis-
cussions of his beer-barrel business of the early 1930's.[21] His business connections revived under Brezhnev in 1973. He admits to
having made business transactions, including a single deal worth

---

16. Lenin, "Report on War and Peace" (March 7, 1918), in *The Lenin Anthology*,
pp. 548-49.

17. Armand Hammer and Neil Lyndon, *Hammer* (New York: Putnam's,
1987), ch. 8.

18. Joseph Finder, *Red Carpet* (Ft. Worth, Texas: American Bureau of Economic Research, [1983] 1987), p. 13. Antony Sutton, *Western Technology and Soviet
Economic Development, 1917-1930* (Stanford, California: Hoover Institution, 1968),
pp. 108, 268.

19. Finder, *Red Carpet*, p. 13.

20. *Ibid.*, p. 17.

21. *Hammer*, pp. 245-46.

over $20 billion.[22] These deals, he asserts, will make Occidental Petroleum the number-one American corporation operating in the Soviet Union until the year 2000.[23] As I write this, in the summer of 1987, Armand Hammer is still trading with the Soviet Union, as well as Communist China. He is almost certainly the only person in the world whose private jetliner is entitled to land in both nations.[24] Hammer told *The Times* of London in 1972, "In fifty-one years of dealing with the Soviets I've never known a better climate for growth. We're moving towards socialism, they towards capitalism. Between us there's a meeting ground."[25] (Notice the dating of 51 years: 1972 minus 51 is 1921: he desperately wants the world to believe that he made his first deal with the Soviets only after having become a millionaire on his own as a risk-taking entrepreneur.)

That same year, 1972, the U.S. Department of Commerce authorized the sale to the Soviet Union of the ball bearing machines that alone make possible the construction of MIRVed nuclear warheads. A single Soviet missile can now launch at least 12 independently targeted nuclear warheads. This made several million dollars for the Bryant Chucking Grinder Corporation of Springfield, Vermont, who had begun petitioning the government to make this sale in 1961.[26] This sale soon brought the one convergence the Soviets had always wanted: the ability to kill 80 percent to 90 percent of all North Americans within 25 minutes after launch.[27]

The only possible convergence of the West with international Communism is in the concentration camp, the mental institution, and the grave. Only to the extent that the West has abandoned

---

22. *Ibid.*, pp. 400-1.

23. *Ibid.*, p. 406.

24. *Ibid.*, p. 458.

25. Cited by Joseph Finder, *Red Carpet* (Ft. Worth, Texas: American Bureau of Economic Research, [1983] 1987), p. 262.

26. Richard Pipes, *Survival Is not Enough: Soviet Realities and America's Future* (New York: Simon & Schuster, 1984), p. 264.

27. Arthur Robinson and Gary North, *Fighting Chance: Ten Feet to Survival* (Ft. Worth, Texas: American Bureau of Economic Research, 1986).

Christianity can it be said to be on the road to convergence. *Convergence means surrender.* It means national disarmament and the transfer of military power to an international central government. This was the stated goal of U.S. State Department Publication 7277, *Freedom from War* (1961), which announced:

> The over-all goal of the United States is a free, secure, and peaceful world of independent states adhering to common standards of justice and international conduct and subjecting the use of force to the rule of law; a world which has achieved general and complete disarmament under effective international control; and a world in which adjustment to change takes place in accordance with the principles of the United Nations.
>
> In order to make possible the achievement of that goal, the program sets forth the following specific objectives toward which nations should direct their efforts:
>
> The disbanding of all national armed forces and the prohibition of their reestablishment in any form whatsoever other than those required to preserve internal order and for contributions to a United Nations Peace Force;
>
> The elimination from national arsenals of all armaments, including all weapons of mass destruction and the means for their delivery, other than those required for a United Nations Peace Force and for maintaining internal order;
>
> The institution of effective means for the enforcement of international agreements, for the settlement of disputes, and for the maintenance of peace in accordance with the principles of the United Nations;
>
> The establishment and effective operation of an International Disarmament Organization within the framework of the United Nations to insure compliance at all times with all disarmament obligations.[28]

The pamphlet proposes a three-stage program of disarmament, culminating with this: "The peace-keeping capabilities of

28. *Freedom from War: The United States Program for General and Complete Disarmament in a Peaceful World*, Disarmament Series 5, Released September 1961, Office of Public Services, Bureau of Public Affairs, Department of State Publication 7277 (Washington, D.C.: Government Printing Office, 1961), pp. 3-4.

the United Nations would be sufficiently strong and the obligations of all states under such arrangements sufficiently far-reaching as to assure peace and the just settlement of differences in a disarmed world."[29]

This three-stage program was taken from the United Nations' own "Declaration on Disarmament," which was reprinted as an appendix in the booklet. This final provision was taken word for word from the UN declaration.

Since the time that this State Department booklet was published, political liberals everywhere have lost faith in the United Nations. But they have not lost faith in the vision of universal disarmament within the framework of an international, one-world order.

Breaking Diplomatic Relations

Diplomacy means working out differences. There is no way to work out differences between nations that are ideologically, officially, and continually engaged at war against each other. Only a nation led by fools or knaves maintains diplomatic relations with rival nations that openly intend to destroy them. The standard argument against breaking diplomatic relations goes along these lines: "We cannot ignore the existence of a superpower like the Soviet Union." Nonsense; diplomatic relations have nothing to do with the public acknowledgment of a nation's existence. During a shooting war, nothing is clearer than a rival nation's existence, but upon either nation's declaration of war, diplomatic relations are mutually severed between them. The issue is pure and simple: formal recognition of a nation means that another nation accepts it as being part of the "family of acceptable nations." This is why the humanist Left has always wanted diplomatic relations with tyrannies, including Nazi Germany until World War II broke out. Even more important is trade, which was also extensive between the United States and the Nazis.[30] The idea of permanent ideolog-

---

29. *Ibid.*, p. 10.

30. Antony Sutton, *Wall Street and Hitler* (Seal Beach, California: '76 Press, 1977); Charles Higham, *Trading With the Enemy* (New York: Delacorte, 1983).

ical warfare until one or the other culture is destroyed or conquered is foreign to those who seek the formal, visible, covenantal unity of mankind. Granting or continuing diplomatic recognition, like breaking recognition and recalling one's ambassador and consulate officials, is a moral and judicial act, an acknowledgement of another nation's moral and legal legitimacy among the community of free nations. It has meaning far beyond the mere acknowledgment of a nation's existence or even its right to exist.

It is interesting that President Roosevelt justified his decision formally to recognize the USSR in terms of needs of the peoples of both nations, rather than the need for State-to-State formal alliances. For "people" not to recognize each other is "abnormal," he said. Here we discover the language of ultimate sovereignty—the sovereign people—covering the heart of humanist foreign policy: conduct between national governments. He wrote to the President of the Soviet All-Union Central Executive Committee in October of 1933:

> Since the beginning of my Administration, I have contemplated the desirability of an effort to end the present abnormal relations between the hundred and twenty-five million people of the United States and the hundred and sixty million people of Russia.
>
> It is most regrettable that these great peoples, between whom a happy tradition of friendship existed for more than a century to their mutual advantage, should now be without a practical method of communicating directly with each other.[31]

Notice that he spoke of Russia, not the Soviet Union. This was deliberate. He was following the lead of his Secretary of State, Cordell Hull. In the fall of 1933, the President had handed Hull a pile of letters addressed to the President regarding the wisdom of recognizing the USSR. They were overwhelmingly opposed, as the President knew. Hull read them and returned to speak with Roosevelt.

---

31. Oct. 10, 1933. *Foreign Relations of the United States: Diplomatic Papers. The Soviet Union, 1933-39* (Washington, D.C.: Government Printing Office, 1952), p. 17.

"I favor recognizing Russia," I said, "although our correspond-
ence reveals that great numbers of people are opposed to it. Russia
and we had been traditional friends up to the end of the World
War. In general, Russia has been peacefully inclined. The world is
moving into a dangerous period both in Europe and in Asia.
Russia could be a great help in stabilizing this situation as time
goes on and peace becomes more and more threatened."

The President, without a moment's hesitation, replied, "I agree
entirely." He then added, "Two great nations like America and
Russia should be on speaking terms. It will be beneficial to both
countries to resume diplomatic relations."[32]

So much for democracy. The American public was wrong
about recognizing the USSR, and should be ignored, they decided. Notice also that Hull went so far as to speak of the long
friendship between the United States and *Russia*. The fact that the
geographical territory formerly known as Russia was being governed by a gang of criminal revolutionary conspirators was seen
by Hull and Roosevelt as utterly irrelevant. It still is, in the eyes
of the foreign policy experts of the world.

Diplomatic recognition is very important to Communist nations. It is a way to demonstrate to the captives at home and
abroad that the West does not intend to do anything to liberate
them. It also helps to convince Communist leaders that the West
is still morally impotent. It is a sign that the West has not yet recognized its mortal danger.

One of the weakest links in Western foreign policy is that it
operates in terms of only two conditions: declared war and peace.
It does not understand that a cease-fire is different from peace.
North Korea and South Korea are not at peace; formally, only a
cease-fire has been in existence since 1953. The two Koreas recognize that a war is in progress; the West does not. Both Hitler and
Stalin gained ground and power at the expense of the West
because, short of a shooting war, the West is compelled by law to

---

32. *The Memoirs of Cordell Hull*, 2 vols. (New York: Macmillan, 1948), I, p.
297.

operate in terms of peace. Military aid to victims of Communist aggression is sporadic and sometimes secret. The West does not recognize military encirclement until the last moment.

If Hitler had not foolishly declared war against the United States on Thursday, December 11, 1941, it is difficult to know what the U.S. would have done. We subsequently committed most of our military resources to the European war, not to the Pacific, where Japan had attacked us. Roosevelt had wanted to take the U.S. into the war in Europe, as published documents from Churchill's secret cabinet speeches revealed thirty years later. For years, American historians had denied this.

> LONDON, Jan. 1 (AP) — Formerly top secret British Government papers made public today said that President Franklin D. Roosevelt told Prime Minister Winston Churchill in August, 1941, that he was looking for an incident to justify opening hostilities against Nazi Germany.[33]

But Roosevelt could not have accomplished his goal without Hitler's help. Even today, hardly any American without an advanced degree in U.S. history or modern European history knows the legal basis of our entry into the war in Europe in 1941. The Soviets are too wise to make a similar error. The encircling process goes on, yet the West extends long-term credits to the Soviet Union as if the Soviet Union were a U.S. ally.

Summary

The humanistic West is engaged in a long-term policy of surrender to totalitarian Communism. Our diplomats are not committed to the survival of the West. They seek peace, but it is the peace of surrender. They hope to attain conditional surrender through convergence. The Communists are more consistent: they seek unconditional surrender, but in bite-sized portions.

There can never be peace in history outside of Christ. There can be temporary cease-fire agreements, but never a lasting

---

33. *New York Times* (Jan. 2, 1972), p. 7.

peace. What Christians must understand is that peace is attained through the preaching of the gospel and the discipling of the nations. There is no other way. God will not permit peace on any other terms. War and peace are always covenantal concepts. As long as God and Satan are engaged in a spiritual, historical, and cosmic battle, so their covenanted disciples will be engaged in spiritual, historical, and earthly conflict.

Foreign policy must be restructured in every Christian nation to reflect this struggle. It, too, must be reconstructed in terms of the Bible. The goal is international peace, but only on Christ's terms.

In summary:

1. A cosmic battle is always going on between God and Satan.
2. These wars are the result of sin in men's hearts.
3. Men universally want peace.
4. Peace cannot be defined neutrally.
5. The Communists have seen this clearly, and define peace in terms of a worldwide Communist victory.
6. God also defines peace in terms of conquest: every knee shall bow to Jesus Christ.
7. Christians can be peaceful warriors.
8. Peace is covenantal and attained through covenant-keeping.
9. The war of this age is a war of first principles: God as God vs. man as God.
10. The West's political leaders refuse to see that such a theological war is going on.
11. Democracies will not admit that a war between two rival systems is going on.
12. The West's humanists seek a convergence between liberalism and Communism.
13. They seek the visible political unification of man.
14. This is a statement of faith: the unity of the godhead.
15. The explanation for the West's policy of détente is found in the West's humanist theology.
16. The ultimate expression of this faith is the doctrine of

unilateral disarmament by the West.

17. The West does not have any formal way to deal with an enemy nation until a formal declaration of war takes place after the shooting has begun.

5

GOD'S LEGACY OF PROGRESSIVE PEACE

He shall judge between the nations, and shall rebuke many people; they shall beat their swords into plowshares, and their spears into pruninghooks. Nation shall not lift up sword against nation, neither shall they learn war anymore (Isaiah 2:4).

The fifth point of the Biblical covenant is inheritance. Inheritance is the basis of continuity in history. Implied in the concept of inheritance is disinheritance. The enemies of God will be cut off finally at the final judgment. They are also disinherited progressively in history.

The goal of foreign policy is peace. This means *peace on God's covenantal terms*. There is no other basis of lasting peace—personally, locally, nationally, or internationally. God does not offer rebellious mankind peace on any other basis. To be at war with God covenantally is to abandon the only basis of peace on earth.

Can international peace happen in history? Yes, for this is the God-inspired prophecy of Isaiah 2:4 and Micah 4:3. There are few, if any, prophecies in the Bible that are more appealing to mankind than this one. International peace is one of life's almost universally acknowledged goals, despite the fact that so little planning for peace goes on in the world, compared with planning for war.

Peace is the fruit of a previous victory. (This victory need not be military in nature; it is covenantal victory, not military victory.) Nothing else but covenantal victory can produce lasting true peace. A peace other than covenantal peace is only a temporary cease-fire. Permanent peace comes only at the final judgment.

121

"For He must reign till He has put all enemies under His feet. The last enemy that will be destroyed is death" (1 Corinthians 15:25-26).

Thus, the search for perfect peace is legitimate, so long as we bear in mind that it cannot be attained in sinful history:

> "We have a strong city; God will appoint salvation for walls and bulwarks. Open the gates, that the righteous nation which keeps the truth may enter in. *You will keep him in perfect peace, whose mind is stayed on You*, because he trusts in You. Trust in the LORD forever, for in YAH, the LORD, is everlasting strength. For He brings down those who dwell on high, the lofty city; He lays it low. He lays it low to the ground. He brings it down to the dust. The foot shall tread it down — the feet of the poor and the steps of the needy" (Isaiah 26:1b-6; emphasis added).

Again, the issue is *faith*, not walls; *ethics*, not weapons. Perfect faith brings perfect peace; and we are to seek perfect faith. We are commanded to be perfect (Matthew 5:48), even though we inevitably sin in history: "If we say that we have no sin, we deceive ourselves, and the truth is not in us" (1 John 1:8). The perfect humanity of Jesus is our standard; we are told to pursue it, to be conformed to the image of God's Son (Romans 8:29). The search for peace goes on, but Christ alone brings perfect peace through *perfect victory*. He gives it definitively to His people when they are converted. He brings it progressively in history. He fulfills it finally at the last judgment.

Jesus did not come to bring us peace in this world. He brings us *peace with God* which assures us of *conflict with God's enemies*. Paul wrote to the church in Rome regarding the coming judgment of their enemies, "And the God of peace will crush Satan under your feet shortly. The grace of our Lord Jesus Christ be with you. Amen" (Romans 16:20). Ethical peace with God brings ethical warfare with the anti-Christian forces of this world. This is why Christ is Prince of peace, but only on His own terms, with peace defined as the victory of Christ's people in history. Anything less than this victory is the world's peace, not Christ's, and He came to destroy this world's peace. Citing Micah 7:6, Christ said:

"Do not think that I came to bring peace on earth. I did not come to bring peace but a sword. For I have come to 'set a man against his father, a daughter against her mother, and a daughter-in-law against her mother-in-law.' And 'a man's foes will be those of his own household' " (Matthew 10:34-35).

Christian foreign policy must begin with this view of peaceful relations among nations. The humanist's peaceful world is a world at war with God.

Swords Into Plowshares

The phrase, "swords into plowshares," was adopted as the title for a book on humanist internationalism back in the late 1950's. The book closes with a ringing declaration of confidence in the United Nations Organization, an organization that has proven to be so hopelessly inept, so overstaffed with overpaid and underworked bureaucrats, so impotent in dealing with the fundamental international issues of our era, that political liberals have begun to regard it as another god that has failed. I shall never forget photographs in the newspaper of U.N. members from Africa dancing on their desks when Red China was admitted over the objection of the United States. I cannot resist quoting the book's conclusion, if only as a reminder of how naive humanists are. It serves as a reminder that Christians should not be overawed at their intellectual opposition. "The United Nations, for all its imperfections and inadequacies, is an achievement of the first magnitude. It is a symbol of the urge to civilization. It is a repository of decent hopes and progressive aspirations. It is a center for the consideration of, and a mechanism for the effectuation of, such plans as governments can agree upon to improve the common human lot and safeguard the common human destiny. It is an instrument for the mobilization of as much good will and good sense as the political leaders of divided humanity can muster for dealing with the critical issues of our time. As such, it draws into its proceedings the representatives of virtually every state which can contrive to obtain membership. The United Nations can be, and is being, abused,

used, and improved. It may not be the last or the best hope of mankind, but it is an indispensable instrument of the human effort to muddle through the crises of the present and rise to the challenges of the future."[1]

The Bible's goal is clear: international peace. Christian nations are to "wage a peace offensive." But how is this "peace offensive" to be pursued? By a "convergence" between East and West, North and South? By unilateral disarmament? By billions of dollars of taxes in foreign aid programs?

The Bible is very clear concerning the nature of peace. It is one of the blessings promised in the blessings section of Deuteronomy 28, the Bible's key passage that deals with the sanctions of God:

> Now it shall come to pass, if you diligently obey the voice of the LORD your God, to observe carefully all His commandments which I command you today, that the LORD your God will set you high above all nations of the earth. And all these blessings shall come upon you and overtake you, because you obey the voice of the LORD your God: Blessed shall you be in the city, and blessed shall you be in the country. Blessed shall be the fruit of your body, the produce of your ground and the increase of your herds, the increase of your cattle and the offspring of your flocks. Blessed shall be your basket and your kneading bowl. Blessed shall you be when you come in, and blessed shall you be when you go out. The LORD will cause your enemies who rise against you to be defeated before your face; they shall come out against you one way and flee before you seven ways. . . . Then all the peoples of the earth shall see that you are called by the name of the LORD, and they shall be afraid of you (Deuteronomy 28:1-7, 10).

This was God's covenantal promise to Israel as a lonely and frequently besieged nation. But with the gospel of Christ spreading throughout the world, this promise can be appropriated by a federation of faithful nations. The promise of peace meant that

---

1. Inis L. Claude, Jr., *Swords Into Plowshares: The Problems and Progress of International Organization* (2nd ed.; New York: Random House, 1959), p. 472.

there would be fewer and fewer enemies willing and able to raise the battle cry against God-protected Israel. It means the same today.

Peace is therefore seen in the Bible *as the ability militarily to wage war successfully, if necessary.* But what about turning swords into plowshares? If peace really means preparation for war, how can swords be converted into plowshares? They cannot be, *until the enemies of God have died on the field of battle, or else have retreated or surrendered.* Christian international relations can seek military disarmament only if Christians affirm the legitimacy of, and work toward, national and international covenantal commitment to God. Only if nations *as nations* affirm the covenant of Christ can international relations progressively attain peace.

In short, if there were no such thing as a Christian nation, there could be no such thing as Bible-defined international peace in this world. We would be condemned to a world of endless military conflict. But we are not condemned to this. Jesus said very clearly that when we hear wars and rumors of wars, the end is not at hand. "And you will hear of wars and rumors of wars. See that you are not troubled; for all these things must come to pass, but the end is not yet" (Matthew 24:7).

What those who cite "swords into plowshares" fail to recognize is that the Bible also calls on the enemies of God to launch a doomed offensive against the protected nation. The Bible calls God's enemies into a losing battle. The Bible teaches plowshares into swords . . . *first.*

Plowshares Into Swords

We are familiar with the phrase, "swords into plowshares." It applies to covenantally faithful nations. But the reverse phrase also appears in the Bible, "plowshares into swords." It applies to covenantally rebellious nations. This is the message of the prophet Joel:

> Proclaim this among the nations: "Prepare for war! Wake up the mighty men. Let all the men of war draw near. Let them come up. Beat your plowshares into swords and your pruninghooks into

spears. Let the weak say, 'I am strong.'" Assemble and come, all you nations, and gather together all around. Cause your mighty ones to go down there, O LORD.

Let the nations be wakened, and come up to the Valley of Jehoshaphat; for there I will sit to judge all the surrounding nations. Put in the sickle, for the harvest is ripe. Come, go down; for the winepress is full, the vats overflow—for their wickedness is great (Joel 3:9-13).

Then Joel promises, "But the LORD will be a shelter for His people, and the strength of the children of Israel" (Joel 3:16b).

It should be clear what is being said here. The wickedness of the nations leads them at last into self-confident contempt for God and God's people. They take up weapons to invade the land of the righteous. They are lured by the illusion of strength, when in fact they are weak—weak compared to God the Judge. It is wickedness that weakens the enemies of God, and it is righteousness that strengthens the people of God. Weakness and strength are not technical concepts, but *ethical* concepts. Judgment is God's judgment, not the warriors' judgment. "Yet I will have mercy on the house of Judah, will save them by the LORD their God, and will not save them by bow, nor by sword or battle, by horses or horsemen" (Hosea 1:7). It is a question of where men place their trust. Who do they believe is the judge? What is the basis of the judgment rendered, including on the battlefield?

Now I know that the LORD saves His anointed; He will answer him from His holy heaven with the saving strength of His right hand. Some trust in chariots, and some in horses; but we will remember the name of the LORD our God. They have bowed down and fallen; but we have risen and stand upright (Psalm 20:6-8).

The tyrants of the world eventually "overplay their hand." They are incapable of judging their own limitations and drawing back in order to consolidate their gains. The Soviet Union has been better than most in following Lenin's policy of two steps forward and one step back, of marching forward until resistance is met. But eventually, God's judgment will fall on them: they will go too far in their confidence in weapons. This is the fate of all empires. They do not know where or when to stop.

Arms Control

There is no goal of foreign policy in the humanistic West more sacred than this one. The humanist elite that sets Western foreign policy will sell anything, or sell out any nation, in order to gain an arms control agreement with the most successful liars in history, the Soviet Union. The West's humanists believe that if both sides in the conflict between the "superpowers" reduce their weapons supply, that peace has a better chance of breaking out. They misread the Bible.

The Bible tells us to put no faith in offensive military weapons. The kings of Israel were commanded not to gather horses (Deuteronomy 17:16), for horses were offensive weapons. Leaders were not to multiply wives, either, or gold (v. 17). They were to make a copy of the law for themselves and read it, in order to keep themselves humble:

> Also it shall be, when he sits on the throne of his kingdom, that he shall write for himself a copy of this law in a book, from the one before the priests, the Levites. And it shall be with him, and he shall read it all the days of his life, that he may learn to fear the LORD his God and be careful to observe all the words of this law and these statutes, that his heart may not be lifted above his brethren, that he may not turn aside from the commandment to the right hand or to the left, and that he may prolong his days in his kingdom, he and his children in the midst of Israel (Deuteronomy 17:18-20).

The prophet Joel called the enemies of God to build up their military arsenal. It seems clear from the context that this call is made toward the end of a long confrontation, not at the beginning or in the middle, when peace might be secured on favorable terms for the righteous. Peace is clearly impossible at this final stage, so the enemy is then goaded by God's prophet to attack, to go on the offensive, to build offensive weapons out of their tools of production. Yet God instructed the kings of Israel to refrain from build-

ing up offensive weapons. They were to avoid displays of great
wealth. They were to study the law of God all of their days, in
order to keep from becoming arrogant. It is arrogance in the face
of God that is the sure path to destruction.

Arms control is a legitimate goal in a Christian commonwealth. Weapons should be defensive. The enemy must know
that an attack will be met with overwhelming resistance, but that
if they leave us alone militarily, they will be left alone militarily.
(They will never be left alone evangelistically; they must live with
that pressure until their conversion or their self-destruction.) The
Bible is confident that the Word of God is sufficiently powerful to
bring down kingdoms. Offensive weapons are not the tools of dominion. The gospel and Biblical law are the tools of dominion.[2]

The call for organized, formal mutual disarmament is nonsense. Each nation is responsible for its own policies. Disarmament schemes in the years between World War I and World War
II benefitted Germany and Japan's war plans, not the West's. The
tyrants built up their war machines, and the democracies let their
military forces rust. Yet as it turned out, the Axis powers lost the
War. This should not be ignored. They gained too much confidence in their weapons. They went on the offensive, and lost.

Is unilateral disarmament appropriate? No, but unilateral
shifting from an offensive strategy and arsenal to a defensive strategy and arsenal is not only legitimate, it is required by God. Humanists refuse to accept this, which is why the West continues to
rely on a policy of nuclear retaliation against civilian populations
—Mutual Assured Destruction (MAD)—rather than on a space-
based defense that would make intercontinental ballistic missiles
strategically obsolete. MAD is not a defense policy, but rather a
revenge policy.

The Bible clearly teaches arms control. Arms control is to be
self-imposed on the king of a righteous nation. Covenantal faithfulness must become the foundation of a successful military

---

2. Gary North, *Tools of Dominion: The Case Laws of Exodus* (Tyler, Texas: Institute for Christian Reconstruction, 1987).

defense program. The Bible calls on God's enemies to build up huge, misleading, bankrupting arsenals. The final showdown in history takes place when the enemies of God surround the faithful, thinking them to be defenseless (Revelation 20:8-10).[3] It is God's supreme irony: in the appearance of weakness there is strength. Note: in the *appearance* of weakness, not in weakness as such. Strength is ethical, not military.

The great danger of arms control programs is that the fearful will put their faith in the piece of paper rather than in God. The tyrants, in contrast, will continue to build up their weapons, but their fear-ridden opponents will do everything possible to conceal this fact from the voters, or de-emphasize the importance of violations of the agreement. We saw this in England and France in the 1930's, and we have seen it in the United States in the 1980's.

Thus, a legitimate goal—strategic realignment from offense to defense—is made illegal or unacceptable to the fearful nation or alliance, which wants to avoid all new risks, while the illegitimate goal of arms build-up is pursued by the empires, making war that much more likely.

The Stated Goal of a War Should Be Victory

The foreign policy of Christian nations should have one goal in mind: the conversion of all national allies into Christian allies, and the conversion of all enemies into either non-Christian allies or Christian allies. There can be no religious neutrality in international relations.

If this conversion process does not take place, and a shooting war begins, then the primary tasks of foreign policy shift to the military: the destruction of the enemy's ability to fight. Foreign policy then becomes military policy. The politicians turn foreign policy over to the chief executive, who in turn tells the generals and admirals what resources they have and what rules to follow. He then spends his time deciding which senior officers to fire or

---

3. Gary North, *Dominion and Common Grace: The Biblical Basis of Progress* (Tyler, Texas: Institute for Christian Economics, 1987), pp. 99-100.

promote, and encouraging voters and allies to stick with the program of military victory.

This is the key, in peace and war, day in and day out: *a vision of victory.* Nothing else will suffice. Any diplomat who is not on the job to make victory possible should be fired. Any foreign policy officer whose goal is not the victory of the West over the Communists should be fired.

Life is covenantal. God's covenant governs a nation's life, or else Satan's covenant does. We wear Christ's yoke (which is light) or else we wear Satan's yoke. There is no life without a covenantal yoke. Life is therefore a war between covenanted societies.

Diplomats or Ambassadors?

Such a vision of victory is rejected by the West's humanists, though not by the Communists. A good statement of this no-victory view is found in a book by Henry Wriston, one of the most influential humanists in United States foreign policy in the twentieth century. He was the father of Walter B. Wriston, the former chairman of Citicorp, the holding company of the largest and most influential bank in the United States. Henry Wriston served as President of the Council on Foreign Relations from 1951 until 1964. The CFR is the United States' most influential foreign policy organization, even more influential than the State Department itself, which CFR members have dominated at the senior positions since 1941. Senator Prescott Bush, father of the Vice President of the United States (1981-   ), said in 1961 to his colleagues in the Senate concerning Dr. Wriston: "He is credited with having 'Wristonized' the Foreign Service of the United States."[4]

In 1956, Wriston introduced his series of lectures at Claremont Colleges in California with these words: "The foreign Service Officer Corps has been virtually invisible throughout the larger part of its half century or more of history. This is not peculiar or abnormal. . . . But their effectiveness is in almost inverse ratio to

---

4. Cited by Dan Smoot, *The Invisible Government* (Boston: Western Islands, [1962] 1977), p. 12.

their conspicuousness. It is not only bad form, it is bad diplomacy, for them to win 'victories.' Such 'triumphs' are hollow, for they are bound to injure domestically the government with which the diplomat has to deal, and make future relationships and negotiations more difficult, needlessly."[5]

Contrast this view of a diplomat with Jesus' Great Commission. Jesus gave the job of kingdom ambassador to the disciples. He was and is God's representative to mankind on earth and in heaven. His disciples are under His discipline, and are responsible to their Commander-in-Chief.

The same should be true of a nation's international ambassadors. They owe allegiance to the nation's political head. They should be hired and fired based on the decision of political authorities, not on the basis of their years inside a closed bureaucracy. Any interference with this system of personal accountability disrupts the chain of command (in this case the authority of the voting public) and eventually creates disastrous situations. There must be *hierarchical accountability*. There must be an unbroken chain of command in government, whether in Church or State.

An ambassador should be polite. He should be diplomatic. But he should not be a professional diplomat. The ambassador should owe his job directly to the Prime Minister or President. He must be fully accountable to a political representative of the voters. Today, this is seldom the case. The diplomat is protected by Civil Service, or by the "old boy network," or by other formal restrictions against his being fired at will, so he cannot be fired by a political representative except for gross malfeasance in office. Until this is changed, there is no hope to restore sanity to foreign policy. An ambassador must represent the political representatives of the people. A diplomat represents the professional foreign policy establishment.

The problem with Western foreign policy is that it is conducted by diplomats for the sake of those elitists who benefit from

---

5. Henry M. Wriston, *Diplomacy in a Democracy* (New York: Harper & Brothers, 1956), pp. 3-4.

continued trade with the enemy.[6] The economic deal-doers have taken control of the policy-making organizations, so the diplomats are paid to avoid confrontations with the Communists. For example, the U.S. Department of Commerce secretly helped to establish a highly secretive non-profit, tax-exempt foundation in the mid-1970's, the US-USSR Trade and Economic Council, located in New York City.[7] Step by step, decade by decade, Western diplomats and Western businessmen have worked hand in hand to strengthen the Communist bloc nations.

Diplomats are specialists in softening rival positions, trading with the other side. The result has been a steady retreat by the West in the face of danger for over two generations. If we count 1933-38, it has been almost three generations.

An ambassador is to represent the national interests of his country. He is not a professional negotiator. Negotiators are useful professionals, but *only when a nation is negotiating with its allies*. They should not be let anywhere near a self-identified enemy. We should not trade with the enemy, so we need to keep specialists in trading—economics or politics—completely out of the picture.

This is not some strange view of foreign policy. Professor Richard Pipes of Harvard, a specialist in the Soviet Union, has pointed out, first, that in the United States, the Constitution designates the President as the person responsible for conducting foreign policy, not the Department of State. Second, the Department of State is concerned with diplomacy, not foreign policy: "The belief that the State Department is the proper instrument of foreign policy derives from the fallacious view that foreign policy is synonymous with diplomacy—which, as has been pointed out, is not the case. The Department of State is the branch of government specifically responsible for diplomacy in all its aspects, and

---

6. Antony C. Sutton, *The Best Enemy Money Can Buy* (Billings, Montana: Liberty House Press, 1986).

7. Joseph Finder, *Red Carpet* (Ft. Worth, Texas: American Bureau of Economic Research, [1983] 1987), pp. 254-60. This book was originally published by Holt, Rinehart and Winston.

this involves, first and foremost, the peaceful resolution of disagreements and conflicts with other sovereign states. This task has a great deal in common with law. And indeed, on closer acquaintance, the Department gives the impression of a giant law firm. . . . Diplomats have an instinctive aversion to violence and an insurmountable suspicion of ideology; the one is to them evidence of professional failure, the other, a hindrance to accords. Foreign Service officers have as much taste for ideas and political strategies as trial lawyers have for the philosophy of law. They squirm at the very mention of the words *good* and *evil*, which in their professional capacity they regard as meaningless."[8] But the conflict between good and evil is what the history of man is all about. To deny this is to surrender in principle to the satanic enemy.

A Spiritual Conflict

We are in a great spiritual conflict. This conflict takes place in history. There *are* covenantal institutions, and civil governments are among these covenantal institutions. Thus, the idea that a nation can never be Christian is preposterous. Nations are clearly Islamic. The State of Israel is Jewish, to be sure, even to the point of imposing a jail sentence on anyone who preaches the gospel of Jesus Christ to an Israeli. The Soviet Union, even the *New York Times* occasionally admits, is a Communist nation. But no nation can ever be Christian, we are assured. Why not? *Because the humanist elites that run the West's nations are anti-Christian.* They do not want to lose their jobs if voters begin voting as Christians. They also do not want to lose power.

Should they ever be in positions of political authority, Christians should insist that no Civil Service protection or other bureaucratic restrictions on the political firing of staffers should be tolerated. We are not talking about the municipal garbage collection agency. We are talking about conducting a war to the death — the death of the West or the death of Communism, preferably by

---

8. Richard Pipes, *Survival Is Not Enough: Soviet Realities and America's Future* (New York: Simon & Schuster, 1984), pp. 273-74.

the triumph of Christians in Communist nations. Time-serving bureaucrats should have no role to play in foreign policy, at least not in any dealings with the enemy.

It is not surprising that the Rockefeller Panel Reports, compiled in the late 1950's and issued in 1961, came to the defense of this most important elite in the U.S. government, the U.S. Foreign Service. The continuing revelations during the 1950's concerning the infiltration of the Foreign Service by Communist sympathizers had created growing public hostility against this humanist monopoly. Therefore, Report I (Dec. 8, 1959), "The Mid-Century Challenge to Foreign Policy," noted:

> In a mature democracy, the Department of State and the Foreign Service require a degree of popular support that has not been regularly forthcoming. The stereotype of a Foreign Service officer as a man in striped pants who trades secrets at cocktail parties has, happily, been modified in recent years. But the public does not yet have a full sense of the skill, dedication, and often self-lessness that are asked of representatives in this field. It still does not set as high a value as it should upon the role of these officials.
>
> A democracy cannot afford to provide them with careers—in terms of opportunity for promotion and in terms of pay—that fall short of the highest careers of public life. The barring of top diplomatic posts to men not endowed with private wealth must be corrected.[9]

And corrected it was! Pressures were subsequently placed on all U.S. Presidents after John Kennedy, and an unofficial agreement was reached—one that the public has never been told about. Today, two-thirds of all ambassadorial posts must be filled by Foreign Service officers, who in turn are selected by the Foreign Service bureaucracy itself, not by the President. The President appoints only one-third of his ambassadors. I did not learn of this quiet arrangement until I discussed the Foreign Service screening system with Morton Blackwell, a former White House liaison

---

9. *Prospect for America: The Rockefeller Panel Reports* (Garden City, New York: Doubleday, 1961), pp. 81-82.

officer for President Reagan, in May of 1987.[10]

There will be no stalemate on the day of judgment. History is to reflect progressively the definitive victory of Christ over Satan at Calvary, developing toward the final victory of Christ over Satan at the last judgment. No compromise with the principle of victory is tolerable. Our victory cannot be total, nor should we offer terms of unconditional surrender, for fallen men in a sin-filled world are in no position to demand total anything or unconditional anything. But the movement of history should progressively reflect God's total victory, both definitive and final. It should progressively reflect God's demand of unconditional surrender.[11]

This is what modern diplomacy has denied since the end of World War II. Hitler was the last internationally acknowledged "devil incarnate." Modern diplomacy is geared to "settling disputes out of court," as Pipes says. The diplomats can work on settling such international conflicts as fishing and water disputes, rescheduling of debts, and so forth. "But," he says, "these issues embrace only a part, and not even necessarily the most important part, of international relations as practiced in the twentieth century; the latter include also military power, ideology, and a host of other matters that are implicit in Grand Strategy and do not lend themselves to resolution by diplomatic means. As soon as international conflict is shifted to this ground, diplomacy is powerless. The natural reaction of diplomats under these circumstances is to minimize the phenomena they are incompetent to deal with, so as to reduce everything to manageable — that is, negotiable — terms, where their particular skills can come into play."[12]

What happens, he says, is that diplomats minimize the ideological statements of totalitarian leaders. They say that such statements are mere rhetoric. They begin a search for the dictator's

---

10. An audiocassette of my 90-minute interview with Blackwell is available from Dominion Tapes, P.O. Box 8204, Ft. Worth, Texas 76124: $10.

11. Gary North, *Unconditional Surrender: God's Program for Victory* (3rd ed.; Ft. Worth, Texas: Dominion Press, 1987).

12. Pipes, *Survival Is Not Enough*, p. 274.

"real" demands. Appeasement has therefore been basic to Western diplomacy throughout this century. Hitler bluffed his way from German military weakness in 1933 to German control over much of Central Europe by 1939, and the European professional diplomats never learned to deal with him.[13] Pipes concludes: "Thus, for both constitutional reasons and reasons connected with the peculiarities of totalitarian politics, the State Department is not the proper agency to formulate and execute foreign policy toward the Soviet Union or any other totalitarian state. These states play by different rules and must be dealt with accordingly. Since they employ Grand Strategy, to the extent that democracies are capable of coordinated foreign policies, these must be undertaken by the chief executive."[14]

Summary

It is the God-assigned task of Christians to render righteous judgments in history, in preparation for the day that we shall judge the angels (1 Corinthians 6:3). Exercising righteous judgment is a difficult task. When Adam failed to judge righteously between the claims of Satan and the claims of God, he fell, and his posterity lives under the curses that God applied in His righteous judgment.

The worldwide task of preaching the gospel and subduing the hearts, minds, and souls of men to Christ is a form of spiritual warfare. It is a war aimed at attaining peace, but only on God's terms. There is no other way to attain peace. Peace is a blessing from God, as are all good gifts (James 1:17). Thus, Christian nations must wage peace. Sometimes this involves preparing for war. But military warfare is always to be defensive; the sword of the Lord is our offensive weapon: preaching. We are to trust God to provide our national defense. A Department of Defense is legitimate; a Department of Offense isn't.

---

13. A. J. P. Taylor, *The Origins of the Second World War* (2nd ed.; New York: Fawcett, [1961] 1965).

14. *Survival Is Not Enough*, p. 275.

A Christian nation is not to seek to impose its national will on other nations. It can legitimately offer to help other nations prepare to defend themselves. It is not the task of a Christian nation to "save another nation from itself." If God is about to bring a pagan nation under judgment, and that nation will neither repent before God nor appeal to God's representative nation or nations for assistance, then it should be allowed to fall to the invader. The empire will eventually overextend itself. The righteous nation will not perish. The problem comes when righteous people live in unrighteous nations. Sometimes, they are carried into captivity for a while.

We need ambassadors who understand the theological nature of the confrontation, and who will press the claims of Christ. Diplomats can negotiate the details with covenanted allies, pagan allies, and even neutrals. They should not be allowed to negotiate with hostile nations. They do not possess the required skills.

We must strengthen our allies and weaken our enemies. We must be guided by a vision of victory. We must work day and night for victory. Nothing else can succeed. There is no compromise with evil. There is no substitute for victory.

In summary:

1. The goal of international relations is peace with God, not peace with Satan.

2. International relations must face the fact that nations seek to impose their will on other nations, just as God seeks to impose His will on His enemies.

3. Christian nations must trust in God, not weapons.

4. We are not to go unarmed into battle, however: David and Goliath.

5. Christian foreign policy is to seek the surrender of the nations of the world to God through an international covenant.

6. Peace is the fruit of a previous victory, though not usually a military victory.

7. Perfect peace comes only at the last judgment.

8. Perfect peace is a legitimate goal in history, but impossible to attain.

9. Perfect peace, perfect victory, and perfect humanity are

found only in the Person of Christ.

10. This perfection is imputed to us definitively at the point of conversion.

11. Peace with God produces conflict with God's enemies.

12. Humanists seek their peace through conquest or international agreement.

13. Swords are turned into plowshares as the enemies of God surrender covenantally and nationally to God.

14. If there is no such thing as a Christian nation, there can be no such thing as international peace in this world.

15. God lures sinful empires to turn plowshares into swords as preliminary acts of aggression against Christian nations.

16. This act of rebellion then brings destruction to the rebels.

17. Tyrants eventually "overplay their hand."

18. Arms control is an illegitimate international goal.

19. What is valid is the conversion of offensive weapons to defensive weapons in Christian nations.

20. Unilateral disarmament is illegitimate Biblically.

21. The goal of a war should be victory.

22. Diplomats are peace-seekers, not people who can deal successfully with war.

23. Christian nations should confine the use of diplomats to relations among nations that are not declared enemies.

24. Ambassadors should press the claims of Christ on every nation.

25. The international goal of history is the unconditional surrender of all nations to God.

6

ALL PEOPLE ARE CITIZENS OF TWO WORLDS

For many walk, of whom I have told you often, and now tell you even weeping, that they are the enemies of the cross of Christ: whose end is destruction, whose god is their belly, and whose glory is in their shame—who set their mind on earthly things. For our citizenship is in heaven, from which we also eagerly wait for the Savior, the Lord Jesus Christ, who will transform our lowly body that it may be conformed to His glorious body, according to the working by which He is able even to subdue all things to Himself (Philippians 3:18-21).

The first point of the Biblical covenant is the doctrine of the true transcendence of God. God is wholly distinct from His creation, yet wholly present with it. All the events of history must be interpreted in terms of God and God's sovereign plan for history. The world centers around God. The world is *theocentric*.

Men are always in the presence of God. He is everywhere. But His presence is always mediated by the covenant. It is not enough that people are always in God's presence; they must acknowledge Him as sovereign. People are required to make a choice in life between two declared sovereigns in the universe: God and Satan. They must make a covenant. There is no escape from the covenant. It is never a question of covenant vs. no covenant. It is always a question of *which* covenant. We are born physically into Satan's covenant, our legacy from Adam. Whether implicitly or explicitly, we affirm his covenant by natural birth. Only by the grace of God are we adopted into God's family (John 1:12).

Only by grace do we become citizens of God's heavenly nation.

God calls all men to change their "citizenship papers." He calls them to leave Satan's covenanted kingdom and join God's covenanted kingdom. There is no neutrality. There is no third choice of spiritual nations. There are only two: God's and Satan's.

This means that all people are citizens of a supernatural nation. Everyone works in history to make manifest his particular supernatural citizenship. He works to manifest heaven on earth or hell on earth. There is no neutrality. There is no possibility of any nation on earth not reflecting one or the other supernatural nation. This is why God will judge the nations at the end of time.

> When the Son of Man comes in His glory, and all the holy angels with Him, then He will sit on the throne of His glory. All the nations will be gathered before Him, and He will separate them one from another, as a shepherd divides his sheep from the goats. And He will set the sheep on His right hand, but the goats on the left. Then the King will say to those on His right hand, "Come, you blessed of My Father, inherit the kingdom prepared for you before the foundation of the world" (Matthew 25:31-34).

Covenant Citizenship Is the Model for All Citizenship

It is obvious that with respect to the final manifestation of God's kingdom, there will be absolute, eternal inclusion and exclusion. There is no universal salvation. There will be saved and lost forever. The saved are resurrected to reign with Christ in the new heaven and new earth (Revelation 21-22), while the unsaved are dumped into the lake of eternal fire (Revelation 20:14).

Our "citizenship papers" are taken out by God in our name when He imputes Christ's perfect humanity to us at the time of our salvation by grace. Christians already possess *in principle* eternal life: "He who believes in the Son has everlasting life; and he who does not believe the Son shall not see life, but the wrath of God abides on him" (John 3:36). The Christian has eternal life *now*, in history. Nevertheless, all Christians will die physically, except those who are transformed in a twinkling of an eye at the coming of Christ in final judgment. (Of course, this too is the death of the old Adam physically, but it comes in a much-preferred form.)

Christians are citizens of two countries: heaven and earth. Anti-Christians are also the citizens of two countries: hell and earth, although I know of no Bible verse that says this as explicitly as Philippians 3:20 says it regarding Christian citizenship. Surely, covenant breakers are dead in trespasses and sins. Surely the wrath of God abides on them in principle *now*: ". . . and he who does not believe the Son shall not see life, but the wrath of God abides on him" (John 3:36b). It does not require a great leap of faith to conclude that covenant-breakers are citizens of hell, in the same way that redeemed covenant-keepers are citizens of heaven.

The dividing issue regarding a people's supernatural citizenship is the covenant-renewing supper. With whom do men partake in their communion meal? With God or with demons? Is their communion holy or unholy? This is what Paul asks in 1 Corinthians 10 and 11. He warns us, "You cannot drink the cup of the Lord and the cup of demons; you cannot partake of the Lord's table and of the table of demons" (1 Corinthians 10:21). People partake of these meals on earth and in history. They are this-worldly events as well as other-worldly. The two meals are at war with each other; the two supernatural kingdoms are at war with each other.

This points to *the* fact of history: the earth is a battlefield between two rival forces, the followers of God and the followers of Satan. This battle is primarily *ethical* in nature. Two rival law-orders are involved: Christ's and Satan's. There can be no ethical neutrality; therefore, there can be no judicial neutrality. Ethical neutrality is a myth. So is natural law (Chapter Three).

God has *already* established the basis of citizenship in His kingdom: ethical perfection. Only Jesus Christ has (or can) achieve this perfection in history. Thus, the basis of the Christian's citizenship in heaven is God's imputation of Christ's perfect humanity (though not His divinity) to those whom He graciously redeems. God the Father declares them "not guilty" because of the work of His Son in history (Chapter Four).

But never forget: we are citizens of earth, too. We are not of the world, but we are *in* the world. We are citizens on earth. More to the point, *the whole concept of earthly political citizenship is based on the Bible's concept of supernatural citizenship.* Heavenly citizenship is the God-required model. God did not invent the category of heavenly citizenship based on the earthly model of citizenship. He did not look to Greece, Rome, or the United States Constitution to discover the proper concept of citizenship to establish in heaven. This may seem silly to stress, but it is vital. Because Christians *implicitly* believe that all citizenship is earth-originated, they adopt as their model of heavenly citizenship this or that pagan political model of what it means to be a citizen.

There can be no religiously neutral society in history. There can be no religiously neutral nation. Nations, like people, are either covenant-breakers or covenant-keepers, as Sodom and Gomorrah learned too late. There can be no people who hold citizenship papers in only one nation, earth. In history, we all hold earthly citizenship papers and supernatural citizenship papers, heaven or hell.

Covenant-keepers are required by God to seek to extend God's kingdom principles on earth: the Great Commission (Matthew 28:18-20). Covenant-breakers are required by Satan to extend anti-Christian, satanic kingdom principles on earth. Thus, earth's nations in history reflect one or the other kingdom. They manifest primarily either heaven on earth or hell on earth. There is no possibility of any nation manifesting a neutral kingdom of man that is neither heavenly or hellish. It is *the humanist lie of permanent political pluralism* that teaches that such earthly citizenship is possible, manifesting neither God's covenant nor Satan's. Yet most Christians have held (and still hold) to concepts of earthly citizenship that are implicitly and even explicitly "single-citizenship papers" theories of political participation. The Marxists know better. This is why they are winning. They have always had a far more consistent theory of earthly citizenship: "Christians need not apply."

Eternal Citizenship: Inclusion Requires Exclusion

Some people are included in God's eternal kingdom, while others are forever excluded. This eternal separation will take place when God judges all people at the last day. He will judge them as members of nations, for He is the Judge of the nations (Matthew 25:31-35).

What must be understood is that this covenant structure is truly covenantal. Many people have interpreted such verses as Matthew 25:31-35 as referring exclusively to individual salvation, but God's covenant encompasses more than simply individual souls. It also involves institutional salvation, meaning restoration. It involves each of the three covenantal institutions ordained by God: church, State, and family. To restrict the meaning of salvation of the human soul is to misread Scripture.

God judges between two kinds of nations. This division reflects the two kinds of people who dominate the nations in history. Paul writes that there are only two kinds of people in this world: covenant-keepers and covenant-breakers.

Covenant-breakers are those who "are the enemies of the cross of Christ, whose end is destruction, whose god is their belly, and whose glory is in their shame — who set their mind on earthly things." Covenant-keepers are those who can honestly say that their "citizenship is in heaven," and who publicly acknowledge that they "eagerly wait for the Savior, the Lord Jesus Christ, who will transform our lowly body that it may be conformed to His glorious body, according to the working by which He is able even to subdue all things to Himself."

There is a final transformation of covenant-keepers at the final judgment. What they are in principle in history they become in fact in eternity.

> Now this I say, brethren, that flesh and blood cannot inherit the kingdom of God; nor does corruption inherit incorruption. Behold, I tell you a mystery: We shall not all sleep, but we shall all be changed — in a moment, in the twinkling of an eye, at the last trumpet. For the trumpet will sound, and the dead will be raised

incorruptible, and we shall be changed. For this corruptible must put on incorruption, and this mortal must put on immortality. So when this corruptible has put on incorruption, and this mortal has put on immortality, then shall be brought to pass the saying that is written: "Death is swallowed up in victory." "O death, where is your sting? O Hades, where is your victory?" (1 Corinthians 15:50-55).

Covenant-breakers also become in eternity what they are in principle throughout history: ethical rebels. At the resurrection, covenant-keepers and covenant-breakers are separated forever. Perfect righteousness has no fellowship with perfect wickedness; only history's imperfect righteousness and imperfect wickedness permits partial cooperation.[1]

Paul writes of a final transformation of Christians' sin-cursed bodies. This takes place when Christ returns in judgment. It is an *instantaneous* transformation, accomplished "in a moment, in the twinkling of an eye." Paul writes elsewhere:

> For the Lord Himself will descend from heaven with a shout, with the voice of an archangel, and with the trumpet of God. And the dead in Christ will rise first. Then we who are alive and remain shall be caught up together with them in the clouds to meet the Lord in the air. And thus we shall always be with the Lord (1 Thessalonians 4:16-17).

The Triumph of God's People in History

Liberals may not like such language of people being caught in-to the air at Christ's coming, but Bible-believing Christians must affirm this future event. This is not some sort of symbolic event. This will really take place as described.

The problem is, Christians have neglected too many of the implications of these passages of final transformation. They have not recognized that as time goes on, Christians mature in Biblical faith, and they are progressively to manifest as "through a glass, darkly" the final ethical perfection of the post-resurrection world. Because of this universal, progressive, *external* ethical maturity,

---

1. Gary North, *Dominion and Common Grace: The Biblical Basis of Progress* (Tyler, TX: Institute for Christian Economics, 1987), ch. 2.

God will even give mankind a sort of down payment ("earnest": Ephesians 1:14) on this period of eternal life to come, when death will have no sting. Covenant-keepers and even covenant-breakers will be given the blessing of long life before the final judgment:

> No more shall an infant from there live but a few days, nor an old man who has not fulfilled his days; for the child shall die one hundred years old, but the sinner being one hundred years old shall be accursed (Isaiah 65:20).

There will still be sinners in the world, so this verse cannot possibly refer to the post-final judgment resurrection of the saints. This prophecy will therefore be fulfilled in human history.

This means that there is to be *progressive Christian dominion in history.* The universally recognized blessing of God, long life, will pour down on all of humanity. This will reflect the fact that all people will have conformed themselves *outwardly* to the fifth commandment: "Honor your father and your mother, that your days may be long upon the land which the LORD your God is giving you" (Exodus 20:12). This outward conformity to God's law brings outward blessings to society at large. This does not mean that every person in that future period of external blessings will be saved eternally, for Isaiah mentions the presence in society of sinners; it does mean that the visible manifestation of God's kingdom will be extended in history, though not in the kingdom's final manifestation of absolute, sin-free perfection, which appears only after the final judgment. Flesh and blood cannot inherit that final, post-resurrection kingdom.

Earthly Citizenship: Inclusion Requires Exclusion

The liberal resents the idea that God excludes some people from His blessings forever. In 1841, the German atheistic philosopher Ludwig Feuerbach ("FOYurbawk") attacked Christianity for its doctrine of eternal exclusion of unbelievers. "To believe, is synonymous with goodness; not to believe, with wickedness. Faith, narrow and prejudiced refers all unbelief to the moral disposition. In its view the unbeliever is an enemy to Christ out of obduracy, out of wickedness. Hence faith has fellowship with believers only; unbelievers it rejects. It is well-disposed towards believers, but ill-disposed towards unbelievers. *In faith there lies a malignant principle.*"[2] Frederick Engels, the co-founder with Karl Marx of Communism, wrote: "Then came Feuerbach's *Essence of Christianity*. . . . Enthusiasm was general; we all became at once Feuerbachians."[3]

Let us return to the language of the United States Supreme Court in defining citizenship for immigrants. It is granted by Congress by means of adoption. Naturalization was defined as "the act of adopting a foreigner, and clothing him with the privileges of a native citizen."[4] We have already discussed briefly various concepts of political citizenship in history (Chapter Two). They all necessarily involve inclusion and exclusion. There is no escape from this, except by adopting a concept of world citizenship. Yet even here, those who have promoted this idea have been forced to deal with the appearance of people who have denied the legitimacy of world citizenship in a one-State world (people like myself). These people ultimately must be kept from influencing those who might rebel against the future one-State humanist world order. They must therefore be *denied citizenship* in this future kingdom of man.

The Communists deny it quite persuasively: by murder and by the concentration camp.

Humanism's Standards for Exclusion

It does not matter what nation we look at: every one of them has a concept of citizenship that involves both inclusion and exclusion. Consider a few of these various forms of citizenship:

---

2. Ludwig Feuerbach, *The Essence of Christianity*, translated by George Eliot (New York: Harper Torchbook, [1841] 1957), p. 252.

3. Frederick Engels, "Ludwig Feuerbach and the End of Classical German Philosophy" (1888), in Karl Marx and Frederick Engels, *Selected Works*, 3 vols. (Moscow: Progress Publishers, [1970] 1976), III, p. 344.

4. *Boyd v. Nebraska ex re. Thayer*, 143 U.S. 135, 162 (1892). See *The Constitution of the United States of America: Analysis and Interpretation* (Washington, D.C.: Government Printing Office, 1973), p. 283.

ancient classical democracy, clan family (brotherhood), Renaissance nation-state, totalitarianism, and modern democracy.

Ancient classical (Greece and Rome) citizenship was based on membership in the family. Only males could participate in the city-state because only males could participate in the family religious rites. Citizenship was through family membership. Women were excluded because upon marrying, a woman moved to her husband's family. Slaves were excluded. Foreigners were excluded. Citizenship was achieved either by birth or adoption. There was no other way. If you were not a citizen, you could not enter into a court of law. Contracts were valid only between citizens. Foreigners were considered outside "humanity." (The best study of classical citizenship is Fustel de Coulanges' *The Ancient City*, published in 1864).

Clan families have been similar. Membership was by birth or perhaps adoption. A man is a brother; outsiders are "others." Ethical rules governing those inside the clan are different from those governing those outside. The Mafia is the obvious modern example of clan citizenship. It is international in scope, but only men of certain regional background (Sicily, southern Italy) are eligible for full Family membership. (Inheritance is through the mother, not the father: "Where was your mother or grandmother born?") Membership is provisional. Only the man who has "made his bones" — murdered someone — is initiated fully ("adopted") into the Family. Murder is the rite of passage, the basis of inclusion.[5] This is the ultimate earthly exclusion of another from membership in any earthly citizenship.

The Renaissance nation-state that developed after the sixteenth century is based on geographical residence. Those living under the jurisdiction of the king are eligible for exercising political power. Usually, membership within the oligarchy was based on birth: royal or noble line. It could be attained through inter-

---

5. I was given this information by a man whose grandmother was born in the region of Calabria, Italy, and who was subtly invited into the Mafia when he became of age. He turned down the offer.

marriage: rich children of businessmen could marry into the nobility. The royal lines were sacrosanct, which is why European royalty was related by marriage. The kings of England, Germany, and Russia in World War I all had the same grandmother, Queen Victoria. Cousins King George V and Czar Nicholas II looked enough alike to be brothers. (As one of the three was rumored to have said, "This war would never have started if Grandmother had been alive.")

The totalitarian State is geographical. Everyone is supposed to vote in elections, but only the Party selects candidates. Membership in the Party is through initiation. High Party officials bring their children into the Party. Citizenship is largely fictional for the masses outside the Party. Their purpose is to legitimize the social order: "Vox populi, vox dei" ("The voice of the people is the voice of God"). It is ritual participation.

Modern democracy is constitutional. The citizen must swear allegiance to the constitution, either explicitly (naturalized citizens) or implicitly (children of citizens automatically become eligible to vote at a certain age). Those who have not sworn allegiance may be residents of the nation, but they are not citizens. Geography is not the deciding issue. For example, the United States government requires U.S. citizens who reside outside the geographical boundaries of the United States and who earn income from non-U.S. sources to pay income taxes to the U.S. government. (There is a minimum income that is not taxed, but high income earners are required to pay.) This is unique in the world, yet fully consistent with the U.S. theory of citizenship: constitutional (covenantal) rather than geographical.

Each system has exclusions. There is no escape from the process of inclusion and exclusion. The only question is: What should be the basis for inclusion or exclusion? The Biblical answer is: the terms of God's civil covenant.

Christian Civil Citizenship

The basis of inclusion in the institutional church is covenantal: baptism, Communion, and outward conformity to the terms of the covenant. The question must then be raised: What about inclusion in the civil covenant?

Over time, men lose faith in the doctrine of natural law. They recognize that ethics can never be neutral, which means that law can never be neutral. Laws include and exclude certain types of behavior. Thus, as the earthly, visible, and institutional development of Satan's kingdom and God's kingdom takes place in history, it becomes more and more difficult for anyone to make decisions consciously outside the two kingdoms. As men seek to live lives consistent with their covenantal status as either covenant-keepers or covenant-breakers, this is reflected in political life. Those who become dominant politically, either through conspiracy or power (the humanist ideal) or through steady conquest through preaching, example, and godly service (the Christian ideal), will eventually seek to exclude their rivals from participating in political affairs.

Exclusion is inherent in any process of inclusion. By defining legal citizenship, a society necessarily must impose some principle of exclusion. For example, in the United States anyone who has been convicted of a felony is prohibited from voting for the rest of his life. This is a pagan recognition of the covenantal status of citizenship. Christians should seek to overturn this law constitutionally. Anyone who has repented publicly ("word") and has made restitution to the victim ("deed") should be restored to full citizenship. This would make visible politically Christ's process of ethical and judicial restoration. But the "church" of modern democracy is often unforgiving.

Elites in Political Life

The elitism of modern democracy is the product of a group of conspirators who have successfully closed membership to the seats of real power. This is the satanic principle of "the inner ring," as C. S. Lewis has called it.[6] Members initiate new members

---

6. C. S. Lewis, "The Inner Ring," in Lewis, *The Weight of Glory and Other Addresses* (New York: Macmillan, 1980).

through certain kinds of performance: illegal acts, immoral acts, the earning of university degrees, or attendance at prestige universities. The Harvard Law School is such an identifying and screening institution in the U.S.; in France, it has been the Ecole Polytechnique since 1795.[7] Another screening device is membership in secret societies, or quasi-secret societies. There have always been elites in man's history.[8] The question is: What is the basis of membership in the ruling elite? Blood lines, military valor, education, religious initiation, membership in a church, or what?

The Bible makes it clear who should rule: those who are covenantally most faithful in public, for all to see:

> Moreover you shall select from all the people able men, such as fear God, men of truth, hating covetousness; and place such over them to be rulers of thousands, rulers of hundreds, rulers of fifties, and rulers of tens (Exodus 18:21).

This process of becoming a lawful ruler is *ethical*. Civil rulers must be "able men, such as fear God, men of truth, hating covetousness." Without a commitment to Biblical law, democracy necessarily degenerates into rule by coercive elites, but always in the name of the People. There is no possibility of attaining long-term human freedom apart from self-government under Biblical law. Only as the citizens of a society seek to conform themselves to God's covenant law will good rulers appear in their midst. But steadily, as covenant-keepers become more consistent ethically and diligent in their labors, they will find righteous people to represent them before God as civil rulers. This is the process of *progressive sanctification in civil government*.

Jesus told the leaders of Israel: "Therefore I say to you, the kingdom of God will be taken from you and given to a nation

---

7. F. A. Hayek, *The Counter-Revolution in Science: Studies in the Abuse of Reason* (2nd ed.; Indianapolis, Indiana: Liberty Press, [1952] 1979), ch. 11.

8. See Philip H. Burch, *Elites in American History*, 3 vols. (New York: Holmes & Meier, 1980). See also G. William Domhoff, *Who Rules America Now? A View for the '80s* (Englewood Cliffs, New Jersey: Prentice-Hall, 1983).

bearing the fruits of it" (Matthew 21:43). This transfer took place at Pentecost and was confirmed by the destruction of the temple in 70 A.D. This kingdom grows in history. After the final judgment, the "nation" of Matthew 21:43 — the Church International — becomes identical to members of Christ's international church. The question is: To what extent does nationhood in history progressively reflect this definitive and final definition of nationhood? Will there be high positive correlation (international theocracy)? Will there be no correlation (random: permanent democratic pluralism)? Or will there be a negative correlation (the triumph of Satan's world religion and empire in a one-State world)?

The historical optimists see the steady spread of the gospel, the expansion of missionary activities, and a bottom-up restoration of all things, as God's kingdom is progressively manifested in history. The political neutralists see political freedom in terms of Western secular humanism's *official* "party line": world liberation through world democracy, though without the triumph of the gospel in history. The pessimists see an overnight imposition of world theocracy under Jesus' physical rule during the millennium, but with political decline into tyranny prior to Christ's coming. The European Christian traditionalists, denying a visible millennium in history, see only political decline into tyranny in history.[9]

Let us choose victory rather than defeat as our goal.

Summary

Because of the covenantal nature of all life, all men are under one of two covenants: God's or Satan's. The cosmic conflict that goes on between the forces of God and the forces of Satan is reflected in every covenantal institution, including national civil governments. The goal of each side is to make manifest in history the religious principles of its respective leader, either God or Satan. Men seek to create either heaven on earth or hell on earth. There is no third option, because there is no neutrality.

---

9. Gary North, *Dominion and Common Grace: The Biblical Basis of Progress* (Tyler, Texas: Institute for Christian Economics, 1987), ch. 4.

There is no escape from citizenship in one of the two supernatural commonwealths. One is born into Satan's or adopted into God's. This supernatural citizenship is the model for earthly citizenship, either godly or satanic. Men are citizens of two commonwealths: supernatural and earthly. There is a continuing struggle throughout history between each side to increase the geographic range of authority of the respective supernatural commonwealth. This battle is primarily ethical. Each side seeks to extend through its covenant the number of those who swear allegiance to the respective supernatural commander.

The nature of this struggle has been concealed by the doctrine of natural law. The quest for ethical neutrality in terms of common-ground principles between the two kingdoms has been a familiar feature of Christian scholarship since the early centuries of the Christian church. As men's faith in natural law has declined, so has the myth of neutrality.

The basis of citizenship in the two supernatural kingdoms is covenantal. So is the basis of earthly citizenship. As time goes on, the nations of the world will be divided more and more in terms of the rival covenants. The hope of discovering neutral terms for these national covenants is fading, except in academic Christian circles. The humanists of the West know better. The humanists who rule in Communist societies know best of all.

Citizenship will progressively include and exclude members of the earthly commonwealths in terms of the rival supernatural covenants. As we approach the final judgment, the rival camps will be more consistent in their imposition of the respective covenant. Satan's forces will grow weaker and lose territory, and Christ's forces will steadily replace them.

The basis of legitimate civil rule is ethical. Humanists substitute power and intrigue for ethics. This creates resistance and suspicion. Steadily in history, ethics replaces power and intrigue as the basis of lawful civil rule.

In summary:

1. Christians are citizens of heaven.
2. Christians are covenanted to heavenly citizenship.

3. God calls on all covenant-breakers to change their citizenship papers to heaven.

4. All people are citizens of either heaven or hell.

5. Each kingdom manifests itself on earth and in history.

6. Political citizenship is modeled after supernatural citizenship.

7. At the final judgment, all people will be separated eternally in terms of their supernatural citizenship.

8. All people are citizens of two countries: supernatural (primary) and earthly (secondary).

9. The communion meal is the major manifestation of the supernatural kingdom to which God's people are covenanted.

10. History is a battlefield between the ethics of two supernatural kingdoms.

11. Jesus Christ in His perfect humanity is the only true citizen of heaven.

12. God imputes heavenly citizenship to those redeemed by Christ.

13. Heavenly citizenship is the morally mandatory model for all earthly political citizenship.

14. There can be no morally and covenantally neutral citizenship in history.

15. Permanent political pluralism is therefore a myth.

16. In eternal citizenship, inclusion requires exclusion.

17. God judges between covenant-keeping nations and covenant-breaking nations.

18. The progressive victory of God's covenant-keeping nations in history is assured.

19. In earthly political citizenship, inclusion requires exclusion.

20. This applies even to the theory of world citizenship: the exclusion of nationalists and localists.

21. Humanism has adopted numerous systems of political exclusion: clan, geography, blood lines, naturalization through law, membership in a political party.

22. Each system involves exclusion.

23. Church membership is by covenant.

24. Christian political citizenship must also be by covenant.

25. Natural law is a myth.

26. Political rule (representation) is elitist.

27. The question is: By what standard should elites rule?

28. The Bible's answer is *ethics*.

29. Covenant-keepers are to replace progressively covenant-breakers in every area of authority, including politics.

30. This will eventually lead to Christian dominion across national borders.

7

MISSIONARIES MAKE THE BEST AMBASSADORS

Now it shall come to pass in the latter days that the mountain of the LORD's house shall be established on the top of the mountains, and shall be exalted above the hills; and all nations shall flow to it. Many people shall come and say, "Come, and let us go up to the mountain of the LORD, to the house of the God of Jacob; He will teach us His ways, and we shall walk in His paths." For out of Zion shall go forth the law, and the word of the LORD from Jerusalem (Isaiah 2:2-3).

The second point of the Biblical covenant is hierarchy. Men covenant with each other under God. They place themselves under the law of God (point three). They also place themselves under a hierarchical authority that can impose sanctions (point four). The point is, they place themselves *under* God and His designated human representatives. They themselves become representatives to others.

The Hebrews were under a sovereign in Egypt: the Pharaoh. They groaned under his rule, and cried out to God (Exodus 3:7). They needed to be delivered from bondage under Pharaoh. God delivered them. After having delivered them from slavery in Egypt, God confronted His people at Mt. Sinai. He announced His law to them. They formally assented to live under the terms of God's covenant (Exodus 19). They went from bondage to Pharaoh to bondage to God.

There is no escape from ethical bondage, either to God or to Satan. "Come to Me, all you who labor and are heavy laden, and I will give you rest. Take My yoke upon you and learn from Me,

155

for I am gentle and lowly in heart, and you will find rest for your souls. For My yoke is easy and My burden is light" (Matthew 11:28-30). A bondservant is under a hierarchy. The bondservant to Christ is under Christ's hierarchy. His sign of bondage is a yoke: the yoke of the covenant.

God's Holy Mountain

The mountain is God's dwelling place, His house. It is the place where He teaches us His ways. Out of Mt. Zion goes God's law. It is the covenant law of God that subdues the nations. This process of subduing the nations begins with self-government under law, but it does not end there.

What is this mountain? Clearly, it is the institutional church. The institutional church preaches God's Word. Out of the institutional church flows the law of God. The passage does not teach that the institutional church will control the world. On the contrary, it is the people who obey the law that flows *out of* the church who will subdue the earth. It is God's Word that brings Christians victory over His enemies. His Word is His sword. Jesus warned: "Repent, or else I will come to you quickly and will fight against them with the sword of My mouth" (Revelation 2:16). Again, "Now out of His mouth goes a sharp sword, that with it He should strike the nations. And He Himself will rule them with a rod of iron. He Himself treads the winepress of the fierceness and wrath of almighty God" (Revelation 19:15). The power of God's Word in history is awesome.

The nations will come into the New Jerusalem, the Church, the true mountain of God (Revelation 21:9-27). This process has already begun. It began at Pentecost. Pentecost was the first public manifestation of the arrival of God's international kingdom. Devout Jews had come to Jerusalem "from every nation under heaven" (Acts 2:5b). The Word of God flowed out to them through the preaching of the gospel in every tongue. The Holy Spirit began His work of international healing. Like the oil that was mixed in with the peace offerings of the Old Testament (Leviticus 7:13), so the Holy Spirit was poured out on these representatives of the nations. Peter told them concerning Christ's absolute authority: "Therefore being exalted to the right hand of God, and having received from the Father the promise of the Holy Spirit, He poured out this which you now see and hear" (Acts 2:33).

When the new converts returned to their respective nations, they did so as representatives of God's heavenly nation. They became ambassadors for Christ. But to become an ambassador for Christ, you automatically become an ambassador for Christ's kingdom on earth. Even Christians who reject the idea that God's heavenly kingdom will be manifested on earth work to soften up men's resistance to the covenantal claims of Christ in history.

It is the missionary who, above all, is to announce to the pagan world the two-fold judgment of God: blessing and cursing. It is therefore the missionary who best represents a Christian nation in a foreign land. He is the full-time servant of Christ's kingdom who is best equipped to mobilize grass-roots support in favor of Christian freedom and against the tyranny of Satan's empire. He is best equipped to begin the *bottom-up process* of evangelism that ultimately leads to the establishment of a covenanted confederation of Christian nations.

To see the gospel missionary as God's primary ambassador to the nations requires that men first understand that God really does intend to bring the nations under His earthly administration. This means that nations are to affirm God's covenant. The missionary is the best representative of a Christian nation because he is God's ecclesiastical representative of the international kingdom of God on earth. Missionaries bring the Word of God to foreign nations in order to subdue all nations under God.

The Witness-Ambassador

Christians are told by God to manifest the power of God's kingdom. "The LORD shall send the rod of Your strength out of Zion. Rule in the midst of Your enemies! Your people shall be volunteers in the day of Your power" (Psalm 110:2-3a). Zion is not a particular civil nation, but the Church International, the place of the preaching of the gospel and the administration of the sacraments, from which all blessings flow. This centrality of the institutional Church is the basis of a fundamental office in the Bible, the office of *ambassador of Christ*. "Therefore we are ambassadors for Christ, as though God were pleading through us: we implore you on Christ's behalf, be reconciled to God" (2 Corinthians 5:20).

This office is the model for civil ambassadors. It is not that the office of civil ambassador for some earthly kingdom has become the model for the Church office of witness-ambassador. On the contrary, the Church office of witness-ambassador is God's model for the civil government's office of ambassador. The witness-ambassador is the person who brings God's covenant lawsuit before the people and kings of rival kingdoms, as Jonah did. It is crucial to notice that Jonah did not ask Nineveh to submit covenantally to Israel. He informed them of God's requirement that they surrender unconditionally to God.[1]

Understand, however, that unconditional surrender to God is not the same as unconditional surrender to some human government. When national leaders insist that other national leaders surrender unconditionally as covenantal representatives of their nations, they are acting sinfully. They are imitating God, pretending that a nation-state is the equivalent of God's sovereign kingdom. It is this demand for unconditional surrender that reveals the paganism of modern statism. Underlying the doctrine of unconditional surrender to a nation-state is the doctrine of the absolute perfection of one nation and the total depravity in history of its rival. Also underlying the insistence on unconditional surrender is a doctrine of unconditional hatred. It is this unconditional international hatred that has repeatedly led to world wars in our era.[2]

The individual witness-ambassador of Christ's kingdom invites the enemies of God to join the family of God, person by person, family by family—adoption into God's family (John 1:12). At

---

1. Gary North, *Unconditional Surrender: God's Program for Victory* (3rd ed.; Ft. Worth, Texas: Dominion Press, 1987).

2. Russell Grenfell, *Unconditional Hatred: German War Guilt and the Future of Europe* (Old Greenwich, Connecticut: Devin-Adair, [1953] 1971).

the same time, as we saw in Chapter Two, in a seriously Christian international world, the national witness-ambassador of a Christian nation invites the representative leaders of pagan nations to enter into a peaceful alliance—though not yet a covenant—with Christian nations, thereby giving time for missionaries from Christian nations to preach the gospel to the pagan nation's people. Then, steadily, as the gospel brings converts into the Church, the once-pagan nation is transformed. Upon becoming officially, covenantally Christian, it is then invited to enter the family of Christian nations on a covenantal basis. It is not asked to subordinate itself to any other nation, but it is asked to subordinate itself to the Christian nations' covenanted appeals court system. This is Christian internationalism, and it is the standard of foreign policy set forth in the Bible.

Baptizing the Nations

If the Word of God is the tool (sword) of dominion, then the Church of Jesus Christ preaches an international Word as well as a national and local Word. The Word of God does not cease flowing from God's mountain just because it reaches a national border. The church is international, for it is called Jerusalem. It is the center of the earth, just as the sacrifices in the Temple were the ritual center of the earth. At the center of worship in Israel was the law of God. It was written on the two copies of the covenant legal document that were deposited in the ark of the covenant (Exodus 20; 34:28; 1 Kings 8:9), which is the reason it was called the ark of the covenant. It rested in the holy of holies of the Temple (1 Kings 8:6). At the center of worship today is the Communion Table, where all Christians unite together to *renew their covenant with God and with each other* at the throne of God.

Covenant renewal requires men to take a public oath promising to submit to the ethical terms of the covenant and also to the sanctions of the covenant—cursings and blessings. These oaths are to be taken in the three covenant institutions that God has established: church, family, and civil government. Covenant renewal in the local church takes place each time members take the

Lord's Supper. But Christians should not believe that this periodic covenant renewal applies only to the local church; it applies to every faithful church when the Lord's Supper is taken. The Lord's Supper has meaning and manifests publicly God's imparting of forgiveness and healing because communing men enter into the presence of God as Judge, and also into spiritual presence in the heavenlies with all other communing (covenant-renewing) Christians, in heaven and on earth. This is the covenantal basis of spiritual Church unity, even though individual churches disagree in history. There is only one body of Christ. There is only one baptism and one Holy Communion. This unity is real because it is covenantal. (If the covenantal unity of bread and wine is not truly a sign and means of unity, then what other continuing act or symbol throughout history testifies to the unity of Christ's body, the Church?)

Similarly, covenant renewal applies to all levels of civil government that are formally covenanted to God: local, regional, national, and international. There is no reason to limit the application of church covenant sanctions to any one congregation. Neither is there any reason to limit the application of civil covenant sanctions to any one town, region, or nation. God's law flows out to all nations. The sanctions apply to all nations. This was Jonah's message to Nineveh, and it is Christ's message to the world. The disciples of Christ are to disciple the nations (Matthew 28:19).

We have already seen in Chapter Three that God's law is the legal basis for uniting the Christian nations of the world. The God-assigned task of Christians is to press steadily the legal claims of Christ in their own nations, as well as in other nations (church missions). Christians serve as ambassadors of Christ to the nations. Our goal is to win the nations to Christ covenantally. Nations are to be baptized. This raises the question: How are nations to be baptized? We baptize people. How can nations be baptized? We cannot understand this process unless we first understand the doctrine of representation.

The Doctrine of Representation

We can find the answer in two New Testament accounts of the same event. They seem to be conflicting accounts, but they are not. Matthew 8 records that a centurion came to Jesus and asked Him to heal his servant. It says that "a centurion came to Him, pleading with Him" (v. 5). But Luke 7 says that Jews came to Jesus in the name of the centurion, and then the centurion's friends came to Him (vv. 3, 6). There is no evidence that the centurion ever actually spoke with Jesus. Is there a conflict here? Does the Bible contradict itself?

No. The centurion spoke with Jesus through representatives. Also, the centurion represented his sick servant in his request that Jesus heal him. The centurion understood the doctrine of representation. He even went so far as to say that Jesus did not have to enter his house in order for the servant to be healed (Luke 7:6b). Then he said, "But say the word, and my servant will be healed" (v. 7:7b). He understood Jesus' authority. He was implicitly testifying to Jesus' position as God's representative, for he compared Jesus' authority to his own position as a representative of Caesar:

> "For I *also* am a man placed under authority, having soldiers under me. And I say to one, 'Go,' and he goes; and to another, 'Come,' and he comes; and to my servant, 'Do this,' and he does it." When Jesus heard these things, He marveled at him, and turned around and said to the crowd that followed Him, "I say to you, I have not found such great faith, not even in Israel!" (Luke 7:8-9; emphasis added).

The Jews spoke to Jesus in the name of the centurion. His friends also spoke in his name. The centurion spoke to Jesus in the name of Caesar (above him) and in the name of his sick servant (below him). Understand, he was publicly subordinating himself to Jesus' authority, despite his official position as Caesar's lawful representative. This took great faith, as Jesus publicly affirmed to the crowd. The centurion recognized that Jesus spoke in the name of God the Father (above Him) and could therefore banish the power of sickness and death (below Him). Jesus *also* was a man under authority. The centurion recognized clearly that Jesus' covenantal subordination to God was the basis of His power over sickness and death, just as the centurion's covenantal subordination to Caesar was the basis of his power over his troops and servants.

We have come "face to face" (representationally through the printed word) to the doctrine of representation: *to speak in someone else's name before God, and to speak to men in God's name.* This is the structural basis of human authority in God's world of plural, hierarchical, institutional authorities.

Baptizing Covenantal Representatives

People are baptized as individuals. They are also baptized as members of families. Fathers are baptized as covenantal representatives of their households, as those who proclaim and enforce God's law in their homes. The baptism of fathers is supposed to lead, Biblically, to baptism of their households.[3] We see this in the baptism of the family of the Philippian jailer. Paul and Silas spoke to the jailer in the name of God (as God's lawful representatives):

> So they said, "Believe on the Lord Jesus Christ, and you will be saved, you and your household." Then they spoke the word of the Lord to him and to all who were in his house. And he took them the same hour of the night and washed their stripes. And immediately he and all his family were baptized. Now when he had brought them into his house, he set food before them; and he rejoiced, having believed in God with all his household (Acts 16:31-34).

There is another aspect of family representation that is important. God sanctifies unbelievers because of their believing spouses. This does not mean that He saves them eternally. It does mean that He *sets them apart covenantally*, treating them as special people, because of their marriage vows (covenantal oaths). "For

---

3. Ray R. Sutton, *That You May Prosper: Dominion By Covenant* (Tyler, Texas: Institute for Christian Economics, 1987), pp. 89-91.

the unbelieving husband is sanctified by the wife, and the unbelieving wife is sanctified by the husband; otherwise your children would be unclean, but now they are holy" (1 Corinthians 7:14). Holiness means sanctification: to be set apart. Obviously, Christianity does not teach regeneration through marriage. It teaches regeneration by grace through faith in Jesus Christ (Ephesians 2:8-9). Therefore, to speak of the unbelieving spouse's being sanctified by the believing spouse points to the existence of a legal, external, covenantal bond. The external blessings given by God to the believing spouse flow to the unbelieving spouse.

So it is with nations. Unbelieving residents and citizens receive blessings because of the believing residents and citizens in their midst. The classic Biblical example is Sodom: as few as ten righteous men in the city would have preserved it from God's fiery judgment (Genesis 18:32). The believers would have served as *representatives* of God to the Sodomites.

We still see traces of the original covenant with God in the taking of oaths. An oath, like baptism, is a covenantal act. (We might also say that baptism is a Biblical oath.) It is not an ecclesiastical covenantal act, but rather a civil covenantal act. Those who testify in a United States civil court are asked to swear: "I promise to tell the truth, the whole truth, and nothing but the truth, so help me, God." A witness places his left hand on a Bible as he affirms that he will abide by this oath. Only in the twentieth century have courts made provisions for those who refuse to swear with their hands on a Bible, but the civil sanctions against perjury still apply, Bible or no Bible. The President of the United States still swears his oath of allegiance to the U.S. Constitution with his left hand on an open Bible, right hand raised. This is a civil covenantal act, even though no one comments on it publicly. (It is a theological embarrassment to humanists.) The President places himself and the nation publicly under God's covenant sanctions: blessing or cursing.

As baptized Christians grow in number, as they seek to extend the dominion of Christ's kingdom in history, they begin to affect politics. Steadily, they begin to take over the operations of the civil realm, just as Christians did in fourth-century Rome under Constantine. This is an inescapable development of the spread of Christianity. Covenant-keeping people exercise dominion in every area of life, not excluding anything that is morally legitimate, and clearly not excluding politics. This is a long-term bottom-up process of comprehensive evangelism: bringing every area of life under God's authority.

Individual baptisms place people under the covenant, and steadily these baptized people become representatives: of their households initially, and then of their nation. The process continues over time (point five of the Biblical covenant: continuity). Eventually, they will be able to bring the whole nation formally under God's covenant. Their nation then becomes officially Christian, in the same sense that the State of Israel is officially Jewish, Saudi Arabia is officially Muslim, and the Soviet Union is officially Communist.

Missionaries as Christ's Ambassadors

Is the unity of churches a legitimate Christian goal? Can Christians legitimately seek a formal (covenantal) church union based on their shared faith in the Bible? Yes. God does not look with favor on the needless splitting of the body of Christ into factions.

The unity of churches internationally (Apostles' creed, Nicene creed) testifies to the unity of God's covenant and the unity of His kingdom. While churches since the Protestant Reformation have been identified primarily as national entities, especially in Western Europe, this tradition was based originally on political and military expediency. To establish a permanent cease-fire at the end of the Thirty Years' War (1618-48), European churches were formally established as the churches of a particular region, based generally on the religious profession of faith by local princes, in order to stop the seemingly endless war between Protestant and Catholic armies. The year 1624 was retroactively agreed to as the year of the boundaries. Protestant churches that were worshipping in Catholic regions in 1624, and Catholic churches that were worshipping in Protestant regions, were allowed to continue worshipping after 1648. This was the outcome of the famous Peace of Westphalia (1648).

Why should an international decision made in 1648 be regarded as theologically binding until the end of time? Why should churches not seek to covenant across borders? Missions work presumes that some nations will take the lead and spread the gospel from a *temporary* home base in a particular nation. Missionaries have no illusions that their converts will attempt to establish legal civil outposts of the missionaries' home nations. The missionaries know that the converts in any region will remain covenanted civilly in their own nations. But what missionaries have tended to forget is that the gospel is intended to bring every institution under the law of God. Thus, the job of the missionary ultimately should be to make a Christian nation out of the pagan nation in which he is operating, just as surely as he is to seek to make Christian individuals and Christian families out of the pagans he is working with.

Is the missionary a citizen of his home nation? Yes. Is he also a citizen of heaven, his ultimate home nation? Yes. "For our citizenship is in heaven, from which we also eagerly wait for the Savior, the Lord Jesus Christ" (Philippians 3:20). Every missionary should self-consciously become an agent of a foreign country: heaven. Similarly, every Christian in a non-Christian nation should also self-consciously become the agent of this same foreign country.

Every missionary knows that if he is perceived as an agent of an earthly foreign nation, his mission work would be jeopardized. This is why the missionary's task is so difficult, for he must honor three nations: heaven, his home nation, and the nation in which he is operating. He must also honor his home church or missions board.

The missionary is in close contact with the people of a foreign nation. He is in far closer contact than any professional diplomat. He knows what the issues are at the local level. He may not know much about the national leaders, but he knows the locals.

The foreign policy establishment of any nation would be far better off relying on the opinions of lifetime missionaries and profit-seeking businessmen than on the opinion of its salaried foreign service professionals, who are moved to new countries every few years. Foreign diplomats spend most of their time with other rival foreign diplomats, and with the particular nation's bureaucrats. A good illustration of this comes from Burton Yale Pines of the privately funded Heritage Foundation in Washington, D.C. He reports that during his 1986 trip as a guest lecturer to the Chinese Communist government, his lectures were attended by many U.S. Foreign Service officials, as well as by Winston Lord, the U.S. Ambassador to Red China and the former President of the Council on Foreign Relations. The American diplomats have few opportunities to meet with actual Chinese government officials, since most of their time is spent with Chinese diplomats.

Ultimately, the missionary is an ambassador of Christ to the nations. He owes his primary allegiance to Christ. He is not the agent of the home government. This is a great advantage to him when the charge of "colonialism" is leveled at him. Nevertheless, as a representative of heaven, he can push God's program of national renewal, not in the name of his earthly home country, but in the name of Christ's kingdom principles. He can impart to his listeners a vision of social transformation that is not the exported ideology of his earthly home nation, but his heavenly home nation.

He does not answer to voters back home, whose vision may be diffused. He does not take their money or owe his allegiance to them. He can speak in the name of God.

He is a representative of God before the nation in which he is bringing the gospel, and he also represents that nation before God, as Jonah did. He represents primarily the kingdom of God to the pagan nation. He represents secondarily his own nation to the pagan nation as a person who is the product of an operating national example of Christ's national covenant. Third, he intercedes before God and the pagan nation, pleading for time and peace to bring the gospel.

The missionary also serves as a representative of a *future* nation of nations, a confederation of covenanted Christian nations. The goal of establishing Christ's international kingdom can be presented to citizens of any nation. The missionary does not ask the citizens of any nation to give up their nation's boundaries. He asks them to incorporate their national boundaries under Christ's kingdom boundaries: the whole earth. This message of the missionary avoids the problems of preaching a disguised form of colonialism, except insofar as enclaves of local Christian believers become colonists of heaven within their own pagan nation. "All nations under God" is a far more compelling vision than a hidden agenda, "Your nation under mine."

Colonialism: God's vs. Man's

God calls all men to covenant with Him. He sends out His disciples to preach the gospel and disciple the nations. There is a nation in heaven, a kingdom that God wants manifested on earth as it is in heaven (Matthew 6:10). Thus, God is the original colonialist. He wants His nation to subdue all human nations.

What God as the owner of the nations chooses to do is His business. The nations are His because He created them. He chooses to subdue them covenantally in history, one by one, or else to destroy them one by one in history. They are His. No man can legitimately complain against God's colonialism.

What happens in history is that covenant-breakers imitate God in His sovereign and exclusive office as the cosmic colonialist. This is an incommunicable attribute of God, for it is based on His position as Creator. Nevertheless, as covenantal agents of Satan, men choose to elevate their own nations to the position of God's heavenly nation. They seek to subdue other nations to conform to their nation's will.

Imperialism and colonialism are the international manifestations of Satan's centralized kingdom. Both rest on the idea that a particular earthly, geographical nation-state should represent the kingdom of man in history. The Bolshevik Communists established the supremacy of white Russians over the nations that today make up the Soviet Union. Then the Soviet Union seeks to establish control over its satellites, but all in the name of international Communism, never in the name of Russian nationalism.

Anti-Communists tend to emphasize the ideology of Communism in explaining this empire; liberals tend to emphasize historic Russian nationalism. The lure internationally is Communism; the reality is Russian nationalism, but a peculiar form of nationalism: one justified by a doctrine of international class solidarity of working people. The messianic impetus of Communist ideology has given the Bolsheviks a far more potent motivational tool for world revolution than Russian nationalism ever did.

British colonialism was also based on empire, but a particular kind of empire. It, too, had to be clothed in the language of ethics and vision. It could not be perceived as simply a British power play. Thus, the ideal of "the Atlantic community" was born, more commonly known as the white man's burden. The accent was on the Anglo-Saxon race and culture. Nazism was a more occult and messianic version of this same colonial vision. It was less subtle, more reliant on power. The goal was the same: dominion by race, with a particular nation best representing the legitimate world-ruling racial culture.

This is the old satanic lure of salvation through blood. The definition of "blood" can be either occult or cultural (or both), but the ideal is the same. It should not be surprising that Hitler was something of an Anglophile.[4] It should also not be surprising that Italian fascism had its share of supporters within the British elite in the 1920's.[5]

Missionaries as Heaven's Colonialists

Those who are redeemed by God are to work to manifest God's kingdom in their lives. They are to disciple the nations. They are not to do this in the name of any earthly nation, but in the name of God's heavenly nation, and its manifestation on earth, the kingdom of God.

Missionaries are the primary international ambassadors of

---

4. A. J. P. Taylor, *The Origins of the Second World War* (2nd ed.; New York: Fawcett, [1961] 1965), p. 213.

5. *Ibid.*, p. 60.

this heavenly colonialism. They call all nations to join a Christian commonwealth of nations. They are not to call other nations to join under the headship of a particular nation, for that would be an imitation of Satan's colonialism. But there must always be colonialism: God's or Satan's. Colonialism is an inescapable concept.

The Biblical standard is that nations must see themselves as missionary bases, just as Israel served Jonah as a base of operations. The goal is spiritual conquest. If God's vision for His kingdom is international, with the goal being the establishment of a covenantal "nation of nations" over time, then no nation can legitimately claim that it is *the* Christian nation, the only valid representative of God's kingdom on earth. Political conquest of one Christian nation by another is illegitimate.

This is not to say that such attempts will never be made. Sin is always a problem. But open borders do reduce tensions: free trade and immigration allow men to achieve in international relations what residents of regions within a nation have achieved. Warfare between states (provinces) has generally disappeared; the same can be true in the future of nations that are in covenant together. Sin will be subdued over time through the preaching of the gospel and the conversion of men and nations.

Of course, anyone who believes that sin will increase because the gospel fails in history will reject the idea that the inheritance of righteous nations increases, while the rebellious nations are cut off in history. The person who accepts such a view of the gospel's effects in history should expect either international anarchy or the rise of a tyrannical empire. Nations will either collapse into anarchy or be swallowed up by some gigantic world empire. But nations as such will not survive.

This is why it is strange that millions of Christians who promote pessimistic eschatologies also tend to be highly nationalistic. It is as if they are putting their earthly political hope in the nation-state as the last, best institutional defense against either world tyranny or world disintegration, despite the fact that their eschatologies ought to tell them the opposite: that of all institutions, the nation-state is the most doomed of all man's political inventions in a time of increasing sin.

If a nation can extend its influence through example and through missions, and if it can seek out markets for its residents' goods without foreign political retaliation, then the twin motivations for empire are reduced: cultural dominance and wealth. The gospel provides the dominance ("all nations under God"), and free trade provides opportunities for increasing every nation's wealth.

Official National Ambassadors

The missionary is the best ambassador; he is not the only one. A head of State needs ambassadors in several nations, though not necessarily every nation. There must be someone who speaks in the name of the national head of State who sets policy. This person deals primarily with the representatives of the nation in which he is assigned.

There is no doubt that long-term diplomats of democratic nations to a single foreign country tend to become spokesmen for the nation in which they are assigned. There is also no doubt that rotating diplomats reduces their effectiveness, especially if a foreign language is involved. The United States constantly rotates its professional diplomatic corps, and ambassadors are politically appointed. This is a major handicap in terms of continuity.

About one-third of United States ambassadors are political appointments who reflect the current administration's policies. The rest are career Foreign Service bureaucrats. There is continuity based on two facts: 1) the Council on Foreign Relations and the Trilateral Commission ultimately control U.S. foreign policy and domestic policy, as the cabinet appointments of every U.S. President indicates; and 2) two-thirds of the ambassadors are lifetime bureaucrats screened in terms of Foreign Service standards. But the faces change: Presidents and ambassadors.

Not so with the Soviet Union. Anatoly Dobrynin served as the Soviet ambassador to the U.S. from the early 1960's until 1986. He was known in Moscow as a well-informed expert on the U.S., and a man who produced accurate, incisive reports to the Soviet

Foreign Ministry.[6] He understood the intended victims. Dictatorships do have great visible continuity over long periods of time.

Heads of State need official representatives to represent them abroad. A head of State cannot be involved in continual confrontations with other heads of State. He needs official representatives who, in a difficult dispute, can always delay committing anything because they "have to contact Washington (or wherever) to get further instructions." Also, in face-to-face dealings, a head of State may give up too much, or grow needlessly obstinate, because of personal reasons. A leader needs official representatives.

What is important is continuity of vision. This is what the West has lost. Missionaries usually have this continuity of vision; democratic majorities do not. Better for the leader of a Christian nation to limit drastically the formal international contacts among nation-states and leave to Christian missionaries the fundamental task of building links among societies. The head of a Christian State can afford to decentralize because God provides national continuity and strength, whatever people's personal failings are. Like the free market, foreign relations do best when they are generally left alone.

What must be insisted on is that the official ambassadors of a nation be completely answerable to the constitutional head of State and to nobody else. This means that the national leader can hire and fire at will. This hiring and firing must be without limits, from the highest-level ambassadorial post to the lowest-level secretary (who in the U.S. embassy in Moscow is likely to be a Russian KGB plant: see Chapter Thirteen). Foreign Service representatives must *represent* the citizens through their elected national leader. They are not to represent some self-appointed elite.

The great advantage of missionaries is that they press the claims of Christ locally. The conflict between Christianity and humanism need not become a source of continual public international confrontations. Public peace becomes possible because the

---

6. Arkady N. Shevchenko, *Breaking With Moscow* (New York: Knopf, 1985), p. 196.

crucial confrontations are going on locally. Public international relations can be limited to settling arguments between pairs of allies, and maintaining no formal relations with nations that are ideologically at war with Western civilization.

The idea that a nation needs a huge, permanent bureaucracy of foreign service professionals is a myth promoted by the very professionals themselves. It is also promoted by the ruling elite who have discovered that control over foreign policy is the institutional key to maintaining power over the political life of a nation. It is time to decentralize by removing the lifetime status of tax-financed ambassadors.

Summary

The goal of any nation's foreign policy should be national self-interest. But it is the primary self-interest of any nation, as with any individual, to extend God's kingdom principles in history. This means that the best ambassador of any nation is the missionary, who works in the name of Christ's kingdom, not in the name of an earthly nation. He is ordained by God by a church, not by a nation. He represents God in the name of the permanent kingdom of God, not the kingdom of some temporary nation.

In this stage of world history, the missionary is a colonist representing heaven, whether living in his home pagan nation or in a foreign pagan nation. He leaves to others back home the task of colonizing his nation for Christ's kingdom. He concentrates on his job: colonizing a foreign nation for Christ's kingdom. He becomes a co-laborer in this task of colonization with his followers abroad. They can be invited into the task of the great commission: colonizing all nations for Christ's kingdom.

To see the missionary as a nation's best ambassador, we must first understand that a nation should be covenantally Christian. Few Christians understand this in today's world of humanistic nationalism. The nation-state is supposed to be free of God's covenant. Thus, to have a seriously Christian foreign policy based on the use of missionaries as the best agents, citizens must first adopt the goal of establishing their Christian nation as a home base for missionaries of Christ's international kingdom.

We are all colonialists. Christians promote the colonization of the world under God. Humanists promote the colonization of the world under Satan. Christians do not promote the colonial ambitions of any single earthly nation, but instead promote the creation of a world Christian civilization. In our era, humanists have promoted either colonialism by open nationalism—which ended in the 1960's—and, in recent years, colonialism by hidden nationalism: either Chinese or Russian Communism. The answer to false colonialism is God's colonialism: discipling the nations under God's heavenly commonwealth.

Any nation that refuses to accept missionaries from a Christian nation should be regarded as having broken all treaties with that nation. No binding covenants with such a nation should be continued after the closing of its borders to the Christian nation's missionaries. A nation that has shut the door to the gospel has established a public covenant with Satan. At that point, the prohibition against making covenants becomes operational.

In summary:

1. The nations will eventually come under the rule of God's law.

2. There is no escape from bondage: to Christ or to Satan.

3. The church, as the mountain of God, is the earthly source of the law of God.

4. Pentecost was the first public sign of this process of internationalizing the kingdom of God.

5. Those foreigners who were converted to Christ at Pentecost returned as ambassadors of heaven.

6. The missionary is the key figure in the establishment of a bottom-up program of building an international kingdom of God on earth.

7. The Word of God applies covenantally to all nations and races.

8. This means that individual nations are formally and publicly to covenant with God in history.

9. Christians must place their first loyalty to Christ—over family, church, and nation.

10. Christians are to baptize the nations.

11. Baptism and communion covenantally link all Christians in the church during history.

12. Formal covenanting of individual Christian nations covenantally link these nations under God's judgment throne during history.

13. Baptism of the nations means baptism of national representatives.

14. God sets pagan citizens aside covenantally to bless them externally for the sake of faithful national representatives.

15. The process of covenanting is a long-term, bottom-up process of evangelism.

16. Missionaries make the best ambassadors because they represent the kingdom of God.

17. They are in close contact with the people of the pagan nation.

18. They are the best source of information about local conditions.

19. They are not identified as an agent of an earthly colonial power.

20. They *are* colonists: colonists representing heaven.

21. A head of State should decentralize foreign policy.

22. God provides national continuity.

23. No missionaries, no covenant.

8

BUSINESSMEN MAKE THE BEST DIPLOMATS

Now as they heard these things, He spoke another parable,
because He was near Jerusalem and because they thought the
kingdom of God would appear immediately. Therefore He said:
"A certain nobleman went into a far country to receive for himself
a kingdom and to return. So he called ten of his servants, delivered to them ten minas, and said to them, 'Do business till I
come'" (Luke 19:12-13).

The third point of the Biblical covenant refers to the legal
terms of God's covenant. These are His laws that He gives to men
in order that they might obey Him, and thereby extend their dominion over their assigned areas of responsibility. Obedience to
God's law is the public sign of men's subordination to God (point
two) and the basis of God's rewards (point four). God's revealed
law is man's tool of dominion (point three).

Christ's parable of the rebellious servants presents the familiar
kingdom picture of a nobleman and his servants. He entrusts to
his servants a sum of money, and tells them to do business with it.
The King James Version translates this last phrase, "Occupy till I
come." By implication, this is what the word means, but not literally. The Greek word is *pragmateuomai*. Interesting, isn't it? The
Greek word for doing business comes from the same root word as
the English word "pragmatic." In English usage, the word *pragmatic*
means "realistic" or "businesslike." The pragmatist asks: "Does this
work?" His answer is governed by what goes on in what we call
"the real world."

The Greek word *pragma* means "affairs," or "business," or

175

"undertaking." These are *worldly* affairs. The pragmatist in this sense is a man of the world, skilled in the practical affairs of men. The word used in Luke 19:13 means "to pursue with vigor." The focus in the parable is profit-seeking business. It is equally revealing that in the Jews' Greek translation of the Old Testament, called the Septuagint (third century B.C.), the same Greek word is used to translate the Hebrew word for "the king's business" in Daniel 8:27, meaning the king's service. To be in the service of the king means that you must be a worldly, wise, practical person, a pragmatist. But a Biblical pragmatist is not a person who denies fundamental Biblical principles. A Biblical pragmatist pursues God's goals for mankind in every area of life, as effectively as circumstances allow him.

Christianity: This-Worldly and Otherworldly

This sounds strange to most Christians. They think to themselves: "Aren't we supposed to be principled people? Aren't we supposed to be Spiritual?" We are indeed. But because few Christians take seriously the Biblical doctrines of creation, providence, and ethics, they mentally create a false conflict between what is principled Biblically and what "really works" in history. They assume that God's law is not designed to be applied in this world. They forget that God created this world, established His laws to govern it, and created man to administer it as His steward in His name (Genesis 1:26-28). They forget that God's law is practical because the God who established it also runs the world. They dismiss as "dead Old Testament doctrine" the specific promises of God to His people, that if they obey His laws as a people, they will receive external, visible blessings as a people (Deuteronomy 28:1-14). They also forget that He has promised to curse His people visibly and externally if they disobey His law (Deuteronomy 28:15-68). On this point, the humanists agree completely.

Both groups—"otherworldly" Christians and "underworldly" humanists—hasten to agree that God's law is irrelevant in New Testament times. Both groups agree that Christians are supposed to be irrelevant in history. They all conveniently choose to forget the first half of Jesus' command: "Therefore be wise as serpents and harmless as doves" (Matthew 10:16b). Harmless as doves, yes, but never wise as serpents!

There is a quiet alliance between humanists and responsibility-denying Christians against those Christians who want to follow Christ's Great Commission to preach the gospel, disciple the nations, and baptize them, bringing them under the requirements of God's covenant law. This alliance has been in effect for almost two thousand years. But as humanists have become more consistent ethically with their God-denying presuppositions, a growing number of responsibility-fleeing Christians have begun to see more clearly what it means to live under God-denying laws and God-denying rulers. They are becoming fearful of where the humanist West is headed. They at last have begun to see that the weak-kneed humanists of the West are no match for the murderous humanists of the Communist empires. Yet it is foreign policy, above all, that is dominated by the weak-kneed humanists who are ready at a moment's notice to bow the knee to the Soviets. The highest-level members of the Council on Foreign Relations and the Trilateral Commission determine U.S. foreign policy.[1] These unelected representatives in fact represent the United States to the world. They are, in the words of one of their most respected leaders, an invisible government.[2]

Christians were horrified in 1979 when an American President kissed the cheeks of the Soviet Premier at the signing of the SALT II treaty (which the U.S. Senate later refused to ratify), for they at last began to understand just where some future President will be asked to kiss symbolically some future Soviet Premier, unless our leaders get some backbone. The President represents his nation, just as the Soviet Premier represents his. The doctrine of representation is part of God's inescapable covenant structure (point two: hierarchy).

---

1. Larry Abraham, *Call It Conspiracy* (Seattle, Washington: Double A Publications, 1985).

2. Henry M. Wriston, *Diplomacy in a Democracy* (New York: Harper & Brothers, 1956), p. 108.

Former world-retreating Christians since 1979 have begun to defect from the traditional humanist-pietist alliance. They have begun to see the light. This has alarmed the humanists, for good reason. The authors of a 1987 article in *The Humanist* magazine lament the influence that the vision of reconstructing this world according to Biblical principles has had on what they call "otherwise fatalistic fundamentalists": "We are already in the third presidential campaign in a row that bears unmistakable witness to the power of politicized conservative religion. We are at this point because we failed to read the Reconstructionists' own honest words about their aims. In Germany, they failed to read and believe the plan set forth in *Mein Kampf*."[3]

They are shocked by the idea that Christians have at last begun to take steps that will enable them someday to bring the Bible to bear on social institutions. They wish Christians would remain safely restricted to the shadows of history, the way it used to be when the humanists' nearly monopolistic control over American society faced no self-conscious challenge from well-informed and increasingly militant Christians. They wish that Christians would go back to their "old time religion" of cultural impotence. They will not get their wish.

Practical Men

The king's servant is supposed to be a man who understands the way the world works — not the physical world, but the world of human affairs. He is to understand how other men accomplish their public tasks. He must understand the competitive pressures of the real world. He must give evidence of his understanding, and the results of his work will come under public scrutiny. He will be judged either by the king or by the competitive market (point four of the Biblical covenant, sanctions). There is no escape from the pressures of the "real world," meaning the world of commerce.

---

3. Frederick Edwords and Stephen McCabe, "Getting Out God's Vote: Pat Robertson and the Evangelicals," *The Humanist* (May/June 1987), p. 36.

The King James translators translated *pragmateuomai* as "occupy." This is not far from the mark. The man of affairs is to take possession of the capital entrusted to him and put it to effective, profitable use for its true owner. If he is successful in his endeavor, he will increase this capital base, as is required in the parable of the talents (Matthew 25:14-30). This parable also tells the story of a rich man who goes on a journey and leaves each of three servants with capital. Then he returns to judge them. This parable is immediately followed by a discussion of Christ's coming to judge the world at the last day. There is no doubt what Christ was talking about: the Christian's walk in this world. The last judgment is discussed by Christ in the most practical of terms: business, profits, and banking.

These are kingdom parables. Christ used these parables to describe the operations of His kingdom on earth and in history. He was not talking about some future kingdom in which He will come to rule in person as the most powerful bureaucrat in history. He was instead talking about a nobleman who goes to a far country and who leaves his servants in charge of operations. They are left "on their own," so to speak, either to use or abuse whatever capital assets that the ruler had entrusted to them. Clearly, Christ was talking about God as a distant ruler, and about men as servants who are left to themselves to prove their capabilities in a highly competitive world.

What has this to do with foreign relations? If anything, modern diplomacy seems to be the reverse. We send our ambassadors abroad to the distant country, and the nation's citizens remain at home. In the United States, the ambassador may be a rich businessman who has given a lot of money to the political party that won the last Presidential election. How does all this fit the parables?

I previously discussed the difference between ambassadors and diplomats (Chapter Five). The ambassador is the public representative of the national leader. He meets with other heads of state or high officials.

The diplomat, in contrast, is the lifetime professional negotiator. He works with diplomats hired by other nations to conduct their detailed negotiations. In most cases, these negotiators are unknown to the general public, or even to the politicians. They are bureaucrats in the classic sense. They hold office for life, except for gross malfeasance in office. They cannot be fired by politicians. They outlast all political policy-makers. The politicians come and go; the foreign service officers remain.

A profit-seeking businessman is also a negotiator, but in a free market society, he is not protected by the government from economic losses and failure. He faces competition. He is not a bureaucrat in a government-protected world. There was a time in Western history when businessmen were the unofficial army of diplomats for European nations, especially Northern European nations. Humanism changed this.

The professional diplomat is not supposed to set a nation's foreign policy. His job is to carry out the delicate task of international negotiations, nation to nation, meaning diplomat to diplomat. In a Christian nation, civil government at the national level would be small. The ability of the central government to tax its citizens directly would be nil; it would be limited by what it can extract from the states or regional governments. The total tax burden of all levels of civil government would be kept under the tithe, meaning under 10 percent of net new income of a nation's residents. So the diplomats would have little to do; the nation could not be heavily involved in major transactions. This has not been the case in the centralized, bureaucratized humanist West, however.

Because government-protected diplomats face little threat of being fired by politicians (who represent the voters), they and a handful of politically appointed specialists in foreign policy actually set the nation's foreign policy except in rare instances. It takes too long for the newly elected national leaders to master the intricacies of foreign relations. By the time they do, they are out of office. They are forced to rely on the highest level diplomats to screen their information and to pursue the details. This in effect transfers to those highest level foreign policy officials the reigns of power.

The key to the exercise of power, then, is to establish control over the professional foreign service officers and diplomats. An invisible government needs to be established, a group of self-appointed men who can maintain their influence for long periods of time, unlike politicians who come and go. This is what the Council on Foreign Relations has done since 1941, and what the Round Table Group did in Great Britain from about 1890. Wealthy Americans used their money as wisely as serpents, recruiting bright young men in college and graduate school, sending them into high-level banking and foreign service careers, getting their essays published in the key intellectual journals (which their members have steadily purchased), and establishing their own journal, *Foreign Affairs*, as the most important single quarterly journal in the West.

Before I offer a Biblical alternative, I want to tell a bit of the story of how the bankers captured the diplomats.

Multinational Bankers and Foreign Policy

Control over national bureaucracies as the basis of power was recognized by a handful of very rich businessmen in the United States immediately after World War I. They saw that the world had entered a new phase in its history, when wars would be fought on a scale never seen before, and where national governments had grown so large and so powerful and so rich that the key to wealth and power would be control over the high-level decisions made by the top political representatives. Thus, they created a highly secretive organization to pursue their decades-long goal of staffing the highest level appointed posts in government, as well as gaining influence over those who advised the President. The organization is the Council on Foreign Relations. By 1941, just before the United States entered World War II, they gained permanent control over the top posts of the State Department. Henry M. Wriston, the most influential figure in the CFR-State Department connection in the post-World War II era, once referred to the CFR as "the invisible government of the United States."[4] This

---

4. Henry M. Wriston, *Diplomacy in a Democracy*, p. 108.

served conservative critic Dan Smoot as the title of the first book ever published about the organization, which did not appear until four decades after the CFR's creation (1962).

The founders of the CFR had a model to follow. In the late nineteenth century, Cecil Rhodes, one of the wealthiest men on earth, used his money and personal influence to create the Round Table groups throughout the British Commonwealth. The goal of the CFR was the same: the creation of permanent access to the decision-making processes of the government, and also to assure members of continuing access to world markets and revenue from government projects.

Moral Vision and Humanist Empire

What must be understood from the beginning is that the vision that originally motivated these elite figures was moral. They saw their task as extending Western ideas and techniques to the downtrodden masses—but at a profit, of course. Their vision, being moral, was also expansionist. They were men who sought dominion: through money, power, indoctrination, politics, and most of all, through an informal network of like-minded men throughout the world.

The initial vision had been provided by John Ruskin, who in 1870 became the first professor of fine arts at Oxford University. Historian Carroll Quigley describes what happened shortly after Ruskin's appointment to this teaching post, a position in fine arts which we might erroneously think would have little impact on anyone. "He hit Oxford like an earthquake, not so much because he talked about fine arts, but because he talked also about the empire and England's downtrodden masses, and above all because he talked about all three of these things as moral issues. Until the end of the nineteenth century the poverty-stricken masses in the cities of England lived in want, ignorance, and crime very much as they have been described by Charles Dickens. Ruskin spoke to the Oxford undergraduates as members of the privileged, ruling class. He told them that they were the possessors of a magnificent tradition of education, beauty, rule of law, freedom, decency, and self-discipline but that this tradition could not be saved, and did not deserve to be saved, unless it could be extended to the lower classes in England itself and to the non-English masses throughout the world. If this precious tradition were not extended to these two great majorities, the minority of upper-class Englishmen would ultimately be submerged by these majorities and the tradition lost. To prevent this, the tradition must be extended to the masses and to the empire."[5]

Quigley goes on to say that "Ruskin's message had a sensational impact. His inaugural lecture was copied out in longhand by one undergraduate, Cecil Rhodes, who kept it with him for thirty years." Rhodes, who died in 1902, discovered and developed the diamond fields and gold mines in South Africa. He and Lord Rothschild monopolized the diamond mines of South Africa as DeBeers Consolidated Mines and Consolidated Gold Fields. He received a million pounds sterling a year—five million dollars—in an era when few families earned 200 pounds a year, yet he was always overdrawn in his bank account. No one knows where this money went. He financed groups to extend the empire along the lines of Ruskin's vision. One such project was the creation of the Rhodes Scholarships, which are still the most prestigious academic awards that American undergraduates can win. These scholarships bring English-speaking people from "the colonies" to study at Oxford.[6] It is also highly significant that Rhodes' model for the extension of the empire was the Society of Jesus (Jesuits).[7]

Dominion? Yes. Moral vision? Yes. Conspiracy? Yes.[8]

The New York Banking Connection

Parallel organizations were established throughout the empire. Prof. Quigley refers to the "Wall Street, Anglo-American

---

5. Carroll Quigley, *Tragedy and Hope: A History of the World in Our Time* (New York: Macmillan, 1966), p. 130.

6. *Ibid.*, pp. 130-31.

7. Frank Aydelotte, *The American Rhodes Scholarships* (Princeton, New Jersey: Princeton University Press, 1946), p. 8.

8. Larry Abraham, *Call It Conspiracy* (Seattle, Washington: Double A Publications, 1985), ch. 5.

axis."[9] Here is a brief summary of what happened. At the end of World War I, the Round Table Group began to extend its influence. It set up national front organizations. The main one was the Royal Institute of International Affairs. "In New York it was known as the Council on Foreign Relations, and was a front for J. P. Morgan and Company in association with the very small American Roundtable Group." The officials with the Morgan banking organization had first met at the Paris Peace Conference earlier that year, in 1919. "The New York branch was dominated by the associates of the Morgan Bank." One of the academic associates linked to the bank was Henry M. Wriston.[10] His son Walter later became the president of Citicorp, the parent holding company for Citibank (formerly First National City Bank), now the largest bank in the United States. Quigley's conclusion is the heart of the matter: "On this basis, which was originally financial and goes back to George Peabody [Co.], there grew up in the twentieth century a power structure between London and New York which penetrated deeply into university life, the press, and the practice of foreign policy."[11]

But the attempts of men to imitate God invariably fail. The Round Table Group's influence disappeared when President Franklin Roosevelt sided repeatedly with Joseph Stalin against Winston Churchill at the Yalta Conference in 1945. George Crocker has described the diplomacy of the war years as Roosevelt's road to Russia.[12] Christian journalist and historian Otto Scott comments: "This was not a conscious, deliberate policy, but a net result of his desire to see an international organization created (the United Nations) that would embody the dream of statesmen and religious leaders through the centuries."[13] The British Empire was thereafter steadily dismantled, piece by piece, from 1945 until 1960. The Soviet Union has gobbled up the lion's

---

9. *Tragedy and Hope*, p. 953.
10. *Ibid.*, p. 952.
11. *Ibid.*, p. 953.
12. George N. Crocker, *Roosevelt's Road To Russia* (Chicago: Regnery, 1959).
13. Otto Scott, *The Other End of the Lifeboat* (Chicago: Regnery, 1985), p. 123.

share of the remains.

Scott's comments on the Round Table Group's efforts are important as a warning.

> The nature of the postwar world was an almost precise reverse of what the group had hoped to accomplish in the busy and powerful years since the 1880's. To expect its members to learn some sort of lesson from that, however, is to underestimate the awesome ability of human beings to rationalize their failures and repeat their errors.
>
> The group was high-minded, but also determinedly secular in its concerns. It still has the Rhodes trust, vast financial interests in South African mining, in copper and zinc, in utility interests through Lazard Brothers; its organizations like the Round Table, Chatham House, the Council on Foreign Relations; its ties with the House of Morgan, its connections and German industrialists, its far-flung connections in academia, its weblike influence in government and society.
>
> To expect the group to have realized its errors and abandon its attempts to direct the lives of others is to expect great pride to grow humble while it still lives in comfort and luxury. In minute but steady stages the group had sought power to do good, and although that good turned out not to be good, its search for power would continue in the postwar world. But power is an idol whose gifts sear the hands of its followers.[14]

He is correct: "In their efforts to create heaven on earth, the group opened the gate to hell."[15]

The making of United States foreign policy has, since the 1890's, been closely linked to British foreign policy. Those who write textbooks on the history of U.S. foreign policy never cease to mention that the success of the "Monroe Doctrine" (1823)— formulated by President James Monroe and his Secretary of State John Quincy Adams (later President)—rested on the strength of the British navy. This was true enough; Britain had helped to initiate the Monroe Doctrine in the summer of 1823. Monroe wrote

---

14. *Ibid.*, pp. 130-31.
15. *Ibid.*, p. 114.

to both Madison and Jefferson in the fall of 1823 for advice regarding Britain's willingness to work with the United States to keep the nations of the Holy Alliance — Russia, Austria, Spain, and France — out of the Americas. Jefferson wrote back to Monroe enthusiastically: at last Great Britain would cooperate! "Great Britain is the nation which can do us the most harm of any one, or all, on earth; and with her on our side we need not fear the whole world." The proposed plan's object "is to introduce and establish the American system, of keeping out of our land all foreign powers, of never permitting those of Europe to intermeddle with the affairs of our nations."[16] Here was the "American system" in a nutshell: *isolationism.*

The Monroe Doctrine was presented in Monroe's December 1823 annual message to Congress. The printed text of the message is twelve and a half pages long;[17] only two paragraphs, about a page and a half in length, deal with subject of Western hemisphere foreign relations.[18] The President warned European powers not to attempt to re-subjugate Latin American nations that had gained their independence and had been formally recognized by the United States. Monroe also stated that European governments would not be allowed to establish *new* colonies in the Western Hemisphere. "With the existing colonies or dependencies of any European power we have not interfered and shall not interfere."[19] Then he issued a mild warning to those nations of the Holy Alliance that might attempt to establish new colonies:

> It is impossible that the allied powers should extend their political system to any portion of either continent without endangering our peace and happiness; nor can anyone believe that our southern brethren, if left to themselves, would adopt it of their own accord. It is equally impossible, therefore, that we should behold such interposition in any form with indifference.[20]

---

16. Robert A. Divine (ed.), *American Foreign Policy* (New York: World, 1960), p. 71.

17. *A Compilation of the Messages and Papers of the Presidents* (New York: Bureau of National Literature, 1897), II, pp. 776-89.

18. *Ibid.*, pp. 786-88.

19. *Ibid.*, p. 787.

20. *Ibid.*, p. 788.

This message placed the United States as a potential military defender of the territorial sovereignty of nations in this hemisphere, although the language of conflict is absent. Monroe's speech produced no negative response by Congress, and his formulation of U.S. foreign policy was continued by John Quincy Adams. Monroe's Doctrine was clearly an act of *regional isolationism*. It was an extension of George Washington's Farewell Address isolationist policy, which President Adams referred to in his March 15, 1826 message to the House of Representatives, and in which he also quoted extensively from Monroe's 1823 speech.[21] He reminded Europe to stay out of our affairs, just as the United States had stayed out of Europe's. If our neutrality is not respected by Europe, "we might be called in defense of our own altars and firesides to take an attitude which would cause our neutrality to be respected. . . ."[22]

Such an "armed and dangerous" isolationist outlook horrifies the Anglophile internationalists who write today's textbooks. "Without the British fleet," the Rockefeller Panel insisted, "Monroe's declaration to protect the hemisphere against European imperialisms would have been merely rhetorical, a promise incapable of being made good." But, the report complains, this fact was somehow forgotten through most of the nineteenth century. It was Britain, not God, who protected the United States, and American statesmen forgot this key fact of international relations: "The American statesmen of those years liked to think that they were favored by providence, not by human arrangements."[23]

The idea that human agreements come as part of God's providence never occurs to them. That God in His grace might providentially favor a covenantally faithful nation is an obscene thought to the humanist. God's visible blessings testify to the existence of a covenant; this covenant also warns of a coming judgment: God's cursing of a covenantally rebellious nation. The

---

21. *Ibid.*, pp. 903-5.
22. *Ibid.*, p. 904.
23. *Prospect for America: The Rockefeller Panel Reports* (Garden City, New York: Doubleday, 1961), p. 10.

humanist puts his faith in other things: military equipment and international agreements. Fearful men see the Babylon of our day, the Soviet Union, and they want to make an alliance with the Egypts of this world for protection. But Egypt does not offer legitimate hope to God's people. As God warned the Israelites through Jeremiah during a similar crisis:

> "Do not be afraid of the king of Babylon, of whom you are afraid; do not be afraid of him," says the LORD, "for I am with you, to save you and deliver you from his hand. And I will show you mercy, that he may have mercy on you and cause you to return to your own land." "But if you say, 'We will not dwell in this land,' disobeying the voice of the LORD your God, saying, 'No, but we will go to the land of Egypt where we shall see no war, nor hear the sound of the trumpet, nor be hungry for bread, and there we will dwell'—Then hear now the word of the LORD, O remnant of Judah! Thus says the LORD of hosts, the God of Israel: 'If you wholly set your faces to enter Egypt, and go to sojourn there, then it shall be that the sword which you feared shall overtake you there in the land of Egypt; the famine of which you were afraid shall follow close after you there in Egypt; and there you shall die'" (Jeremiah 42:11-16).

Free Market Internationalism

The major players in the Round Table-CFR-Trilateral Commission networks are initiated from the top of the social and intellectual hierarchy: academia, business, law, the military, and the media. But the dominant interest is banking. Until the world adopts a Biblical system of money and banking, there will be continuing economic and political problems with international finance capital. What is needed is a system of honest weights and measures and a prohibition against all fractional reserve banking. (See my book in the Biblical Blueprints Series, *Honest Money: The Biblical Blueprint for Money and Banking.*)

Nevertheless, we must begin to reform this world, not a millennial world. The primary solution to the growth of conspiratorial networks of influential people who control national policy, especially foreign policy, is to subject them to the full pressure of international market competition. These people must learn to compete in a world with low or no tariffs, import quotas, export bounties, government-guaranteed loans, and similar restrictions on trade.

Market competition is a form of internationalism. Perhaps the best known and most successful mechanism of free market internationalism was the gold standard, 1815-1914. It kept national inflationists under tremendous pressure for a century. Wholesale prices in England were about 20 percent lower in 1914 than they had been in 1821, the year Britain introduced a full gold coin standard, with relatively little variation in between.[24]

Free trade with allies and neutral nations — meaning peaceful free trade with citizens everywhere — is perhaps the greatest incentive for contacts between missions-minded societies and those that are still pagan. It was Israel's key location on the trade routes of the ancient world that enabled them to demonstrate to many foreign visitors the wonders of Biblical law (Deuteronomy 4:5-8).

This is not necessarily an argument for trading with self-declared enemies of the West, which the Communist empires surely are. Yet, even in this case, for a Christian nation that is self-consciously on the offensive, free trade with identified enemies during peacetime could become a successful weapon. Just as we send medical missionaries abroad, just as we allow the Red Cross to send medicine to all combatants, so the gospel can penetrate enemy nations through their demand for goods and skills produced in productive Christian societies. The decision to trade or not to trade with a self-identified enemy should be made by the Commander-in-Chief of the armed forces, on the advice of senior military experts, subject to legislation to the contrary by the legislature. The decision should not be made by the foreign policy professionals. (It is not surprising that the Council on Foreign Relations systematically recruits our senior military

---

24. Edwin Walter Kemmerer, *Gold and the Gold Standard* (New York: McGraw-Hill, 1944), pp. 188-91.

officers, including the Commandants of West Point.)[25]

There would be this requirement for an identified enemy nation to be granted trading rights with a Christian nation or a covenanted group of Christian nations: the enemy would agree to allow Christian missionaries to enter the nation and establish churches without any interference, and that agreement would have to be honored. Like skid row bums who are required to listen to a sermon before they are handed their bowl of soup, so will the identified enemy nations be required to allow missionaries to preach the gospel to their people in order to gain access to Christian markets. We will find out how hungry they really are for the products of the free market.

Businessmen as Diplomats

We need an army of skilled, practical people to take the message of freedom to the whole world. They need not be professionally trained diplomats. In fact, they *must not* be professionally trained diplomats, for the humanists long ago captured the key training institutions. What we need are people who can offer the pagan world what the pagans want: the prosperity that Western capitalism has produced. They want Western science and technology. Christians must learn and never forget the history of Western science and technology: it was the product of Christianity.[26]

The businessman understands the ways of market competition. The free market is God's way to expand the honest man's wealth. The free market grew out of Christianity, and *only* out of Christianity. This proven fact of history[27] outrages most humanists and their Christian allies in theologically compromised Christian colleges, whose faculty members all attended humanist-

25. Susan Huck, "Lost Valor," *American Opinion* (October 1977); "Military," *ibid.*, (July/August 1980).

26. Stanley Jaki, *The Road of Science and the Ways to God* (Chicago: University of Chicago Press, 1978); *Science and Creation: From eternal cycles to an oscillating universe* (Edinburgh and London: Scottish Academic Press, [1974] 1980).

27. Max Weber, *The Protestant Ethic and the Spirit of Capitalism* (New York: Scribner's, [1904-5] 1958). See also Gary North, "The 'Protestant Ethic' Hypothesis," *Journal of Christian Reconstruction*, III (Summer, 1976), pp. 185-201.

controlled universities in order to earn the doctorates that the little Christian colleges require them to earn if they want to get hired in the first place. Naturally, this has led to the increasing theological and political liberalism of those colleges.[28]

What diplomats need are *real-world skills*, not college classroom skills. The U.S. State Department deliberately screens out people with these real-world skills by imposing the most rigorous academic exam required by any branch of civil government, the foreign service examination. It is strictly acad_mic. Thousands of highly educated college graduates take the exam each year. Only about 200 pass. A committee decides what kind of exam is administered, and then conducts interviews to determine which of the few applicants who pass the exam actually get into the ranks of the 3,700 Foreign Service Officers.

Those who survive are virtually all academic types. The academic institutions are controlled by liberal humanists. Thus, a self-perpetuating liberal bureaucracy controls access to the diplomatic corps.

The Biblical answer is to fire most of this corps, and replace them with informal, unofficial diplomats whose talents are precisely what a diplomatic corps needs: practical business skills that the whole world wants. We want to make the world capitalist, and then our witness-ambassadors will have greater freedom to bring the gospel. We want to show the so-called Third World how to feed and clothe itself, and at the same time tell them of the God who has made their wealth possible. We need to take the Bible's warning seriously:

> What does it profit, my brethren, if someone says he has faith but does not have works? Can faith save him? If a brother or sister is naked and destitute of daily food, and one of you says to them, "Depart in peace, be warmed and filled," but you do not give them the things which are needed for the body, what does it profit? (James 2:14-16).

---

28. James Davison Hunter, *Evangelicalism: The Coming Generation* (University of Chicago Press, 1987), pp. 165-80.

What does it *profit* indeed? And if a person possesses the knowledge of how to do business, and this knowledge is the only means in man's history by which the vast majority of people who have adopted this way of life have escaped the threat of starvation, what does it profit you if you never tell the starving masses of the world how to escape starvation? Prof. Bauer is correct: it is contact with the West that stimulates economic growth in backward societies. The fewer the contacts, the poorer the societies.[29]

We are to give food to people in order to give them time and energy to learn the skills of growing food and feeding themselves. This means we must tell them of the liberation offered by Christ, and the economic liberation offered by Christ's social order.[30]

What does the State Department tell them? Morton Blackwell, a former White House aide under President Reagan, relates this story:

> In the spring of 1980, in a briefing at the U.S. embassy in Guatemala City, an embassy staff member stressed to me that the United States must force Guatemala to break up all large farms and to nationalize all banks and the export industry.
>
> I responded, "It sounds to me as if you are saying we must force Guatemala to adopt Marxism in order to save it from Marxism."
>
> The briefer, one Arnold M. Isaacs, replied haughtily, "I am describing the policy of the United States."
>
> And Mr. Isaacs, whom I met in Guatemala in 1980, is still going strong in the State Department. Today he's in Foggy Bottom itself[31] at the State Department's Board of Examiners, interviewing and evaluating people who have applied to join the Foreign Service.[32]

---

29. P. T. Bauer, *Dissent on Development: Studies and debates in development economics* (Cambridge, Massachusetts: Harvard University Press, 1972), pp. 300-2.

30. Gary North, *Liberating Planet Earth: An Introduction to Biblical Blueprints* (Ft. Worth, Texas: Dominion Press, 1987), ch. 9.

31. Foggy Bottom is the place in Washington, D.C. where the State Department is located.

32. Morton C. Blackwell, "Can the United States Have a Winning Foreign Policy?" *The Constitution* (Feb. 1987), p. 8.

It is not enough to clothe people if they do not learn the economic laws through which God says that men must clothe themselves: work, thrift, planning, personal responsibility, meeting the economic needs of others, etc.[33] It is also not enough to make them wealthier if they do not honor God:

> "You have sown much, and bring in little; you eat, but do not have enough; you drink, but you are not filled with drink; you clothe yourselves, but no one is warm. And he who earns wages, earns wages to put into a bag with holes." Thus says the LORD of hosts: "Consider your ways! Go up to the mountains and bring wood and build the temple, that I may take pleasure in it and be glorified," says the LORD. "You looked for much, but indeed it came to little; and when you brought it home, I blew it away. Why?" says the LORD of hosts. "Because of My house that is in ruins, while every one of you runs to his own house. Therefore the heavens above you withhold the dew, and the earth withholds its fruit" (Haggai 1:6-10).

Who will tell them? Humanists in the Foreign Service? Of course not. Christian businessmen must do it. This requires that some Christians become skilled, successful businessmen. They must learn fluency in a foreign language. They must learn the ways of transmitting the practical gospel of Christ into a foreign culture, by way of business skills that must also be imparted. I think this is why Christians have been willing to walk away from personal responsibility: a huge inferiority complex. They do not believe that they can compete, because they do not believe that covenantal faithfulness to God's law works. In short, they are not Christian pragmatists. They refuse to do business (*pragmateuomai*) until He comes. They prefer to let State Department humanists represent their nation, meaning the citizens of their nation, to the world. And since these Foreign Service Officers are dedicated humanists, this means that Christians are ready to allow these men to represent this nation in the name of the God-denying theology of humanism.

---

33. Gary North, *Inherit the Earth: Biblical Blueprints for Economics* (Ft. Worth, Texas: Dominion Press, 1987).

Official National Diplomats

There is still a minor role for professional diplomats, as servants to the drastically reduced number of official ambassadors. These people must be as loyal to the national head of State as any ambassador. There must be no employment protection for anyone in the foreign service. Politics, not bureaucratic rules, must govern the diplomacy of nation-states, for the diplomacy of nation-states must always be conducted in terms of national interests, as expressed by politics.

Those who write international agreements for nations come from the same New York law firms that write the agreements among businesses. Clearly, there is a need for specialists in this field, but such services can be hired when needed like any other professional service. There is nothing in these law firms that says that incompetents cannot be fired. Offers can be made to employees at rival law firms. Competition is good for contract-writing. It is good for treaty-writing, too.

The initiation of formal diplomacy must always come from the top. This is the service that a head of State must perform, as the military Commander-in-Chief. Diplomacy is always related to the issue of war. The diplomat, like the soldier, must work at the pleasure of his Commander-in-Chief.

Summary

We have seen how the humanists captured the foreign service organizations of Great Britain and the United States by a systematic program of buying influence and capturing the institutions of higher learning. They also captured the screening process of the foreign service bureaucracies. Thus, the trained professional diplomats are in fact representatives of a tiny, wealthy, self-selected elite of humanist planners. The richest corporations and the super-rich businessmen have used the monopolistic power of civil government to further their ends, which include making the free world into a top-down centralized bureaucracy. This is always Satan's goal: the creation of a top-down bureaucracy to replace God's bottom-up decentralized kingdom.

Christianity can prosper only if it adheres to God's revealed law in every area of life. When Christian businessmen do this, they will prosper. Eventually, they can carry the story and the skills of the gospel to foreign nations that may hate God but who want the economic fruits of righteousness. Perhaps the most successful social export of the United States in the twentieth century is the Rotary Club.[34] Why wasn't it the Christian church? *Because Christians have lost the Biblical vision of victory in history.*

The first step in reducing the influence of our humanist enemies in foreign policy is to cut drastically the budgets and the size of the government-operated diplomatic corps of Western nations, and replace them with thousands of businessmen who will serve as unofficial, unpaid diplomats. Then it will be our job as Christians to raise up the skilled businessmen and businesswomen necessary for this world-transforming task. There is no shortcut to success.

It is imperative that the elected representatives of the nation establish guidelines regarding valid trade policies. There should be no trade whatsoever with nations inside a hostile, expansionist empire, except to get Christian missionaries inside the country. It is not the task of businessmen to determine which nations are legitimate trading partners and which are not, any more than it is the task of professional salaried diplomats to make this determination. Once the decision is made, however, businessmen rather than foreign service bureaucrats should spearhead both contacts and contracts between residents of the nations.

In summary:

1. Christians are to become Biblical pragmatists.
2. Christians are to become skilled workers in the affairs of life.
3. Otherworldly Christianity resents this vision of full-scale Christian responsibility in this world.
4. The humanists who now are in control agree with these

---

34. The classroom opinion of conservative sociologist-historian Robert Nisbet.

otherworldly Christians.

5. God's servants are supposed to be practical people.

6. Christians are told to increase the capital that God has given them as His stewards.

7. Diplomats are negotiators.

8. Businessmen are negotiators.

9. Diplomats today are professional bureaucrats, protected from being fired by law.

10. Businessmen are not protected by law from bankruptcy in a free market economy.

11. Politicians do not control foreign policy because it takes too long to master the details.

12. Thus, the key to power here is the capture of the intellectual allegiance of the professional foreign service corps.

13. The humanists have done this through capturing the universities and the examination screening system of the foreign service.

14. Cecil Rhodes and his associates captured British foreign policy in the late nineteenth century.

15. In the United States, super-rich bankers and the large businesses that they controlled began this process of capture in 1919, and it was completed in 1941.

16. Such a capture is motivated by a moral vision: either humanist or Biblical.

17. The proper form of internationalism is Christian internationalism.

18. Free market competition is a system designed by God to open foreign mission fields to the gospel.

19. Trade becomes a way to open the door to missions.

20. The world wants the real-world skills of Western business, science, and technology.

21. Western business, science, and technology grew out of Christianity.

22. The pagan world therefore wants the cultural fruits of Christianity.

23. Christians must take the lead in every area of life, in order to prove the workability of Biblical Christianity.

24. Christians must then take the whole counsel of God to foreign nations.

25. Humanism has sapped the courage of the West.

26. We need to return to God and His law in order to regain our courage.

9

ALLIANCES ARE NOT COVENANTS

"You shall make no covenant with them, nor with their gods" (Exodus 23:32).

Then one who had escaped came and told Abram the Hebrew, for he dwelt by the terebinth trees of Mamre the Amorite, brother of Eshcol and brother of Aner; and they were allies with Abram (Genesis 14:13).

The fourth point of the Biblical covenant is the doctrine of sanctions: cursings and blessings. A covenant is established by an oath. The oath-taker places himself and all those under his lawful authority (point two) under the ethical terms (point three) of the covenant. He calls upon God to be his witness (point four) that he will obey the terms of the covenant (point three). In a covenanted institution, all the members take such an oath. For such an oath to be valid covenantally, all those making the oath must agree that it is the God of the Bible who established it (point one), set forth its requirements (point three), and enforces it (point four).

This Old Testament prohibition against covenants with foreign nations referred specifically to covenants between the Israelites and the nations of Canaan. By implication, it now prohibits any formally covenanted Christian nation from establishing a covenant with any non-Christian nation.

The Biblical covenant has five points:

1. An affirmation of the transcendence and presence of God
2. A hierarchical system of appeals courts
3. Biblical law
4. A system of sanctions (blessings and cursings)
5. A system of inheritance or continuity

197

Thus, to make a covenant with a pagan foreign nation, the Christian nation would have to affirm formally the equality of the pagan nation's god with the God of the Bible. This is why all covenants between pagan nations and Christian nations are abominations.

In the ancient world, warfare between cities necessarily involved warfare between the gods of those cities. To establish a peace treaty between cities, the two had to establish an alliance between their respective gods. A sacrifice was required, exactly as the sacrifice of Jesus Christ is necessary to establish a permanent peace treaty between God and rebellious men. Fustel de Coulanges wrote in 1864 of these ritual treaties: "When a war did not end by the extermination or subjection of one of the two parties, a treaty of peace might terminate it. But for this a convention was not sufficient; a religious act was necessary. Every treaty was marked by the immolation of a victim. To sign a treaty is a modern expression; the Latins said, strike a kid. . . . The ceremony of the treaty was always accomplished by priests, who conformed to the ritual. . . . These religious ceremonies alone gave a sacred and inviolable character to international conventions."[1]

For several generations, Christians have avoided thinking deeply about the theological aspects of treaties. One way that they have avoided such intellectual problems is by refusing to acknowledge the legitimacy of the idea that any nation can be identified as a Christian nation. If no nation can ever be identified covenantally as a Christian nation, then Christianity has nothing to say one way or the other concerning the theological distinctions between permanent covenants and impermanent alliances among nations, or concerning proper and improper treaties (covenants). Such treaties are assumed to operate in terms of a hypothetical "law of nations" or "national self-interest," both of which are hypothetically neutral theologically and covenantally. The myth of neutrality again rears its ugly head in the affairs of Christian men.

---

1. Numa Denis Fustel de Coulanges, *The Ancient City: A Study on the Religion, Laws, and Institutions of Greece and Rome* (Garden City, New York: Doubleday Anchor, [1864] 1955), pp. 207-8.

If we begin with the presumption of the necessity of covenantally neutral nationhood, then we will end with the presumption of covenantally neutral international relations.

Christians are to seek peace. The basis of peace in history is the same as the basis of peace in eternity: *subordination to God*. The Bible calls for peace through victory. It does *not* call for peace through moral stalemate, or peace through geographical containment of the enemy, or peace through formal treaties, or peace through isolationism. Covenantal warfare will never end in history, for sin is always present in history, but progress toward peace can be achieved.

Christ's Peace Only Through Christ's Covenant

The increase of public peace accompanies the increase of Christ's institutional rule on earth. This institutional rule is extended by means of the covenant. God has established covenantal representatives of Christ on earth. Christians are Christ's *representatives*. The doctrine of covenantal representation is basic to understanding Christ's rule in history. Christ's representatives bring covenant sanctions in His name. Christians understand that Christ need not be physically present with them in order for them to have progressive victory over sin in their personal lives, their families, their churches, and their businesses. Yet as soon as anyone begins discussing victory over sin in the realm of civil government, 99.9 percent of them say either that such victory is not possible (European traditionalism) or can only be achieved when Christ returns physically to establish His international, top-down, bureaucratic kingdom (American fundamentalism).

As soon as modern Christians begin talking about civil government, they self-consciously assure the listener that they have abandoned the doctrine of representation and hierarchy (point two of the Biblical covenant model). What they forthrightly affirm as binding in personal life, family life, and church life—*theocracy* (rule by God)—they have been persuaded by generations of humanists is invalid and even immoral in civil life. They write such statements as this one: "We must not confuse the Kingdom of God with our country. To say it another way: 'We should not wrap Christianity in our national flag.' "[2]

Of course we must not wrap our national flag around Christianity. Instead, we must work toward that day when we can fly our national flag *under* Christianity's flag. We must not confuse the kingdom of God with our country, for the kingdom of God is international and above all nations: "Behold, the nations are as a drop in the bucket, and are counted as the small dust on the balance" (Isaiah 40:15a). This is why each Christian should work all his life to do whatever he can to lead his business, his children's school, his family, his church, his local community, and his country under the international kingdom of God in history. This is what it means to abandon as Satan's lie the myth of neutrality.[3] This is also what it means to pray in faith and confidence, "Thy kingdom come. Thy will be done in earth, as it is in heaven" (Matthew 6:10, KJV). If Jesus did not expect this prayer to be answered in history, He would not have told us: "Ask, and it will be given to you; seek, and you will find; knock, and it will be opened to you" (Matthew 7:7).

When Christians deny the Biblical legitimacy of a national Christian covenant, they necessarily are proclaiming the myth of neutrality, the myth of natural law, the myth of permanent political pluralism, the myth of "equal time for Satan." There is no logical escape from this conclusion. If neutrality is a myth, then there is a cosmic war going on between Christ and Satan, between Christ's kingdom and Satan's empire, between Christ's law and Satan's counterfeit laws. There exists no neutral court of appeal to which representatives of both covenants can receive impartial, neutral judgment from someone above both God and Satan. *But covenant-breaking man wants to decide between God and Satan*, just as Adam wanted to test the reliability of God's word or Satan's word

---

2. Francis Schaeffer, *A Christian Manifesto* (Westchester, Illinois: Crossway, 1981), p. 121.

3. For an extended critique of Rev. Schaeffer's attack on theocracy, see Gary North and David Chilton, "Apologetics and Strategy," *Christianity and Civilization*, No. 3 (1983), pp. 116-31.

regarding the forbidden fruit. Self-proclaimed autonomous man says he seeks only a neutral court in which man's autonomous word will be upheld. He thereby proclaims that God is not sovereign in history.

Rev. Schaeffer, despite occasional language to the contrary, never broke with natural law theory. He was inconsistent. On the one hand, he spent his career criticizing humanism because it produces a dying culture; on the other hand, he never wrote a book outlining what the God-required Biblical alternatives to humanism are. He rejected Biblical covenantal law, so he had no Bible-revealed standards for public institutions. This is also why his published followers still publicly proclaim political pluralism in the name of Christianity. *They think they can successfully cut a temporary political deal with the humanists in order to buy the Church enough time until Jesus comes again physically to set up His international bureaucratic kingdom.* This is why Rev. Schaeffer could write: "There is no New Testament basis for a linking of church and state until Christ, the King returns."[4] He did not trust Christians to be able to run anything outside their families and local churches; thus, he in principle turned the political world over to Satan until Jesus comes again. He dismissed the Biblical covenant with the clever phrase, "We should not wrap Christianity in our national flag."

Meanwhile, the humanists are using humanist "flags" to wrap every aspect of public life and much of private life in a legal straightjacket. The 7 to 2 decision of the U.S. Supreme Court in the summer of 1987 that forbids states from requiring the teaching of six-day creationism in public high schools that teach evolution is a recent example. The humanists work diligently to establish their theocracy, the kingdom of autonomous, God-denying man. What terrifies the humanists is that millions of Christians may someday figure out that our national flag, like our nation, should be wrapped in Christianity. This obvious discovery has not taken place yet. Christians applaud this expansion of Christ-denying humanist "neutrality" in the name of political pluralism. Once

---

4. *A Christian Manifesto*, p. 121.

again, we find the myth of natural law and common morality, which Christians believe means "equal time for Jesus (and therefore also for Satan)," but which the humanists know has to mean "no time for Jesus anywhere in tax-financed life." Then the humanists work to make every aspect of life tax-financed. Public school-educated Christians vote for compulsory wealth-redistribution schemes in the name of religiously neutral humanitarian charity, and thereby finance the removal of Jesus Christ from every area of public life. Say one word against this process of covenantal deception, and both Christians and humanists stitch a scarlet "T" on your shirt.

Every aspect of life must come under the public rule of Christ (1 Corinthians 15:24-25). This is why the basis of progressive public peace (though never perfect peace on sinful earth) is the successful waging of spiritual warfare by Christians. Public peace can only be established in history through public covenantal (representative) conquest by Christ the King. All other forms of peace are either temporary cease-fire agreements or deceptions by the enemies of Christ. International relations must be governed by this fundamental Biblical principle of history.

Covenants Are Binding

When a nation signs a treaty with another nation that promises such things as mutual military defense pacts, it has entered into a covenant. The survival of each nation is at stake, yet the terms of survival are specified far in advance by the document. Once the external conditions appear, a nation is committed, unless it simply breaks the covenant.

World War I began because the major European powers were bound by such covenants. Once hostilities began at the fringes of Europe, the leaders had almost no time to decide what to do: all the armies had drawn up offensive and defensive plans that were governed by train schedules. Any hesitation would mean defeat.[5]

---

5. A. J. P. Taylor, *War by Time-Table: How the First World War Began* (New York: American Heritage Press, 1969).

A military alliance such as the North Atlantic Treaty Organization (NATO) is a covenant, but not a strong one. Member nations are pledged to support the others in case of war with the Soviet Union-Warsaw Pact nations. NATO cannot compel its member nations to contribute troops or money. Still, it stands as the major unifying bond of the Western nations militarily.

It is clear from most of the writings of modern theorists of international relations that NATO, SEATO, and the other alliance-covenants are supposed to serve as models for other, more powerful covenants in the future. Nelson Rockefeller was quite open about using these military alliances (covenants) as stepping stones to a one-world government: "Unity in the West implies an act of political creation—comparable to that of our Founding Fathers—and perhaps of even greater originality, daring and devotion. In our time, the challenge leads us, inspires us, toward the building of our great North Atlantic alliance, our 'regional grouping,' into a North Atlantic Confederation—looking eventually to a worldwide Union of the Free."[6]

Each nation is to give up much (or all) of its sovereignty to some future international organization or organizations. But these organizations will not be governed by permanent ethical standards, for Darwinian humanism denies that such standards are possible in an evolving world. We see this perspective of ethical relativism applied to foreign relations in Robert Osgood's college textbook of the early 1950's, which is still in print, *Ideals and Self-Interest in America's Foreign Relations* (1953). Ideals, yes, but no permanent morality. The book's subtitle is also interesting: *The Great Transformation of the Twentieth Century.* Indeed, it was!

Don't these humanist scholars at least understand that nations, like individuals, are marked by certain ultimate moral commitments? Don't they understand that there are fundamental ethical principles that divide men permanently? Don't they understand that the story of the Tower of Babel really tells us a

---

6. Nelson A. Rockefeller, *Unity, Freedom & Peace: A Blueprint for Tomorrow* (New York: Random House, 1968), p. 146.

fundamental truth about the limits on men's ability and willingness to join together politically? No, they don't. There is only one overarching ethical premise for them, one which unifies all mankind: *the brotherhood of man*. This must eventually lead to a new *community of man*. It must lead to a New World Order.

In history and political science departments around the country, this commitment to *pragmatic ethical flexibility* has also long been recognized as the highest moral ideal for nations. The manipulators and the academicians share rhetoric because they share basic principles. Principle Number One: "There are *no* ethical norms that inherently divide the community of man." (Principle Number Two: "Don't go out of your way to aid the career of anyone who rejects Principle Number One, unless you are trying to work some sort of short-run deal.") Here is a major myth of modern evolutionary humanism: *ethics without permanent norms!* Here is an ethical ideal dear to the hearts of pragmatists—and also to thieves, traitors, and other skilled professionals in search of new victims.

Prof. Osgood builds his case for internationalism on the brotherhood of man. He forgets that the brotherhood of covenant-breaking man is best seen in Cain's murder of Abel. "Idealists must recognize as a basic condition for the realization of the liberal and humane values the creation of a brotherhood of mankind in which all men, regardless of physiological, social, religious, or political distinctions, will have equal partnership and in which human conflicts will be settled by reason, morality, and law rather than by physical power, coercion, or violence."[7] *The equal partnership of all mankind*, "regardless of physiological, social, religious, or political distinctions": here is the humanists' version of the covenant bond.

What Osgood wants is a New World Order, although this term was not in use in academic circles back in 1953. He wants to

---

7. Robert E. Osgood, *Ideals and Self-Interest in American Foreign Relations: The Great Transformation of the Twentieth Century* (Chicago: University of Chicago Press, 1953), pp. 6-7.

see it established, however, in the name of what he thinks should be (but obviously is not) acceptable to good, realistic, pragmatic Americans, meaning *people without fixed moral principles*. Flexible people. Deal-doers, but of a very special variety: *deal-doers who do deals with our declared mortal enemies*. These were the kind of people who sold repeating rifles to the Sioux Indians in 1875. When General Custer got killed a year later, the salesmen no doubt blamed Custer for foolhardiness. No doubt today's generals would agree. They have learned from General MacArthur's experience — and, indirectly, from General Singlaub's[8] — that critics of today's U.S. foreign policy, which is designed to assist the rifle salesmen, do not survive either the Indian chiefs or their Commander-in-Chief.

The next step is "internationalism by sacrifice" — the sacrifice of each nation's sovereignty to the needs of others: "The pursuit of a universal goal may demand the practice of that extreme form of idealism, national altruism, according to which men dedicate themselves to the welfare of other nations and peoples without regard for their own nation's welfare. But the ultimate form of idealism is national self-sacrifice, which demands the deliberate surrender of one's own nation's self-interest for the sake of other nations and peoples or for the sake of some moral principle or universal goal. Every ideal demands that nations place some restraints upon egoism and renounce the more extreme forms of self-interest, but the ideal of self-sacrifice must countenance even the surrender of national survival itself."[9] Even the surrender of national survival is legitimate. Here is the humanists' one-State world order.

It is a powerful vision. The Communists possess it. The liberal humanists also possess it. Christians have been unsuccessful in challenging it because they have adopted the views of the isolationist humanists or the humanist nationalists. They have forgot-

---

8. Major General John Singlaub protested once too often against Jimmy Carter's announced intention to pull U.S. troops out of South Korea. Singlaub's career ended, but the troops stayed.

9. Osgood, *Ideals & Self-Interest.*, p. 7.

ten that Christ called His people to subdue the nations under His covenant. They have forgotten that it is the vision of victory that the church offers to redeemed mankind that is *the* model for all humanist internationalism, not a one-State world, but a one-world Christian confederation. Covenants without God's standards are evil. Christian nations must avoid them. But they must not abandon the vision of world victory that motivates humanist internationalists, whether Western or Communist.

Distinguishing Friends from Enemies

There is no neutrality. We are in a total war; it is going on in every area of life. This does not mean that Christian societies should be in perpetual shooting wars. It means that we are all in a life-long, millennia-long war with organized satanic forces of evil. We are warriors as well as ambassadors. We are Christian soldiers. We sing the psalms, and some of them are war songs of the Prince of Peace (such as Psalm 83).

The best way to attain peace is to defeat your enemy without a battle (Deuteronomy 20:10-11). Moses knew this half a millennium before Chinese strategist Sun Tsu established his supreme principle of war: "For to win one hundred victories in one hundred battles is not the acme of skill. To subdue the enemy without fighting is the acme of skill."[10] Christians captured the Roman Empire spiritually and politically; they could not have captured it militarily. The goal is to erode without violence your enemy's will to resist. This is the strategy being used by the Soviet Union against the West. It is the strategy that the West must adopt against every enemy and potential enemy. We must destroy their will to resist the gospel — the job primarily of missionaries. Ours is not a military conquest; ours is a job of national defense, with missionaries of all sorts acting as the offensive specialists.

In a war, we must distinguish between allies and enemies. The West has not done this successfully. We are told that this ability

---

10. Sun Tsu, *The Art of War*, translated by Samuel B. Griffith (New York: Oxford University Press, [1963] 1982), p. 77.

will be characteristic of the millennial triumph of Christianity:

> The eyes of those who see will not be dim, and the ears of those who hear will listen. Also the heart of the rash will understand knowledge, and the tongue of the stammerers will be ready to speak plainly. The foolish person will no longer be called generous, nor the miser said to be bountiful; for the foolish person will speak foolishness, and his heart will work iniquity: to practice ungodliness, to utter error against the LORD, to keep the hungry unsatisfied, and he will cause the drink of the thirsty to fail. Also the schemes of the schemer are evil; he devises wicked plans to destroy the poor with lying words, even when the needy speaks justice. But a generous man devises generous things, and by generosity he shall stand (Isaiah 32:3-8).

Evil people will remain evil, but they will be readily identified, and their schemes will fail. When Christians at last learn the skills of judging between evil and good, between lies and falsehoods, then they will be able to exercise dominion. God the Judge calls His people to make judgments—accurate, God-honoring, Bible-based judgments. Matthew 7 calls us to make judgments with the judgments we want to receive; we are to judge positively, in terms of the Bible, so that we are not judged falsely because we have judged others falsely (Matthew 7:1-2).

Alliances to Spoil Satan's House

A Christian nation should distinguish between six types of nations: 1) Christian nations that are covenanted with each other; 2) Christian nations that for some reason are outside the covenanted group or groups; 3) pagan allies that are nonetheless on the side of God's representative nation or nations if war with pagan empires breaks out; 4) pagan neutral nations that are sitting on the fence, weighing costs and benefits of choosing one side or the other; 5) pagan nations that are aligned with the empire; and 6) pagan empires that are determined to serve as international satanic leaven.

The Bible forbids us to make covenants with His enemies. "Covenant" is not some vague concept in the Bible. A prohibition against making a covenant with another nation means that we may not establish permanent legal pacts with them that possess the five characteristics of the Biblical covenant: 1) common constitution (source of authority); 2) common political or legal hierarchy; 3) common law-order; 4) common courts and common confession of faith; and 5) common citizenship.

This does not mean that Christian nations are not allowed to make temporary alliances for specific purposes with non-Christian nations. Like a Christian who purchases the services of non-Christian specialists, so can the Christian nation legitimately purchase services from other nations, services such as military aid in a crisis. There is a continual process of buying and selling going on in international relations. This is normal. This is legitimate. What is not legitimate is the creation of covenantal bonds, especially any on-going pact that is equal in authority to the constitution or fundamental law of a Christian nation, and which therefore takes precedence over the legislation of a Christian nation.

This is perhaps the most glaring weakness in the United States Constitution: treaties are not explicitly said to be subordinate to the Constitution. The President, with a two-thirds vote of *those present* for a vote by the Senate, can establish covenantal bonds with foreign nations that take precedence over national legislation. A treaty seems to become equal to a ratified amendment of the Constitution. It is still a legally open question as to whether or just how a ratified treaty is to be dealt with by the Supreme Court or Congress if it is not in conformity to the Constitution.[11] The Supreme Court has never held a treaty to be unconstitutional.[12] It held that a treaty does supersede the Tenth Amendment, which lodges in the states all powers not delegated to the United States.[13] Senator John Bricker of Ohio attempted in the early 1950's to add an amendment to the Constitution that would have required the provisions of any treaty to be conformable to the Constitution. It was defeated in the Senate by one vote in 1954, and was never

---

11. *The Constitution of the United States of America: Analysis and Interpretation* (Washington, D.C.: Government Printing Office, 1973), pp. 495-500.

12. *Ibid.*, p. 495.

13. The case that stated this was *Missouri. v. Holland* (1920).

offered to the public for ratification.[14] The humanists spotted this weakness in the Constitution and have worked hard to overturn the Constitution by Supreme Court interpretation (a tradition established by Supreme Court Chief Justice John Marshall in the early nineteenth century) and by international treaties. This is why control over the Foreign Service is crucial in the United States.

Abram made an alliance with Sodom and Gomorrah in order to battle the invading army of Chedorlaomer. The invader had kidnapped his nephew Lot (Genesis 14). After the victory, Abram refused to accept Chedorlaomer's captured goods from the hand of the king of Sodom, because he did not want to become in any way publicly beholden to a pagan king rather than publicly dependent to God (vv. 21-23). He had established a temporary defensive alliance with Sodom, not a covenant.

Divide and Conquer

We are allowed to strengthen our allies in order to weaken our enemies. We acknowledge the common grace of God in restraining some pagans and some pagan nations from becoming ethically consistent with their God-hating first principles.[15] As some pagan nations do become satanically consistent and seek to create Satan's empire in history, we are allowed to seek to divide his kingdom. The principle of "divide and conquer" is taught in the Bible. When Jesus healed a demon-possessed man, the Pharisees complained:

> "This fellow does not cast out demons except by Beelzebub, the ruler of the demons." But Jesus knew their thoughts, and said to them: "Every kingdom divided against itself is brought to desolation, and every city or house divided against itself will not stand. And if Satan casts out Satan, he is divided against himself. How

---

14. See Justus D. Doenecke, *Not to the Swift: The Old Isolationists In the Cold War Era* (Lewisburg, Pennsylvania: Bucknell University Press, 1979), pp. 235-38.

15. Gary North, *Dominion and Common Grace: The Biblical Basis of Progress* (Tyler, Texas: Institute for Christian Economics, 1987).

then will his kingdom stand? . . . Or else how can one enter a
strong man's house and plunder his goods, unless he first binds the
strong man? And then he will plunder his house" (Matthew
12:24-26, 29).

It is our job as Christians to work constantly to plunder
Satan's house, in every area of life. This is what dominion means.
It is what serving as the leaven of God's kingdom means (Matthew 13:33). It is what it means to be an ambassador for Christ, a
disciple of Christ, disciplining the nations. This involves pitting
Satan's less consistent followers against his more consistent followers. In foreign relations, this is the equivalent of exorcising
demons. But it necessarily involves exercising good judgment. We
must distinguish between friend and foe. This is what the foreign
policy of the West, and especially the United States, has failed to
do for over two generations.

Strengthening Our Allies

Having made the distinction between friend and foe, our foreign policy establishment must do whatever it can to strengthen
the confidence of our allies and weaken the support the world
gives to our enemies.

This support must recognize degrees of reliability and wor-
thiness. In the face of aggression from a true tyranny, we can give
limited verbal support to a local dictator. A domestic tyrant is less
of a threat to a godly nation than an expansionist empire is. Anyone who cannot understand this should play no role in the corps of
foreign policy specialists. Unfortunately, the vocal elements of the
legislature, the universities, the media, and the entire foreign policy establishment in the West has great difficulty in grasping this
elementary principle.

In such alliances, the direction of policy must always be primarily in the hand of the Christian nation. We are not to rely on
dictators. We are not to become dependent on them. We are to
make calculated good use of them as buffers against invasion. If a
dictator stands between our borders and the expanding Communist empire, we must do what we can, *cost-effectively*, to strengthen

him while we strengthen our home defenses.

Something received must be accompanied by something given up. The price the dictator pays is continued openness to missionaries. If he shuts the door to the gospel, he takes the risk of sinking or swimming alone. He must learn that Christianity is not the threat to him that the pagan empire is. If he hates God more than he fears the empire, let him fall. Every nation that refuses to accept missionaries from a Christian nation should be regarded as having broken its treaties with the Christian nation. Any continuing alliance is established on a "strictly business" *ad hoc* basis.

We must make judgments regarding the reliability of our allies. If they are generally reliable *for the Christian nation's interests*, then Christian foreign policy should refrain from pressuring them to conform to our outlook and practices at the expense of their perceived national interest. Only if we have our own house in order can we in good conscience offer assistance to an ally regarding his ethical weakness. Again, Matthew 7 is the place to begin discussing making good judgments:

> "Or how can you say to your brother, 'Let me remove the speck out of your eye'; and look, a plank is in your own eye? Hypocrite! First remove the plank from your own eye, and then you will see clearly to remove the speck out of your brother's eye" (Matthew 7:4-5).

We must teach by example, giving our allies confidence that we take God's law seriously, and that God therefore takes us seriously. Nations, like people, are more easily persuaded by success than by shouting. Imitation is entered into more enthusiastically than necessary submission. Japan's post-War revival economic-ally is proof that they took Western capitalism far more seriously than the mixed-market, part-socialist capitalist West took it.

Most of this "speck-removing" process should be private rather than public, quiet rather than loud. Missionaries, businessmen, technicians, medical care specialists, teachers, and other privately financed professional servants should spearhead peaceful change. Free trade is also a good teacher. Solomon hired Hiram of Tyre to supervise the craftsmen of Tyre to build the temple itself; he bought cedars from Lebanon (1 Kings 5). Privately funded charities of all kinds should be sent to nations that need it. Elisha healed Naaman the Syrian (2 Kings 5). Christian nations should have the reputation of being filled with good Samaritans. Again, this is evangelism through visible success (Chapter Three).

We must give allies every sign that our word is reliable, that we do not abandon them when the shooting starts. The West has conveyed the opposite impression for at least two decades, and if you count the fall of free China to the Communists, four decades.

Weakening Our Enemies

If we can peacefully break the support that the leaders of enemy nations receive at home, this is a wise policy. Our enemy is that nation's leadership, not its domestic victims, until a shooting war breaks out.

If our enemies are evil, we must say so: publicly, repeatedly, and to anyone who will listen. If they are truly worse than we are, we must say so. It is one thing for me to have a "mote" (plank) in my eye; it is quite another for you to have a plank in your eye if I have only a speck in mine. We must make judgments, after all. My speck-hampered eye is in better shape than some enemy's plank-filled eye. Hitler was worse than some Central American dictator. Stalin was worse than anyone, even Hitler, for he murdered vastly more of his own people than Hitler ever did— between 20 million and 30 million[16] and he had too many allies within the West's intelligentsia. He was a greater threat to the West. Yet, we relied on him to defeat Hitler. Solzhenitsyn warned: "Do not call a wolf to help you against the dogs."[17]

Undiplomatic Warfare

We are in a battle with the Soviet Union. Soviet leaders have made this plain from the beginning. Lenin was clear about the in-

---

16. Robert Conquest, *The Great Terror: Stalin's Purges of the Thirties* (rev. ed.; New York: Collier, 1973), p. 713.

17. *Solzhenitsyn: The Voice of Freedom* (Washington, D.C.: AFL-CIO, 1975), p. 10.

tentions of the Communists: to rule the world. He was the apostle of the most successful satanic imitation of Christianity since Islam: a conquering religion that offers salvation through bloody revolution.[18]

Lenin began to discuss the need for preparing for the war we are now facing. In March of 1918, he delivered a secret report to the Seventh Party Congress, which was not published until 1923. In it, he said: "But to start a revolution in a country in which capitalism is developed, in which it has produced a democratic culture and organisation, provided it to everybody—to do so without preparation would be wrong, absurd. We are only just approaching the painful period of the beginning of socialist revolutions. This is a fact."[19] He stated his position even more clearly that same year —this time, in public: "Either the Soviet government triumphs in every advanced country in the world, or the most reactionary imperialism triumphs . . . which is throttling the small and feeble nationalities and reinstating reaction all over the world—Anglo-American imperialism which has perfectly mastered the art of using the form of a democratic republic. One or the other, there is no middle course."[20]

Thirty years later, the Soviet line had not changed: "Thus the dictatorship of the world proletariat is an essential and vital condition precedent to the transformation of world capitalist economy into socialist economy. This world dictatorship can be established only when . . . the newly established proletarian republics . . . have grown finally into a World Union of Soviet Socialist Republics uniting the whole of mankind under the hegemony of the international proletariat organized as a state."[21]

---

18. Gary North, *Marx's Religion of Revolution: The Doctrine of Creative Destruction* (Nutley, New Jersey: Craig Press, 1968).

19. Lenin, "Report on War and Peace" (March 17, 1918), in *The Lenin Anthology*, edited by Robert C. Tucker (New York: Norton, 1975), p. 545.

20. Lenin, "Valuable Admission of Pitirim Sorokin" (1918), in *Selected Works* (New York: International Publishers, 1943), Vol. VIII, pp. 148-49. Cited by Anthony Trawick Bouscaren, *Soviet Foreign Policy: A Pattern of Persistance* (New York: Fordham University Press, 1962), p. 11.

21. P. Fedoseev, "The Marxist Theory of Classes and Class Struggle," *Bolshevik*, Vol. 14 (July 1948); cited in *ibid.*, p. 10.

I may be belaboring the obvious, but the majority of those who are in charge of American foreign policy do not take these words seriously. They do not believe that there is any necessary relationship between Soviet tyranny and oppression at home and Soviet foreign policy. They think the two can be separated. They always have believed this, as Lenin pointed out months before the Soviets captured the Russian Revolution: "No idea could be more erroneous or harmful than to separate foreign from domestic policy. The monstrous falsity of this separation becomes more even monstrous in war-time. Yet the bourgeoisie are doing everything possible and impossible to suggest and promote this idea."[22]

Over and over, they have warned us: "We will bury you!" And over and over, our national leaders have dismissed such warnings as empty rhetoric.

Today, that rhetoric is no longer empty. Neither are their missile silos.

There is only one answer: to place ourselves under God's covenant. We must become subordinate as a nation and a civilization under God and His law. But from a military standpoint, it would be best if the President himself takes the first public step, for he is Commander-in-Chief, and he is also this nation's covenantal representative before God. Civil magistrates are called *ministers of God* (Romans 13:4). (See Gary DeMar's book in the Biblical Blueprints Series, *Ruler of the Nations: Biblical Blueprints for Government*.) As a minister, he should publicly reaffirm our authority and responsibility as a covenant people to spread the message of the gospel, and also reaffirm this nation's responsibility before God and men to preserve freedom through military preparedness, so as to allow God's servants to evangelize the world.

If this is not our goal for freedom, then we will surely lose it.

Summary

The immediate problem facing the Christian who strives to develop a Christian foreign policy is that modern man believes

---

22. Lenin, "The Foreign Policy of the Russian Revolution," *Pravda* (June 1917), in Tucker (ed.), *Lenin Anthology*, p. 537.

that ours is a religiously neutral world. Thus, men do not seek to impose Biblical principles in every area of life. They do not acknowledge God's covenantal claims on every family, church, and civil government. They do not acknowledge that God requires Christians to work toward the formal and public affirmation of every covenantal institution under the terms of the Biblical covenant.

This continuing faith in the myth of neutrality has led us to the present crisis. Christians are being represented by civil magistrates who are agents of Satan, at least implicitly. "He who is not with Me is against Me, and he who does not gather with Me scatters abroad" (Matthew 12:30). National civil magistrates have bonded nations covenantally through treaties. The foreign policy of the democratic West is a complex system of treaties, alliances, and power blocs, none of which is governed by the Biblical covenant, but all of which come under the terms of the covenant in history, just as men do, whether or not they affirm the covenant. God brings His judgments in history against His enemies, both personal and collective. He divides the national sheep and goats progressively in history, in preparation for the final dividing at the final judgment (Matthew 25:31-33).

We must recognize that a war is in progress, and we must strive to establish Christ's kingdom of God in history. This will involve the triumph of Christian nations, not as individual nations that seek to establish the kingdom singlehandedly as God's sole kingdom representative, but in covenant with other Christian nations. This requires leaders of Christian nations to make distinctions among nations. We must distinguish between permanent covenants and permanent war. Alliances with pagan nations are cease-fires with enemies who do not threaten us immediately, and they are part of a systematic, dedicated, long-term strategy of war: the conquest of Christianity over its rivals. We must prepare for war by making covenants and alliances.

In summary:

1. Christian nations are not to make covenants with non-Christian nations.

2. Biblical covenants have five points.

3. To make Biblical a covenant among institutions, the representatives must formally profess faith in the trinitarian God of the Bible.

4. In the ancient world, a treaty between cities always involved a ritual bond between the gods of the cities.

5. Modern Christians avoid thinking about such issues.

6. They assume that no nation can be covenantally Christian.

7. They implicitly accept the myth of neutrality.

8. Every institution must be brought into conformity with the Bible's requirements for it.

9. There will be no peace on earth until this is accomplished in history.

10. Peace between nations with rival gods is therefore a cease-fire, not Biblical peace.

11. National leaders must distinguish covenanted friends from enemies, and temporary professed allies and neutrals from permanent enemies.

12. Temporary alliances with temporarily friendly non-Christian allies can be used to spoil Satan's household.

13. The principle is "divide and conquer."

14. We must teach by example.

15. We must work to weaken our enemies.

16. We are at war.

17. We must cease capitulating to Soviet demands.

10

GOVERNMENT FOREIGN AID
DISINHERITS THE FAITHFUL

A good man leaves an inheritance to his children's children, but the wealth of the sinner is stored up for the righteous (Proverbs 13:22).

The fifth point of the Biblical covenant is inheritance. The blessings of God are cumulative over many generations. God shows mercy unto thousands of generations of those who love Him and keep His commandments (Exodus 20:6).

Who is the man that fears the LORD? Him shall He teach in the way He chooses. He himself shall dwell in prosperity, and his descendants shall inherit the earth (Psalm 25:12-13).

Clearly, the inheritance of the earth by the covenant people of God is a long-term process. It is cumulative. It necessarily involves a transfer of assets from the unjust to the just. Those who obey God's covenant laws steadily inherit the inheritance of those who disobey God's covenant laws. Thus, the covenantal process of cumulative inheritance necessarily involves the covenantal process of cumulative disinheritance.

This is the visible manifestation of God's covenant sanctions in history: blessings and cursings (point four). Covenant law, covenant sanctions, and covenant inheritance go together. They cannot be separated in history. Responsibility-denying Christians and power-seeking humanists deny that such a fixed covenantal relationship exists, but this denial is itself an act of covenantal rebellion against God. God may dispossess one or more generations

217

of Christians for allying themselves theologically with the humanists, while He builds up the power and wealth of the humanists for a few generations so that His judgments against them in history might be greater, serving as a more effective warning to other God-haters.

> "Woe to Assyria, the rod of My anger and the staff in whose hand is My indignation. I will send him against an ungodly nation, and against the people of My wrath. I will give him charge, to seize the spoil, to take the prey, and to tread them down like the mire of the streets. . . ." Therefore it shall come to pass, when the LORD has performed all His work on Mount Zion and on Jerusalem, that He will say, "I will punish the fruit of the arrogant heart of the king of Assyria, and the glory of his haughty looks" (Isaiah 10:5-6, 12).

Satan's Deception of Christians

Satan does what he can to reverse this covenantal process of inheritance and disinheritance in history. He seeks ways to thwart this spoiling of his kingdom by God through God's human representatives, the Christians.

To do this, he must first find ways to persuade Christians that the operations of this God-created world are hostile to Christian faith. He seeks to persuade them that long-term obedience to God's law brings defeat (disinheritance) in history, whereas affirming humanistic laws leads to victory (inheritance) in history. He persuades them that there is no system of ethical cause and effect in history. Whenever he is successful in this deception, God's covenantal transfer of Satan's captured inheritance back to Christians is delayed. Satan retains control for one or more generations.

Because the breaking of God's covenant law cannot go on indefinitely without covenantal cursings, Satan's restraining of this transfer does not go on indefinitely. Eventually, three or four generations after Satan's successful deception of Christians (Genesis 15:16; Exodus 20:5), the bills come due, and the humanist society that practiced the deception is smashed, its people expropriated, and Christians are given another opportunity to rebuild the civilization.

We are at the tail end of one of these lengthy periods of successful satanic deception. We therefore face a cultural crisis. This one threatens to be worldwide for the first time since the Noachic Flood. It threatens every human institution. The deception was comprehensive; the judgment will be equally comprehensive.

To delay the coming destruction, Satan seeks to persuade Christians to allow his representatives to confiscate the assets of Christians and transfer them to his most corrupt, perverse, unsuccessful, God-cursed followers. He persuades a majority of them to vote in favor of State-enforced wealth-distribution schemes that are operated by and for humanists. Anyone who sees through this deception is therefore outvoted, and he has his children's inheritance taken from him despite his protests. Coercion whips covenantally faithful Christians into line. It is the technique of the Pharaoh. And Pharaoh can always call upon a group of Christian foremen to speak in his name and defend these forced wealth transfers in the name of Jesus.[1]

Within a nation, this wealth-transfer process is called welfarism. It is designed to reduce personal responsibility on the part of those who would otherwise support private charities and also those who would receive this voluntary assistance. (See George Grant's book in the Biblical Blueprints Series, *In the Shadow of Plenty: The Biblical Blueprint for Welfare*.)

Internationally, this process used to be called foreign aid. Today, it is called multilateral assistance, whether government-financed or (far more likely) bank depositor-financed.

National and international, government-financed and depositor-financed, humanism's welfarism is Satan's program of subsidizing evil at the expense of the productive. It leads inevitably to dependency and bankruptcy. God eventually imposes His inevitable negative sanctions in history.

---

1. David Chilton, *Productive Christians in an Age of Guilt-Manipulators: A Biblical Response to Ronald J. Sider* (4th ed.; Tyler, Texas: Institute for Christian Economics, 1986).

Subsidizing Evil

The first and most important point in understanding government-operated foreign aid programs is that they are *government-to-government programs*. They are not foreign projects that have been investigated by private charitable or profit-seeking organizations in a wealthy country, and then financed by representatives of that nation's donors or investors. Instead, these projects are submitted by a foreign nation's political leaders or by a foreign bureaucracy, for consideration by bureaucratic functionaries in another nation. If approved by the financing nation's bureaucrats, and if put into the budget by the decision-making politicians, money collected by taxation is then transferred to the foreign nation's bureaucrats. The money may or may not be spent on the agreed-upon project, but the money will invariably strengthen the control of the recipient government's bureaucrats at the expense of that nation's private sector, whether charitable or profit-seeking.

The bureaucrats on both sides of the border proclaim the moral necessity of aid "with no strings attached." What this means is aid with no responsibilities to the taxpayers and voters of either nation. It means *no strings attached on bureaucrats in the recipient nation*. This is what every bureaucrat seeks, as surely as businessmen want to begin projects without competitors. The free market does not allow businessmen to achieve their goal; political coercion does allow government bureaucrats to achieve it, at least for a while.

P. T. Bauer, a Jewish scholar who converted to Roman Catholicism late in life, is the Western economist who more than any other scholar has pursued the implications of government-to-government foreign aid. He became a member of the House of Lords in Britain late in life. Bauer writes: "Foreign aid augments the resources of recipient governments compared to those of the private sector, thereby promoting concentration of power in the recipient countries. This effect is much reinforced by the preferential treatment in the allocation of aid of governments engaged in comprehensive planning, a criterion based, at any rate ostensibly, on the ground that such a policy is a condition of economic development. . . . At the same time the continued low living standards and the persistent economic difficulties of centrally planned economies in underdeveloped countries serve as justification for continued aid."[2]

The formerly underdeveloped nations of the Far East that are now noted for their rapid economic growth have received little government foreign aid from the West: Hong Kong, Taiwan (Free China), Singapore, South Korea, and Malaysia. What they have received is access to Western consumer markets. More than any other single factor, the primary cause of economic development of backward nations has been their commercial contacts with the West. The farther away one gets from Western contacts, the poorer the nations become.[3]

Contact with the West raises hopes among those people in backward nations who are willing to sacrifice present consumption for future income. This will initially be a minority of the population. As success proves the point—that contact with the West and adopting Western economic techniques brings prosperity—Western attitudes begin to penetrate the general population. Their own future-orientation, thrift, and hard work have brought them prosperity. Hong Kong is the classic example. A tiny area south of China, a region with no known natural resources, overpopulated by Western standards, Hong Kong is so competitive that manufacturers all over the Western world cry for tariff barriers and import quotas against the "unfair competition" of this tiny crown colony.[4]

They have adopted the Protestant work ethic without Christianity, while the West was abandoning the work ethic, having already abandoned the Protestant work ethic. But God is faithful: He rewards with external blessings those who are externally obe-

---

2. P. T. Bauer, *Dissent on Development: Studies and Debates in Development Economics* (Cambridge, Massachusetts: Harvard University Press, 1972), pp. 106-7.

3. *Ibid.*, pp. 300-2.

4. P. T. Bauer, *Equality, the Third World and Economic Delusion* (Cambridge, Massachusetts: Harvard University Press, 1981), ch. 10: "The Lesson of Hong Kong."

dient to the principles of Biblical law. To sustain this outward obedience, however, they will require a public increase of God's special grace: conversions to Christianity. Common grace requires
the sustaining pressure of special grace.[5] This is why these nations
are ripe candidates for the gospel.

Any discussion of "Third World poverty" should begin with
the recognition, as Bauer says: "The one common characteristic of
the Third World is not poverty, stagnation, exploitation, brotherhood or skin colour. It is the receipt of foreign aid. The concept of
the Third World and the policy of official aid are inseparable. The
one would not exist without the other. The Third World is merely
a name for the collection of countries whose governments, with
occasional and odd exceptions, demand and receive official aid
from the West. . . . Thus, the Third World is a political and not
an economic concept."[6]

What has been the result of this official foreign aid in the field
of international relations? Almost universal hostility to the West.[7]

Another great irony is that poorer people are taxed in the West
in order to finance bureaucratic projects that employ as managers
and technicians the upper classes of the poverty-stricken nations.
This is Robin Hood in reverse: robbing from the poor to give to
the rich.

An even greater irony is that several major studies of the
growth process indicate that direct material aid has contributed
relatively little to the economic growth of the recipient nations.
The key elements are personal and ethical: outlook toward the
future, self-discipline, management techniques, and better use of
existing resources.[8]

The overall percentage of international aid is extremely small.
Government aid to large Third World nations (China, India, etc.)

---

5. Gary North, *Dominion and Common Grace: The Biblical Basis of Progress* (Tyler,
Texas: Institute for Christian Economics, 1987), ch. 6.

6. P. T. Bauer, *Reality and Rhetoric: Studies in the Economics of Development* (Cambridge, Massachusetts: Harvard University Press, 1984), p. 40.

7. *Ibid.*, p. 41.

8. *Ibid.*, p. 44.

accounts for under 1 percent of the recipients' national income—too small to measure statistically.[9] Aid to smaller nations has a greater impact, of course, but so do business investments.

Thus, foreign aid hurts taxpayers in the "donor" nations, hurts the private sector in the recipient nations, strengthens the power of the State in both donor and recipient nations, and cannot be shown to increase per capita wealth significantly.

Foreign aid is simply a way for Satan to postpone briefly the triumph of covenantally faithful people over covenant-breakers. But as a symbolic gesture to evil, it suits his purposes.

The Banking Crisis

Beginning in the 1970's, the large multinational banks began to loan huge quantities of OPEC oil money deposits to the Third World. This money, along with the deposits of national residents, has led to about a trillion dollars, worldwide, in loans to Third World nations. Estimates of bad loans now run as high as 50 percent, though no one really knows. About 40 percent of the trillion dollars in loans are in Latin America, which makes this money unlikely ever to be repaid. What everyone knows is that in early 1987, Brazil, in debt to the West by over a hundred billion dollars, suspended payments on this debt. Other nations may follow Brazil's lead. Eventually, there will be a default. These nations cannot repay. The key questions are these: When, under what form, and how will the banks cover the losses?

Citicorp, the largest bank in the United States, and about tenth largest in the world (the top four banks are Japanese), admitted in early 1987 that $3 billion of its $15 billion portfolio of foreign loans are unlikely to be repaid. As a result, it "wrote down" (admitted to a loss of) $2.5 billion in the second quarter of 1987. This may only be the beginning of major problems for the bank. (This is the "Wriston bank." Walter B. Wriston masterminded its growth in the late 1960's and 1970's by emphasizing foreign loans over domestic loans. He is the son of Council on Foreign Rela-

---

9. P. T. Bauer, *Equality, the Third World and Economic Delusion*, p. 101.

tions leader Henry Wriston, who "Wristonized" the U.S. Department of State in the 1950's. His father was his main role model.)[10] Other multinational U.S. banks will follow. One expert, Felix Rohatyn of the influential merchant banking firm of Lazard Freres, has said, "It's a fissure running up and down the walls. Right now, you can't tell how far it's going to go."

What happened? Bankers had to lend out huge quantities of OPEC money very fast in the 1970's. It is far easier to arrange a one billion dollar loan to a government or government-operated company (such as Mexico's nearly bankrupt Pemex oil monopoly) than it is to arrange a thousand one million dollar loans to distant foreign firms. Besides, the loan is "government-guaranteed." A sure thing! The problem is, the government may be Brazil or Mexico. A sure default!

Good Risks?

Governments look reliable. This is an illusion, but bankers, being the products of the same elite universities that train foreign policy experts, trust governments. The Communists have made good use of this weakness of Western vision, and Soviet bloc nations have run up bills to the West of over $80 billion since 1960.[11] This short-sightedness is revealed in a 1964 verbal exchange between David Rockefeller, chairman of Chase Manhattan Bank, and Soviet Premier Khrushchev:

> "Ours is a firm that will never collapse," Khrushchev boasted. "We are careful with our payments."
>
> Rockefeller replied: "You have always been extremely good in dealings with the Chase Manhattan Bank."[12]

Rockefeller was in a position to know. Chase had been making loans to the Soviet Union since the 1920's.[13] As he said in one long

---

10. "Building a Life After Citicorp," *New York Times* (April 21, 1985).

11. Richard Pipes, *Survival Is not Enough: Soviet Realities and America's Future* (New York: Simon & Schuster, 1984), p. 261.

12. Cited by Joseph Finder, *Red Carpet* (Ft. Worth, Texas: American Bureau of Economic Research, [1983] 1987), p. 185.

13. *Ibid.*, p. 184.

sentence during a 1980 television documentary, "Well, I have to say that having been in this business now for 33 years, I find one has to be very pragmatic and flexible about these things, and that relations with governments regardless of the political label that's attached to them depends to a large extent on people and human relationships, and just because a country is technically called communist doesn't mean that a capitalist institution such as the Chase Bank can't deal with them on a mutually beneficial basis, and indeed we do deal with most of the so-called communist countries of the world on a basis that has worked out very well, I think, for both of us."[14] Such remarkable language! The Soviet Union is just a "so-called communist" country.

The television broadcast also observed: "Private citizen David Rockefeller is accorded privileges of a head of state. He is untouched by customs or passport officers and hardly pauses for traffic lights. Rockefeller is the supreme example of how multinational companies do business."[15]

In the super-secret *Journal of the US-USSR Trade and Economic Council* (Oct./Nov. 1977), General Electric Corp president Reginald H. Jones warmly admitted that his firm's business dealings with the Soviet Union stretched back to 1922. He also affirmed: "It is our experience that the Soviets are meticulous in observing every contractual provision, once a contract has been signed, and they expect the same from a supplier. This has a great deal of positive significance for a supplier, particularly as it affects the specified terms of payment" (p. 17).

The Communists are wise as serpents. They pay their bills on time. They therefore get the external blessings of God to that extent: cooperation from the biggest corporations and banks in the West.

Yet the $80 billion never seems to get repaid. So Western banks make more loans to them, at interest rates below the free

---

14. Transcript, "Bill Moyers' Journal: The World of David Rockefeller," produced by WNET, New York, p. 12. Public Broadcasting System air date: Feb. 7, 1980.

15. *Ibid.*, p. 19.

market rates, many of which are guaranteed by the U.S. govern-ment-financed Import-Export Bank. Should we be surprised that the head of the Import-Export Bank in 1972, the year that the Department of Commerce authorized the sale to the Soviet Union of the ball bearing machines that made possible the building of MIRVed nuclear warheads, was Wall Street lawyer William J. Casey, a former associate of Armand Hammer?[16] And should we be surprised that Mr. Casey was appointed head of the Central Intelligence Agency (CIA) in 1981 by President Reagan? (Mr. Casey died in May of 1987 of a stroke, not long before he was to testify to Congress concerning his involvement in the controver-sial secret program of supplying weapons to Iran.)

The Goods Are Gone Forever

Thus, the multinational banks have used their depositors' money to continue providing foreign aid to insolvent nations that cannot and will not repay them. This has allowed the various na-tional governments to reduce the far more visible foreign aid transfers. The depositors' money was spent by the recipients; the purchased goods of the capitalist world have been transferred to the Third World, and now the loans and the entire banking sys-tem are in jeopardy. The banks have made their money (so far); the foreign governments have spent this money; exporting West-ern businesses have profited from the purchases; and the eco-nomic future of the depositors has been put into jeopardy. It was inevitable that they be sacrificed, either as taxpayers or as depositors.[17] They had already sold their spiritual birthrights for a mess of humanist pottage. They ignored God, and in their time of financial crisis, God may ignore them.

If national governments had prohibited fractional reserve banking, and if the U.S. government had not authorized a *private* corporation (the Federal Deposit Insurance Corporation) to

---

16. Antony Sutton, *The Best Enemy Money Can Buy* (Billings, Montana: Liberty House Press, 1985), p. 25.

17. On the magnitude and inevitability of the bankruptcy, see Lawrence Malkin, *The National Debt* (New York: Henry Holt, 1987).

promise to guarantee the deposits of most depositors with money it does not have (but which the U.S. government can create in a crisis), bankers would have been more careful with depositors' money. The foreign aid program continues, as banks roll over the loans, reschedule payments, and play other accounting games, but the end is in sight: the destruction of the West's debt-based, fractional reserve banking economy. (See my book in the Biblical Blueprints Series, *Honest Money: The Biblical Blueprint for Money and Banking*.)

God will not be mocked . . . not at zero price to the mockers, anyway.

How to Aid Besieged Allies

Is it ever legitimate for nations to send money to other nations except to wartime allies? Yes. But to do so, the transfer of money or goods must be based on military considerations. The main purpose of national civil government is to defend its territory militarily. This is what all defenders of the modern welfare State deny. If anything, they resent military expenditures. They resist them. They also resist sending money to foreign nations for exclusively military purposes (Israel excepted).

The problem is that the West finds it almost impossible publicly to identify an enemy without actually declaring war, meaning a shooting war. Short of war, the Constitution of the United States and the traditions of other Western nations restrict the imposition of sanctions. The Communists recognize this fact and have exploited it for three generations. They finance surrogates (representatives), send in "military and technical advisors," and thereby finance "wars of national liberation." But the Soviets never get blamed in public. No sanctions are ever applied by the West. If anything, the West capitulates further. Thus, Communist nations are difficult to deal with.

In the United States, nationally legislated trade restrictions on Communist nations do exist, but their purpose is to *restrict* access to Communist markets and *allocate* this access, not eliminate it. The real reasons for these legislated restrictions are almost exclusively domestic: *to exclude small firms from the market.* Only the biggest U.S. corporations in the West have the lawyers and political connections to get their products out of the U.S. legally and then inside the Soviet bloc nations. These trade restrictions serve only to create monopoly opportunities for a handful of politically favored Western corporations. The so-called "most-favored-nations" trade agreements are in fact *most-favored corporation agreements* for those doing business with those Communist nations that are not on the most-favored-nations list. The favored corporations are discreetly silent about their special immunities. For example, the membership list of the secret tax-exempt foundation, the US-USSR Trade and Economic Council,[18] is impossible to obtain legally. All we know is that major U.S. corporations advertise in its journal, which is also extremely difficult to locate. (I have photocopies of sections of this journal in my files, but not a complete set.)

Thus, it is difficult to aid allies to fight wars against Soviet-financed national liberation movements (revolutions). On what basis could wealth transfers be made by a Christian nation? First, by identifying enemies before a shooting war breaks out. They should be dealt with as if war had broken out, except for actual armed intervention. Thus, aid could be sent to allies who are at war with such an enemy. We would then treat them as surrogates (representatives) of our interests, fighting on their soil before we have to fight on ours.

Second, in our day, foreign aid would be handled only by the military services. All funds would come directly out of service budgets. It would be clearly an aspect of military defense. Military services could buy information from foreign intelligence services, such as Israel's Mossad. The Navy could pay to lease bases on foreign soil. In short, the military services would buy foreign cooperation the same way they buy hardware. This would remove foreign aid decisions from the peacetime bureaucracies. (When the government of the Philippines suggested in June of

18. Joseph Finder, *Red Carpet*, pp. 254-60.

1987 that the U.S. should pay for its military bases there, Secretary of State George Shultz vehemently rejected such a suggestion, insisting that the bases are for the defense of the Philippines, and therefore are not space that the U.S. should lease. He may have recognized that such leases would transfer power from the Department of State to the Department of Defense.) Foreign aid would be part of legitimate military operations rather than a program of deliberately subsidizing evil with funds extracted from the righteous on threat of violence.

Private Wealth Transfers

These should take two forms. First, open charity that is distributed by privately financed voluntary organizations. Missionaries should take the lead here. Second, capital investment abroad.

This is no different from what should operate in a nation's domestic economy: voluntary charity and capital formation. The tithe and the free market are the two economic engines of Christian dominion through inheritance. This keeps responsibility in the hands of those spending their own money or serving as responsible individuals (trustees) who represent others. Their actions are restrained either by the donors or by the profitability of their business ventures. They cannot steal capital from the righteous in order to give to unrighteous, socialistic foreign governments or petty dictators.

The goal of charity is to build up the *deserving* poor, not the lazy poor. Poverty is God's judgment on lazy people and unrighteous societies. The Book of Proverbs is filled with warnings against laziness. The Book of Deuteronomy is filled with warnings against national rebellion.

Capital will always flow into societies that do not confiscate property though heavy taxation. A nation that honors the Biblical principle of private property and equality of foreigners under the law will have no trouble attracting foreign investment capital. Investors are always seeking out places where their investments will be legally protected. Capitalists are willing to take market risks if civil governments will allow them to keep any profits produced by risky ventures.

Government-to-government foreign aid goes to nations that have confiscatory rates of domestic taxation, and restrictions on taking profits out of the country. These nations need government money from the West because their own policies of socialistic wealth redistribution have prevented the creation of wealth. To send these governments money is positively evil.

Covenantal Adoption

The Biblical principle of covenantal adoption is basic to this program of evangelism and international healing. The Christian's goal is to further the adoption of all people into the spiritual and covenantal kingdom of God, without regard to race, color, or national origin, but with great regard to creed. The goal is to expand the family of redeemed mankind at the expense of the family of fallen mankind through a program of covenantal adoption. The marks of this adoption are a person's profession of faith and his visible covenantal faithfulness: baptism, the Lord's Supper, and publicly moral behavior as defined by the Bible.

Thus, Christian internationalism is based on a doctrine of brotherhood: *the covenantal brotherhood of redeemed mankind.* Wealth transfers that are governed by the principle of the tithe or the principle of profit-seeking investment are not made at the expense of the next generation; they are made in order to finance the building up of the next generation. Money need not go only to Christians, but donors should seek out those who are truly needy, not those who are under the judgment of God personally because of their laziness or debauchery.

What is immoral are the compulsory schemes of government-enforced wealth transfers. These schemes are tactics in the humanists' war with the family of redeemed mankind. The result is the growth of incompetence and the squandering of the capital of the righteous.

Summary

The humanists in power have sought to transfer the inheritance of Christians and externally honest people to State-approved failures who have repeatedly broken God's laws. They have done this in the name of charity, humanitarianism, national self-interest, and sound banking practice. Whatever the excuses, the policies have been wicked. Thus, they have also been impractical and economically suicidal. Biblical Christianity is practical. Covenant-breaking is impractical. When the judgment of God comes, Christians had better remind themselves and those in power that God is in control, that He governs by a hierarchy, that He governs in terms of His law, that He brings judgments in history, and that the wealth of the wicked is in the long run stored up for the just.

The covenant-breakers have been given enough rope to hang themselves with. It is said that Lenin said that if the Communists announced that they would hang all capitalists tomorrow, they would trip over each other today to sell Lenin the rope. What even Lenin did not predict is that they would sell it for long-term credits at below-market interest rates.

The satanic deception of the West is about to be exposed in a wave of crises. The wicked will not keep the inheritance of the righteous. But it may take the righteous several generations of covenantal faithfulness after the crisis to earn back what is rightfully theirs as adopted sons of God. They have allowed wicked people to act as representatives of the Evil One, and transfer their inheritance to those under God's curse. They will pay dearly for their silence.

In summary:

1. The wealth of the wicked is stored up for the righteous.
2. Covenant-keepers are supposed to inherit the earth.
3. During periods of rebellion, covenant-breakers appear to triumph.
4. God eventually cuts them down.
5. Satan fights this inheritance transfer process in history.
6. He deceives Christians into believing that there is no ethical

cause and effect in history.

7. When he is successful in this deception, the transfer process is delayed.

8. This deception cannot go on indefinitely, for God eventually brings external judgment on the receivers.

9. Today, Satan has persuaded Christians to accept and even vote for programs of compulsory wealth redistribution.

10. This wealth transfer subsidizes evil.

11. Government-to-government aid strengthens the control of governments on both sides of the transaction.

12. Economic growth is therefore retarded in the recipient nations.

13. The fastest growing underdeveloped nations have had free markets and relatively little economic aid from foreign governments.

14. They have accepted the Protestant work ethic.

15. The concept of "Third World" is created by foreign aid programs.

16. The banking crisis is really a foreign aid crisis.

17. Government-protected banks have loaned depositors' money to insolvent backward nations.

18. Bankers have trusted foreign governments rather than foreign private borrowers.

19. By making interest payments on schedule, foreign governments have borrowed ever-more money.

20. The principal can never be repaid.

21. The goods of the West have been transferred.

22. The economic future of the West is in jeopardy.

23. Christians will suffer because they allowed humanists to represent them, as politicians, bureaucrats, and bankers.

24. Foreign aid should be limited to military aid.

25. The military services should finance it.

26. They should buy services they need from allied nations.

27. Foreign policy should distinguish between allies, neutrals, and declared enemies that have not yet begun shooting at us.

28. Foreign aid should be private: charity and business investment.

29. The goal is to extend the kingdom through a program of covenantal adoption.

30. Compulsory foreign aid is an attack on the redeemed family of man.

CONCLUSION

Therefore, if anyone is in Christ, he is a new creation; old things have passed away; behold, all things have become new. Now all things are of God, who has reconciled us to Himself through Jesus Christ, and has given us the ministry of reconciliation, that is, that God was in Christ reconciling the world to Himself, not imputing their trespasses to them, and has committed to us the word of reconciliation. Therefore we are ambassadors for Christ, as though God were pleading through us: we implore you on Christ's behalf, be reconciled to God (2 Corinthians 5:17-20).

Christians are *ambassadors of reconciliation*: primarily, the reconciliation of man to God, and secondarily, the reconciliation of covenant-keeping men to each other. Christians are assigned the task of announcing to the whole world that the gospel of Christ alone offers hope to the world. God is reconciling the world to Himself in history through His Son, Jesus Christ. This is God's program for healing the nations. No other program, no other faith, no other plan can work. This is the only basis of permanent peace that God offers to men and nations in history.

The Church of Jesus Christ has never fully believed this, but especially in the twentieth century. Christians have always proclaimed one or another version of natural law theory as the proper basis of reconciling covenant-breakers to covenant-keepers in history: intellectually, politically, culturally, and internationally. To this extent, their message of God's reconciliation has been compromised. The gospel is not designed to reconcile permanent covenant-breakers to God or to covenant-keepers. *The gospel is intended to create a society that subdues covenant-breakers externally,* making

233

them useful to covenant-keepers until the day of eternal wrath begins.[1] *The gospel is designed to extend the dominion of covenant-keepers as God's authorized representatives on earth*, not to create the basis of a permanent cease-fire agreement between covenant-keepers and covenant-breakers until Jesus comes to judge the world. The gospel is not the manifesto of a stalemate religion.[2]

Twentieth-century Christians have become even less confident about the power of Christ's gospel to transform society. They have lost the vision of international victory that used to motivate Christian missions programs. The vision of the international kingdom of God that captured the minds of evangelists in the early Church (Mark 16:15), continued through the Middle Ages, and even lasted well beyond the Protestant Reformation,[3] faded rapidly with the coming of Darwinism. The growing cultural inferiority complex of Christians combined with the growing cultural superiority complex of Darwinists to create a perverse coalition against consistent, world-transforming Christianity, which preaches the existence of progressive earthly manifestations of the kingdom of God in history, in every area of life.

A Defensive Mentality

Christians, especially conservative Protestant Christians, have adopted a defensive mentality. They see the theological savages all around them, and they want to "form a circle with the wagons." First, they want the boundaries of church walls to form a barrier, and they are willing to confine the effects of the gospel inside those walls in order to placate the savages (temporarily), who deeply resent such an invasion of their culture. Second, they trust in national boundaries to protect them from foreign-based un-

---

1. Gary North, *Dominion and Common Grace: The Biblical Basis of Progress* (Tyler, Texas: Institute for Christian Economics, 1987), chaps. 7, 8.

2. Gary North, *Backward, Christian Soldiers? A Manual for Christian Reconstruction* (Tyler, Texas: Institute for Christian Economics, 1984), ch. 11: "The Stalemate Mentality."

3. J. A. De Jong, *As the Waters Cover the Sea: Millennial Expectations in the Rise of Anglo-American Missions, 1640-1810* (Kampen, Netherlands: J. H. Kok, 1970).

pleasantness: cheap foreign imports, low-wage immigrants fleeing Communism or socialism, Communist terrorists, and Communist troops. (Borders do not restrain the AIDS lentivirus: judgment is still coming.) They cling to humanist nationalism — founded on the two-fold myth of permanent pluralist politics and unbiased judicial neutrality — as fiercely as drowning men grasping at life preservers. But humanistic nationalism is a life preserver with a leak in it, the product of a splintered sixteenth-century church and eighteenth-century Enlightenment ideology.

There can be no "equal time for Jesus" in a pluralist society, for Jesus demands covenantal obedience rather than parity with Satan. So covenant-breakers who have control over the legislatures and courts always strive to keep the effects of the gospel tightly controlled. In any case, humanist nationalism is being overwhelmed historically by humanist internationalism, in the form of the Communist world empire. Humanist nationalism is a weak reed to lean on.

Christians have lost a vision of earthly victory. They have no vision of a world progressively transformed by the gospel, or nations brought under Christ's covenant, one by one, or the Church of Jesus Christ speaking with one voice, as it did in Acts 15, or a confederation of Christian nations welcoming newly converted nations into the commonwealth of redeemed mankind. They have no confidence in the Bible as a reliable intellectual weapon against the self-certified humanists who occupy the seats of influence and power in every nation. They view their earthly labors as historically futile, to be swallowed inevitably by the triumph of anti-Christian forces throughout the world. They are afraid even to announce the covenant of Christ as morally binding on their own nations, let alone on the whole world.

They have become confused by the inescapable choices that God's providential history imposes on them. They have accepted the humanists' lie that Jesus Christ has no legitimate authority over the civil affairs of men, or none that men can ever perceive in history. They write: "There have been times of very good government when this interrelationship of church and state has been present. But through the centuries it has caused great confusion between loyalty to the state and loyalty to Christ, between patriotism and being a Christian."[4] (The same can be said about loyalty to the family, the clan, the school, and every other institution that is not structured in terms of God's covenant law.) They explicitly and forthrightly deny that covenantal loyalty to God the Father requires Christians to work to build a civil commonwealth that is publicly covenanted to Christ. Therefore, in order to reduce their humanism-induced divided loyalty, they recommend covenantal loyalty to the humanists' version of religiously neutral patriotism rather than covenantal loyalty to God the Father. The result is obvious all around us: the temporary but widespread triumph of humanism.

International Relations

Nowhere can this temporary triumph of humanism over Christianity be seen more clearly than in the world of international relations. The humanists replaced Christian missions with an elite corps of foreign policy professionals, especially during and after World War I. While the Christian world missions movement has continued, the humanists long ago captured the mainline hierarchical denominations. Theological liberals have become advocates of *mission*—singular rather than plural—a key word that marks the takeover of Christian missionary activities by the liberals. Liberation theology has been offered as a substitute for Christianity. (See my book in the Biblical Blueprints Series, *Liberating Planet Earth*.)

Since the late-nineteenth century, deeply humanistic foreign policy professionals, self-certified and self-screened, have dominated the formal structure of international relations. This dominance led to World War I, the Communist take-over of Russia, the imposition of reparations against Germany, the rise of Hitler, World War II, and the Cold War. Since then, we have seen the steady retreat of the West and the progressive conquest of the

---

4. Francis Schaeffer, *A Christian Manifesto* (Westchester, Illinois: Crossway, 1981), p. 121.

world by Soviet and Chinese Communism,[5] a humanist religion that retains a satanic imitation of the five-point Biblical covenant structure. First, Communism announces a god, the materialist forces of dialectical history, and holy scriptures, the writings of Marx, Engels, and Lenin. Second, it has hierarchy: the Communist Party, which interprets and applies the infallible word of Marxism-Leninism. Third, it has Communist law, Communist economics, and Communist military strategy as the basis of world conquest. Fourth, it has a doctrine of sanctions: the inevitable world Communist revolution. Fifth, it has a doctrine of continuity: the inevitable triumph of the working class through the forces of dialectical history.[6]

The stronger humanist religion is on the offensive. The weaker humanist religion is on the defensive. Christians in the West have bet their futures on the competence of the weaker humanism to defend them from the new Assyrians. Christians have transferred political and cultural sovereignty to the soft-core humanists by default, through their adoption of a limited gospel of partial reconciliation. They have proclaimed that "Jesus is Lord," but only over individual hearts, Christian families, a handful of churches, and underfunded Christian schools. Satan is the prince over everything else, they believe.

But Satan, like Jesus, is not content with partial victory. Satan, like Jesus, wants it all. The Communists articulate Satan's demands much better that the soft-core humanists of the West do. So God is in the process of delivering His people into the hands of these Assyrians, because Christians have already in principle and in fact defaulted to the soft-core humanists. Until Christians start taking the offensive by preaching the whole counsel of God, the absolute sovereignty of God, and the gospel of comprehensive redemption, they will remain covenantal subordinates to the retreating humanists of the West. They will remain on the side of the losers.

---

5. Jean François Revel, *How Democracies Perish* (Garden City, New York: Doubleday, 1984).

6. F. N. Lee, *Communist Eschatology* (Nutley, New Jersey: Craig Press, 1974).

Because the West has lost its faith in God, it has lost its faith in the future. It has steadily abandoned the fifth point of the covenant: continuity. Only with a revival of covenantal Christianity is the West likely to reverse the drift into despair. Such a revival is possible, and there are signs that it is coming.[7] The Communists are suffering from their own waning of faith in Marxism, as Solzhenitsyn has said repeatedly. The problem is, when there is a contest between two empires, or two non-Christian systems, the one that has greater self-confidence and overwhelming military superiority to back up this confidence, is likely to be the winner. The escape religion (Western humanism) is no match for the power religion (Communist humanism).

Defense Is Not Enough

The most famous foreign policy position paper in United States history after George Washington's Farewell Address was State Department diplomat George Kennan's unsigned "X" article, published in the Council on Foreign Relations' highly influential journal, *Foreign Affairs*, in the summer of 1947. Almost immediately, the intellectual world knew who had written it. *Life* and *Reader's Digest* reprinted large sections of it, making it available to middle-class America.[8] In it, Kennan proposed a doctrine of containing Soviet Communism.

Soviet Communism, he correctly recognized, is expansionist but relies on the doctrine of inevitable victory over the capitalist West. Therefore, "the Kremlin is under no ideological compulsion to accomplish its purposes in a hurry. Like the Church, it is dealing in ideological concepts which are of long-term validity, and it can afford to be patient."[9] There was no immediate threat from

---

7. Nisbet, *History of the Idea of Progress* (New York: Basic Books, 1980), pp. 356-57.

8. George Kennan *Memoirs, 1925-1950* (Boston: Little, Brown, 1967), p. 356.

9. X, "The Sources of Soviet Conduct," *Foreign Affairs* (Summer 1947); reprinted in *Readings in American Foreign Policy*, edited by Robert Goldwin, *et al.*, 3 vols. (5th ed.; Chicago: American Foundation for Political Affairs, [1952] 1957), II, p. 80.

the Soviet Union to the peace of Europe, Kennan believed. "In these circumstances it is clear that the main element of any United States policy toward the Soviet Union must be that of a long-term, patient but firm and vigilant containment of Russian expansive tendencies."[10] He continued: "In the light of the above, it will be clearly seen that the Soviet pressure against the free institutions of the western world is something that can be contained by the adroit and vigilant application of counter-force at a series of constantly shifting geographical and political points, corresponding to the shifts and manoeuvers of Soviet Policy, but which cannot be charmed or talked out of existence. The Russians look forward to a duel of infinite duration, and they see that already they have scored great successes."[11]

Foreign policy is to become a kind of giant chess game, with an infinite series of defensive maneuvers on the part of the West. Kennan neglected the obvious: the Soviets are the world's most dedicated chess players. With the exception of the independent and unpredictable recluse genius, Bobby Fisher, no American chess player has taken the world championship in a generation. And no American President seems capable of containing the Soviets. Nevertheless, "containment" was the key U.S. foreign policy doctrine from the 1950's until the U.S. retreated militarily in Vietnam. The Rockefeller Panel insisted in 1959: "In any case, the free world, as a basic tenet of policy, must not permit the Communist states to extend their rule."[12] Not a word about *rolling back* the Communist empire is permitted in any of the influential humanist publications. Former Secretary of State Dean Acheson, Kennan's friend, stated the position in one sentence: "There must be no further diminishment of that part of the world which now lies outside the dominion of Russian or Chinese communism."[13]

---

10. *Ibid.*, II, p. 81.

11. *Ibid.*, II, p. 82.

12. *Prospect for America: The Rockefeller Panel Reports* (Garden City, New York: Doubleday, 1961), p. 40.

13. Dean G. Acheson, "The Premises of American Policy," *Orbis* (Fall 1959); reprinted in Walter F. Hahn and John C. Neff (eds.), *American Strategy for the Nuclear Age* (Garden City, New York: Anchor, 1960), p. 411.

No further diminishment: here is a true counsel of despair. This policy has failed—in Africa, in Asia, in Central America, and in the Middle East.

Kennan knows it has failed. In his memoirs, he insisted that he really had meant, "not the containment by military means of a military threat, but the political containment of a political threat."[14] Here we see the problem: the Soviets, as he recognized, are an ideologically grounded civilization. This includes every aspect of human life: art, religion, military, economics, politics, etc. But Kennan's humanistic liberalism led him to make the standard Western error: that such a threat is "merely" political, or primarily political, rather than truly ideological and deeply religious.

Western liberals in general and diplomats in particular believe that the principles of humanistic liberalism can deal with political threats, and all threats are by definition political. Of course, there can be occasional setbacks, but the future is bright. Losing politically is seen as little more than losing the next Presidential election: a temporary setback. They do not really see today's conflict as a life-and-death struggle for civilization in which one side could really lose permanently, except, they insist, in a nuclear war, where both side would lose—a truly great myth. The fact is, only one side would unquestionably lose: the United States.[15] They certainly do not see the foreign policy conflict as grounded in a supernatural conflict between Christ and Satan, and therefore they do not see the solution to the problem as clear-cut spiritual and institutional victory of one side over the other. But the Soviets do, and always have. And this means that they have never deviated from their commitment to victory in foreign policy.[16]

By the mid-1960's, in the face of the Vietnam war, Kennan retroactively washed his hands of the whole thesis. "If, then, I was the author in 1947 of a 'doctrine' of containment, it was a doctrine that lost much of its rationale with the death of Stalin and with the

---

14. Kennan, *Memoirs*, p. 358.

15. Arthur Robinson and Gary North, *Fighting Chance: Ten Feet to Survival* (Ft. Worth, Texas: American Bureau of Economic Research, 1986).

16. Anthony Trawick Bouscaren, *Soviet Foreign Policy: A Pattern of Persistence* (New York: Fordham University Press, 1962).

development of the Soviet-Chinese conflict. I emphatically deny the paternity of any efforts to invoke that doctrine today in situations to which it has, and can have, no proper relevance."[17] He had learned first-hand the lesson of Western chess players: *the Soviets cannot be permanently contained by their enemies' defensive maneuvers.* His implicit (though undeclared) solution: retreat in the face of Communist expansion. He had become an isolationist. Not a "bright example," "city on the hill" isolationist of an earlier, self-confident America, not a "build up the defense industry" modern conservative isolationist, but an "avoid confrontation for a while longer, for all is lost in the long run" liberal isolationist. He is an "eat, drink, and be melancholy, for tomorrow we die" liberal. Most of the liberal humanist intellectuals—with the exception of New York Jews (many of whom were ex-Marxists) who began to see the light in the mid-1960's[18] —joined him in this shift.

In 1979, the Soviets invaded Afghanistan. Kennan, by now a confirmed isolationist who saw the faint outlines of the handwriting on the wall for Western civilization, criticized U.S. politicians' critical reaction for "a disquieting lack of balance . . ." He pointed out that Afghanistan shares a border with the USSR, as well as sharing "ethnic affinity on both sides of the border," which has created "political instability." These specific factors all suggest "defensive rather than offensive impulses," he concluded.[19] Defensive measures? Did the Soviets fear an invasion by Afghanistan? (Few Americans know that their tax dollars paid for the building of the modern roads in 1966 down which Soviet tanks rolled in December of 1979—U.S. foreign policy in action!)[20]

By 1980, Kennan's "doctrine" of containment had become the doctrine of delaying the inevitable defeat of the West. Thus,

---

17. Kennan, *Memoirs*, p. 367.

18. See, for example, Norman Podhoretz, *The Present Danger: "Do We Have the Will to Reverse the Decline of American Power?"* (New York: Simon & Schuster, 1980).

19. George Kennan, *The Nuclear Delusion: Soviet-American Relations in the Atomic Age* (New York: Pantheon, 1982), p. 162.

20. "Rugged Afghan Road Jobs Fill Gaps in Trans-Asian Network," *Engineering News-Record* (Nov. 3, 1966).

remarked Solzhenitsyn in 1980: "By means of his essays, public statements, and words of advice, all of which are supposedly rooted in a profound understanding of Soviet life, George Kennan has for years had a major detrimental influence upon the shape and direction of American foreign policy. He is one of the more persistent architects of the myth of the 'moderates' in the Politburo, despite the fact that no such moderates have ever revealed themselves by so much as a hint. He is forever urging us to pay greater heed to the Soviet leaders' pronouncements and even today finds it inconceivable that anyone should mistrust Brezhnev's vigorous denials of aggressive intent. He prefers to ascribe the seizure of Afghanistan to the 'defensive impulses' of the Soviet leadership."[21]

There is no neutrality in the battle between Communism and capitalism. There will be no peace until one or the other system triumphs in history. The goal for the West must be victory over Communism. But until the essentially religious, supernatural basis of this conflict is understood by citizens of the West and their elected representatives, the West will continue to capitulate. The humanists who make the decisions have lost the will to resist. The West has succumbed to the fifth stage of Greek religion, the failure of nerve.[22]

The Humanist West's Loss of Faith

The foreign policy of the humanist West is in the process of disintegration. This is understandable, because the humanist West is itself disintegrating—religiously, socially, economically, medically (AIDS), and in most other ways. Even the advances in science and technology are now posing a threat to some nations' continued survival: nuclear war, chemical and biological war. The promised cursings of Deuteronomy 28:15-68 were comprehensive; so are the crises of the humanist West.

---

21. Aleksandr Solzhenitsyn, "Misconceptions About Russia Are a Threat to America," *Foreign Affairs* (Spring 1980), p. 806.

22. Gilbert Murray, *Five Stages of Greek Religion* (Garden City, New York: Anchor, [1925] 1955), ch. 4.

No one has articulated this despair better than George Kennan. His life has been spent brooding over the West, filling vast State Department files with his doubts and fears.[23] His biographers comment: "Whereas [Averill] Harriman was thick-skinned, businesslike, and nearly oblivious to matters he felt unworthy of his focus, Kennan indulged himself as an anguished and sensitive intellectual, tormented by slights and disappointments both real and imagined."[24] His anguished imagination is still running away with him. Nevertheless, he views his early years as optimistic; compared with his views today, perhaps they were. He admitted in 1976:

> I am an American and, like all of us, and especially all of us who were born at the time I was born and brought up — before World War I — I grew up with a certain faith in American civilization and a certain belief that the American experiment was a positive development in the history of mankind, that it was a good thing that the United States had come into being and developed as it had developed. I now see all these assumptions crashing to pieces around us. I do not think that the United States civilization of these last 40-50 years is a successful civilization; I do not think that our political system is adequate to the needs of the age into which we are now moving; I think this country is destined to succumb to failures which cannot be other than tragic and enormous in their scope. All this, of course, is not an easy thing to live with.[25]

Who was in control of the United States during these years? George Kennan and his colleagues, as the fat book, *The Wise Men* (1986), shows so well. These men were failures. Urbanized Kennan calls for a return to agrarianism, to the past he never lived in: "This society bears the seeds of its own horrors — unbreathable air, undrinkable water, starvation — and until people realize that we

---

23. This is a continuing theme of the book by Walter Isaacson and Evan Thomas, *The Wise Men: Six Friends and the World They Made* (New York: Simon & Schuster, 1986), pp. 152, 157, 172.

24. *Ibid.*, p. 228.

25. "A Conversation with George Kennan," *The Alternative: An American Spectator* (November 1976), p. 5. Excerpted from *Encounter* (Sept. 1976).

have to get back to a much simpler form of life, a much smaller population, a society in which the agrarian component is far greater again in relation to the urban component—until these appreciations become widespread and effective—I can see no answer to the troubles of our time." Spoken like a man who spent his life behind a typewriter—and toward the end, an electric typewriter—in air-conditioned luxury, sipping sherry rather than tap water. Yet this man was the primary State Department intellectual for at least five decades.

He says that we face one of two catastrophes: nuclear war with the Soviets, or ecological catastrophe in the next five decades. He neglects another: political conquest by the Soviets, which he dismisses as unlikely because the Russians have suffered reversals everywhere. "The Russians are not in a good position to take advantage of our great weaknesses today."[26] He concludes: "Compared to the dangers which confront us on the ecological and demographic front, the possibility of Soviet control of Western Europe, even if one thought that this was a likely thing to happen (which I don't) would strike me as a minor catastrophe. After all, people *do live* in the Soviet Union. For the mass of people there, life is not intolerable."[27] He should read *What to Do When the Russians Come: A Survivor's Guide* (Stein & Day, 1954), by Jon Manchip White and Robert Conquest, the scholar whose book on Stalin's purges of the 1930's is the definitive work, *The Great Terror*. That was a decade in which 20-30 million people did not survive the politics of the Soviet Union. China lost perhaps 60 million in the 1950's. Cambodia continued this political tradition in the 1970's, and Ethiopia continues it today. But Kennan worries about smog.

Western Europe is decadent, he says, "far too addicted to its material comforts." Pornography is everywhere. "This betrays a terrible lack of self-confidence and a total confusion of values."[28]

---

26. *Ibid.*, p. 8.
27. *Ibid.*, p. 12.
28. *Ibid.*, p. 8.

He sees the problem, but he has no answer except quietism and retreat from international responsibility: "But as things are, I can see very little merit in organizing ourselves to defend from the Russians the porno-shops in central Washington. In fact, the Russians are much better in holding pornography at bay than we are."[29] No doubt they are; they control access to paper and ink. They are also effective at keeping Bibles out of the hands of the population.

He has become an isolationist. "My main reason for advocating a gradual and qualified withdrawal from far-flung foreign involvements is that we have nothing to teach the world. We have to confess that we have not got the answers to the problems of human society in the modern age."[30] This is the death-rattle of a civilization, or at least of its present leadership: its intellectuals no longer see anything in it worth defending or promoting.

The Yoke of Fear

The West has long believed that freedom, peace, and prosperity are available on a permanent basis completely apart from the God who establishes the ethical foundations of freedom, peace, and prosperity. Christians have also defended this view for a century by continued reliance on natural law theories and the humanist doctrine of permanent political pluralism. The West has believed that evolution has overwhelmed every system of permanent ethics, so that no one can speak in the name of God's permanent principles. The Communists believed the same thing, but because they officially replaced the West's fading faith in God with Marxism-Leninism, they were able to delay the loss of faith longer. Solzhenitsyn and other Russian critics insist that this Marxist faith in now dead behind the Iron Curtain, but it still is alive inside Third World revolutionary movements and in many Western college classrooms.

The West has lost its faith in progress. The Soviets have lost

---

29. *Ibid.*, p. 12.
30. *Ibid.*, p. 9.

their faith in Marxism. What keeps the Soviets on the offensive? The quest for power. They still believe in the power religion, even if they have lost faith in the details of Marxism-Leninism. In contrast, the West is in the process of adopting the escape religion. Solzhenitsyn has sounded the warning, but no one in Washington's highest circles has heeded it: "This is very dangerous for one's view of the world when this feeling comes on: 'Go ahead, give it up.' We already hear voices in your country and in the West — 'Give up Korea and we will live quietly. Give up Portugal, of course; give up Japan, give up Israel, give up Taiwan, the Philippines, Malaysia, Thailand, give up ten more African countries. Just let us live in peace and quiet. Just let us drive our big cars on our splendid highways; just let us play tennis and golf, in peace and quiet; just let us mix our cocktails in peace and quiet as we are accustomed to doing; just let us see the beautiful toothy smile with a glass in hand on every advertisement page of our magazines.' "[31]

This is the mentality of slaves. It is God's curse on covenantally rebellious people to allow them to become enslaved. This was God's message to Israel and Judah: "Disobey Me, and I will sent Assyria and Babylonia to enslave you." If Christians want deliverance, it can come only through a new form of servitude: *service to God.* It must come from leaders who stand fearless before men because they are fearful of God. We no longer have such leaders, as Solzhenitsyn knows. "Long years of appeasement have invariably entailed the surrender of the West's positions and the bolstering of its adversary. Today we can assess on a global scale the achievement of the West's leading diplomats after 35 years of concerted effort: they have succeeded in strengthening the U.S.S.R. and Communist China in so many ways that only the ideological rift between those two regimes (for which the West can take no credit) still preserves the Western world from disaster. In other words, the survival of the West already depends on factors which are effectively beyond its control."[32]

---

31. *Solzhenitsyn: The Voice of Freedom* (Washington, D.C.: AFL-CIO, 1975), p. 12.
32. Solzhenitsyn, *Foreign Affairs* (Spring 1980), p. 807.

The Israelites in the wilderness feared death more than they loved the idea of winning the promised land. What did God give them? Death in the wilderness. If we fear the wrath of men more than God, then God will deliver us into the hands of fearfully wrathful men. We must heed the warning of Jesus:

> "And do not fear them who kill the body but cannot kill the soul. But rather fear Him who is able to destroy both soul and body in hell" (Matthew 10:28).

The Rockefeller Panel on foreign policy correctly assessed what the West needs to survive: "Tenacity of purpose as well as capacity for sacrifice, sustained over a long period, will be needed to meet the present challenge."[33] Unfortunately for the deal-doing humanists, the West has run out of both: tenacity of purpose and capacity for sacrifice.

Chambers' Vision

Whittaker Chambers saw the crisis of the humanist West in 1925. He described in 1952 his 1925 "moment of truth" that led him to join the Communist Party. He was sitting on a bench at Columbia University in New York City. "I was there to answer once for all two questions: Can a man go on living in a world that is dying? If he can, what should he do in the crisis of the 20th century?" I have never seen the crisis of this century summarized more eloquently.

> There ran through my mind the only lines I remember from the history textbook of my second go at college—two lines of Savinus', written in the fifth century when the Goths had been in Rome and the Vandals were in Carthage [St. Augustine died at age 76 in 430 A.D. in North Africa during this Vandal conquest— G.N.]: "The Roman Empire is filled with misery, but it is luxurious. It is dying, but it laughs."
>
> The dying world of 1925 was without faith, hope, character, understanding of its malady or will to overcome it. It was dying but it laughed. And this laughter was not the defiance of a vigor

---

33. *Prospect for America*, p. 48.

that refuses to know when it is whipped. It was the loss, by the mind of a whole civilization, of the power to distinguish between reality and unreality, because, ultimately, though I did not know it, it had lost the power to distinguish between good and evil. This failure I, too, shared with the world of which I was a part.

The dying world had no answer at all to the crisis of the 20th century, and, when it was mentioned, and every moral voice in the Western world was shrilling crisis, it cocked an ear of complacent deafness and smiled a smile of blank senility—throughout history, the smile of those for whom the executioner waits.[34]

May God grant to His people in this generation the wisdom, perception, and courage not to turn a deaf ear to the world's crisis, and to wipe the smile of blank senility off their faces. It is late in the century, yet it is difficult to distinguish the Christians from the humanists with respect to their perception of the crisis and their ability to formulate solutions to it.

The Silent Christian Majority

The Christians of the West have remained silent, generally unaware of what is going on in international relations, unconcerned about it, and unwilling to present the claims of Christ on foreign policy, trade policy, and civil government in general. Christians have been watchmen on the walls who have not recognized that the enemy long ago infiltrated and bought off the leadership of the once-faithful nation, nor do they know what to do, now that the enemy's main army is nearing the gates of the city. They comfort themselves with an obvious illusion: that the morally defeated humanist leaders within the gates know what to do, despite three generations of failure. Christians have sounded no warning for three generations; they have forgotten how to blow the trumpet.

> Again the word of the LORD came to me, saying, "Son of man, speak to the children of your people, and say to them: 'When I bring the sword upon a land, and the people of the land take a man

---

34. Whittaker Chambers, *Witness* (New York: Random House, 1952), p. 195.

from their territory and make him their watchman, when he sees the sword coming upon the land, if he blows the trumpet and warns the people, then whoever hears the sound of the trumpet and does not take warning, if the sword comes and takes him away, his blood shall be on his own head. He heard the sound of the trumpet, but did not take warning; his blood shall be upon himself. But he who takes warning will save his life. But if the watchman sees the sword coming and does not blow the trumpet, and the people are not warned, and the sword comes and takes any person from among them, he is taken away in his iniquity; but his blood I will require at the watchman's hand'" (Ezekiel 33:1-6).

The blood of this civilization is presently on the hands of Christians, who have been too timid, and too unsure of themselves, to propose any alternatives to humanist foreign policy in the name of Christ and in terms of the Bible. God set them on the towers as His representatives to a fallen world, and they have remained silent. They have thought it only natural that humanists should control every aspect of foreign policy, and that the nation-state should constitute the heart, mind, and soul of international relations. Now a time of vast international crisis lies ahead — military, economic, political, and biological (AIDS).[35] The banking policies of the West assure us all of a coming economic catastrophe. It can be deferred; it cannot be avoided.[36]

In that day of multiple crises, Christians will not escape unscathed, any more than righteous Hebrews escaped Assyrian and Babylonian captivity. When ungodly men are allowed by the righteous to speak as representatives of a nation (point two of the Biblical covenant model), then that nation will eventually experience judgment. There is a cause-and-effect relationship in history between covenantal standards and covenantal judgments.

Christians have defaulted on their responsibilities. They have assumed that covenant-breaking humanists can and should speak for them. They have not cared to see God's covenant publicly

---

35. Gary North, *The Scourge: AIDS and the Coming Bankruptcy* (Ft. Worth, Texas: American Bureau of Economic Research, 1987).

36. Lawrence Malkin, *The National Debt* (New York: Henry Holt, 1987).

affirmed nationally. Thus, the twentieth century has been the most bloody century since the Noachic Flood.[37] It has become the age of totalitarianism, bureaucracy, and massive international tyranny, all in the name of (principle of representation) humanism's false god, the sovereign autonomous people.

The result will be default by the ruling pagans on their responsibilities to the West, the default of Western civil governments on their economic promises to the voters, the default of the commercial banks, and the default of private pension plans. The twentieth century has been a century of moral and religious default, and sometime during the lifetimes of most of those who read this book in the 1980's, there will be a default by humanist institutions on a scale unimaginable today.

These looming crises offer hope for Christian reconstruction of a humanist civilization that is on its deathbed. But if Christians default once again, refusing to sacrifice their lives and fortunes for the crown rights of King Jesus in every area of life, then a new dark age of tyranny is the obvious alternative. There is no neutrality. We face these choices today: the kingdom of God on earth or the kingdom of Satan on earth. We face freedom under Christ or the Communist concentration camp. We face life in the Son or death by nuclear annihilation.

As Elijah asked the representatives of the tribes of Israel:

"How long will you falter between two opinions? If the LORD is God, follow Him; but if Baal, then follow him" (1 Kings 18:21a).

Let us not be like those pragmatic Israelites, who wanted to see on which altar the fire would fall:

But the people answered him not a word (1 Kings 18:21b).

Baal or God, humanism or Christ, the kingdom of God or the kingdom of Satan: choose this day whom you will serve. The fire will soon fall, and those who choose wrongly could become living sacrifices in history. Do not defer a decision on the assumption

---

37. Gil Eliot, *Twentieth Century Book of the Dead* (New York: Scribner's, 1972).

that God will rapture you out of all problems. He did not rapture Israel when the Assyrians came, or Judah when the Babylonians came, or the Greeks when the Turks came. Lenin's spiritual heirs are coming:

> As long as Capitalism and Socialism exist, we cannot live in peace; in the end, one or the other will triumph—a funeral dirge will be sung over the Soviet Republic or over world capitalism.[38]

The battle between two kingdoms rages, yet Christians in the West pretend that it is somehow all very distant, and all very spiritual, confined to distant lands and invisible worlds where angels battle demons beyond the perceptions of men.

The battle is in fact very close—no farther away than six minutes, as the submarine launched missile flies.

He Shall Overcome

We know there is only one kingdom of God, and it has many enemies in history:

> Then comes the end, when He delivers the kingdom to God the Father, when He puts an end to all rule and all authority and power. For He must reign till He has put all enemies under His feet. The last enemy that will be destroyed is death (1 Corinthians 15:24-26).

The final overcoming of all rival authorities by Jesus Christ comes at the last judgment, when He triumphs over His enemies and delivers His kingdom to God the Father. Christ's kingdom at last absorbs all other kingdoms. But the word "absorbs" is metaphorical, related to some organic process. The expansion process of Christ's triumphant kingdom in history is neither mechanical nor organic. It is *covenantal*.

The kingdom of God is real. It is a factor in human history. It is something that Christ literally delivers to God. Such a transfer of authority is covenantal. Christ subdues the earth through His

---

38. Lenin, "Speech to Moscow Party Nuclei Secretaries" (Nov. 26, 1920); cited by Bouscaren, *Soviet Foreign Policy: A Pattern of Persistence*, p. 11.

representatives, members of His Church; then He transfers this subdued earth to God the Father. This transfer is a kind of dowry which Christ pays to the "Father of the Bride," His church. His inheritance from God becomes the "bride price" for His church, a visible payment at the end of history that was in principle paid for covenantally at Calvary. This payment is *definitive, progressive,* and *final.*

There is of necessity a disinheritance at that time. Like the inheritance concept, and also like the bride price concept, this disinheritance is also definitive (Calvary), progressive (historical), and final. "Let both [wheat and tares] grow together until the harvest, and at the time of harvest I will say to the reapers, 'First gather together the tares and bind them in bundles to burn them, but gather the wheat into my barn'" (Matthew 13:30). The tares are finally and eternally disinherited at the final judgment. The nations will be divided at that time (Matthew 25:31-35).

The Process of Overcoming

It is obvious that this overcoming of His enemies is progressive over time. The last enemy to be subdued will be death. So His enemies are not subdued all at once. This process of overcoming takes place in history.

With respect to the nations, there can be little doubt of how the kingdom of God will be manifested: through confession and covenanting together. Confessing Christ ecclesiastically means confirming both the local and international Church covenant through baptism and renewing it weekly through the Lord's Supper. Confirming Christ in the realm of civil government means a periodic public affirmation of God's covenant law (Exodus 31:10-13). There is no legitimate escape from the covenant and its ethical requirements. Just as a magistrate or other civil officer in the United States swears with his left hand on the Bible, promising to uphold the U.S. Constitution, so should he swear on the Constitution, promising to uphold the Bible. So should those who elect them (Exodus 19). A civil covenant ratification and renewal process is fundamental for a Christian nation. An election is such a renewal event, when the voters pass judgment on their representatives. The covenant renewal aspect of voting is recognized by Communist nations, which compel voters to vote, and which experience voter turnout rates well above 95 percent.

It is this covenant process, with periodic renewal, that serves to bind the members of a Christian nation. So should this process bind Christian nations into a visible civil kingdom that reflects the heavenly kingdom.

As men strive together in national covenant to work out their salvation in fear and trembling (Philippians 2:12), they extend Christ's kingdom on earth. As they become covenantally faithful by honoring God's law in word and deed (James 1:19-27), God's visible, external blessings cover the covenanted society. These blessings are clearly national and external: military (v. 7), weather (v. 12), and finances (v. 12) (Deuteronomy 28:1-14). The rain will not fall only on the spiritually converted, after all. The focus of covenant blessings is the *nation*.

This means that nations as covenantal institutions will eventually overcome the enemies of Christ. The *positive feedback* of covenantal blessings produces wealth, authority, and influence for covenantally faithful institutions: churches, civil governments, and families. These external, visible blessings are designed to reinforce men's faith in the reliability of God's covenant promises in history: "And you shall remember the LORD your God, for it is He who gives you power to get wealth, that He may establish His covenant which He swore to your fathers, as it is this day" (Deuteronomy 8:18).

The humanist socialists have adopted a slogan, "The rich get richer, and the poor get poorer." This is a lie. The Bible teaches that in the long run, the *covenantally faithful* get richer, and the *covenantally rebellious* get poorer. This is denied by the humanists, who want no sign of God's covenant judgments in history, and also by Christian pietists and retreatists, who also want no sign of God's covenant judgments in history. God's covenant system of blessings and cursings is designed to produce long-term victory for Christ's people in history. This steady increase in Christians' personal responsibility to extend God's dominion on earth is opposed by both humanists and Christian pietists. The humanists do not want Christians to inherit authority in history, for they want to retain monopoly power over history. Christian pietists also do not want Christians to inherit authority in history, for with authority necessarily comes responsibility.

Men are responsible before God, and this means that we are responsible *in terms of permanent standards*. This means God's law. The more authority Christians inherit from God, the harder they must strive to see God's revealed laws in the legal codes of each nation. A Christian society's legal order should reflect the requirements of revealed Biblical law. So should the international legal order that is established progressively by Christian nations. The implicit covenantal division between sheep and goats — national entities — must be made increasingly visible over time, "in earth as it is in heaven" (Matthew 5:10b).

This is the basis of Christ's progressive overcoming of His enemies in history: the steady expansion of His people's authority on earth. This is the principle of *leaven*. God's holy leaven steadily replaces Satan's unholy leaven in history. "And another parable He spoke to them: 'The kingdom of heaven is like leaven, which a woman took and hid in three measures of meal till it was all leavened'" (Matthew 13:33).

God triumphs in history through the expansion of Christ's kingdom. "Now when all things are made subject to Him, then the Son Himself will also be subject to Him who put all things under Him, that God may be all in all" (1 Corinthians 15:28). This is not pantheism; it is covenant dominion. God is not infused into His creation; His kingdom in heaven becomes covenantally identified with Christ's kingdom on earth. Our prayer is answered at the end of history: "Thy kingdom come. Thy will be done in earth, as it is in heaven" (Matthew 6:10, KJV).

Beating Something With Something Better

Christians possess the Bible and the Holy Spirit. They have the law of God and the power of God at their disposal. They have the doctrine of the covenant in all its God-given authority. Yet they ignore all this, and instead proclaim Jesus as Lord of all the Church, but not of all the earth; Jesus as sovereign Master of the family, but not the civil government; Jesus as the Healer of a remnant but not healer of the nations.

They send out missionaries, but not to baptize nations. They send out pamphlets, but not handbooks for exercising godly rule. The send out physicians of the body and the soul, but not of the body politic. They have turned the world over to the devil by default (and sometimes in the name of New Testament theology), and then have vainly sought to persuade the devil's power-holding representatives to allow equal time for Jesus. Why should they allow equal time for Jesus? Does Jesus intend to allow equal time for Satan in eternity?

Christians have denied the covenant. They have denied with all their heart, mind, and soul that Jesus intends them to disciple the nations, including their own nations. They have denied the greatness of the Great Commission.[39] They understand the consequences of such covenantal failure, but they have hoped in a last-minute rescue by God's cavalry. They have denied the comprehensive redemption offered at Calvary, and instead hope in a supernatural deliverance in the midst of the international failure of Christianity.

Did God intervene miraculously to bail out Jesus as He walked toward Calvary? Did He intervene to save Stephen from the stones of his adversaries (Acts 7)? No. Then why should He bail out today's Christians, who show none of Christ's courage in the face of death, and none of Stephen's taste for verbal confrontation with the Christ-hating rulers of his day? If God refused to bail out those who, in the midst of crisis, have preached the Church's vic-

---

39. Kenneth L. Gentry, Jr., "The Greatness of the Great Commission," *Journal of Christian Reconstruction*, VII (Winter, 1981).

tory in history, why should he bail out those who, in the fatness provided by modern capitalism, preach the Church's defeat in history? If the Israelites who feared to die in the wilderness all died in the wilderness, and only those two men who were ready to fight from the beginning did survive to enter the land, what can modern Christians expect? A bed of roses? Or lilies on their caskets?

We possess all that is needed to put our enemies to flight. But to do this, we must pick up the spiritual weapons that God has provided. Saul's armor of natural law theory, permanent political pluralism, the myth of neutrality, and anti-covenantalism will not fit us, and if we try to confront Goliath with such armor as our defense, we will lose our heads.

People who live in God's house need to throw stones.

Part II
RECONSTRUCTION

A decline in courage may be the most striking feature that an outside observer notices in the West today. The Western world has lost its civic courage, both as a whole and separately, in each country, in each government, in each political party, and of course, in the United Nations. Such a decline in courage is particularly noticeable among the ruling and intellectual elites, causing an impression of a loss of courage by the entire society. There remain many courageous individuals, but they have no determining influence on public life. Political and intellectual functionaries exhibit this depression, passivity, and perplexity in their actions and in their statements, and even more so in their self-serving rationales as to how realistic, reasonable, and intellectually and even morally justified it is to base state policies on weakness and cowardice. And the decline in courage, at times attaining what could be termed a lack of manhood, is ironically emphasized by occasional outbursts of boldness and inflexibility on the part of those same functionaries when dealing with weak governments and with countries that lack support, or with doomed currents which clearly cannot offer any resistance. But they get tongue-tied and paralyzed when they deal with powerful governments and threatening forces, with aggressors and international terrorists.

Must one point out that from ancient times a decline in courage has been considered the first symptom of the end?

Aleksandr Solzhenitsyn (1978)*

Solzhenitsyn at Harvard (Washington, D.C.: Ethics and Public Policy Center, 1980), pp. 5-6.

11

WHAT THE CHURCH CAN DO

"I do not pray for these alone, but also for those who will believe in Me through their word; that they may be one, as You, Father, are in Me, and I in You; that they also may be one in Us, that the world may believe that You sent Me. And the glory which You gave Me I have given them, that they may be one just as We are one: I in them, and You in Me; that they may be made perfect in one, and that the world may know that You have sent Me, and have loved them as You have loved Me" (John 17:20-23).

In the Introduction to this book, I stated that the Church International—the institutional, international Church—is to serve as the model of what a nation is and should be. The Church International is that nation which inherited the kingdom of God from Jesus Christ (Matthew 21:43). Thus, what the Church International is in principle, the Christian-influenced world will become in history. What the Church International is at any point in history, the Christian-influenced world will not yet have attained, even under the best of circumstances.

If the members of the Church International are at peace, the Christian-influenced world will be headed in the direction of peace. If the Church International is at war internally, the Christian-influenced world will soon imitate. If the Church International through sin is losing its influence, then the progressively *less* Christian-influenced world will be increasing its influence.

The Church International is the world's proper role model. Whatever the Church International does with the gospel at any point in history, it can expect the Church-influenced culture to imitate.

259

If the world is in deep trouble, we know where to start looking for causes. We also know where to start working out the solutions. It does very little good to begin a program of Christian reconstruction in the field of international relations if the Church International is in national institutional fragments. Yet, that is where we are in history.

"Love One Another"

Jesus could not have made it plainer to His disciples: the institutional Church's unity of confession and ethical walk is basic to a successful program of world evangelism. He prayed for God to bring unity to the disciples, "that they may be made perfect in one, and that the world may know that You have sent Me, and have loved them as You have loved Me." It is clear that during any period in which the institutional Church remains fragmented and mutually hostile, the world will not know "that You have sent Me, and have loved them as You have loved Me." A divided Church produces a divided testimony; divided testimony misleadingly points to a divided God. But God is one, and Jesus is God, so the institutional Church should "be one, as You, Father, are in Me, and I in You." Any permanent division within the Church is a form of false testimony, for it points to a division within the Godhead, and it also misleadingly testifies to the non-divinity of Jesus Christ.

Christians forget about the historical setting of this prayer. This was the Last Supper. John 13-17 is a record of their discussion in between the completion of the Last Supper (13:2) and their departure to the garden of Gethsemene (18:1), and these words came at the end of His final instructions to them. His public prayer to His Father was the culmination of His pre-resurrection teaching ministry. His final message to them? Unity!

It has been over 1,900 years since He prayed that prayer. The institutional Church seems no closer to the fulfillment of Christ's prayer than ever. If anything, it seems farther away. Unity was greater a thousand years ago. It was far greater the night He prayed that prayer. There is perhaps no aspect of the Christian

Church, other than this increase in disunity, that stands as a greater condemnation of the Church. Our creeds have improved (at least until the mid-seventeenth century). Our charitable giving has improved. Our missions have improved. Our technical means of communicating the gospel have improved. More people can hear the gospel in one evening because of television satellite broadcasts than could have heard it in a century of missions. These improvements have not been straight-line phenomena, but there has clearly been general improvement.

The exception? The Church's failure even to pursue the ethical and institutional goal of Church unity. Here the Church has been a public failure. The pagan world uses it against Christ. "If the gospel were clear, you people wouldn't be at each other's throats all the time!" The Church has been such a failure for so long in this area of its ministry that Christians seldom even discuss disunity as a major area of failure. They praise local church independency and denominational independency as if independency were God's preferred way. They look at this awful failure that keeps getting worse, and call it a blessing. "Praise God! We Christians give divided testimony to the world!"

Until there is visible evidence that the churches of this world are heading toward cooperation, we know that the hoped-for millennial blessings of God are not close at hand. There will be no worldwide comprehensive blessings without worldwide comprehensive obedience by Christians. We are told to be at peace with each other, to love one another. Evangelicals turn to the Gospel of John as their most effective witnessing tool. What did John tell us?

> "A new commandment I give to you, that you love one another; as I have loved you, that you also love one another. By this all will know that you are My disciples, if you have love for one another" (John 13:34-35).

> "This is My commandment, that you love one another as I have loved you" (John 15:12).

> For this is the message that you heard from the beginning, that we should love one another (1 John 3:11).

> And this commandment we have from Him: that he who loves
> God must love his brother also (1 John 4:21).

Christians preach the coming of the kingdom of God. What is this kingdom? Paul said that "the kingdom of God is not food and drink, but righteousness and peace and joy in the Holy Spirit" (Romans 14:17). "Therefore let us pursue the things which make for peace and the things by which one may edify another" (Romans 14:19).

Precision Through Division

But here we encounter the first problem: the pursuit of two goals that have long divided Christians. We are to pursue both peace and edification. But as we have sought to edify and clarify, we have found that others do not see things our way. One Christian's clarification is another Christian's proof of heretical deviation.

The Bible is a complex book. It baffles the best and the brightest. Its message of salvation is clear enough for children to grasp, Jesus said repeatedly, but it is also sufficiently complex as to divide the greatest minds in the history of the Church.

The progress of the creeds, which is one of the best pieces of evidence for the progress of the Church in history, has also come at the expense of unity. In fact, warfare — literal and figurative — has been a major motivation for improving the creeds. They have served Christians as intellectual and even cultural weapons against heretical enemies, and these enemies have sometimes not been readily identifiable as non-Christians. In fact, the creeds have always come as a means of exclusion as well as inclusion. The writers have, in effect, drawn lines in the dirt and have announced: "Step across that line and you're out of the game." Then the others draw their lines in the dirt and say the same thing. Millions upon millions of people have stepped across each other's lines for about 2,000 years. If we were to take each other's excommunications seriously, all of us are out of the game, and always have been.

Still and all, the lines in the dirt harden. Unlike lines in the dirt, these are more like lines in fresh cement. They get harder over time. No one ever goes back to erase them. They just move onto new ground and draw more lines in their own fresh cement. This is progress. It is high-priced progress, but it is progress. We might call it *precision through division.*

What can overcome this tendency of precision through division? We do not know. So far, the churches have found no solution. But there is one. Actually, there are two. One is called love. We have known about it from the beginning. It has not worked yet.

The other is called fear. We are to avoid fear. Perfect love casteth out fear (1 John 4:18). Nevertheless, when Christians in the Soviet Union are thrown into some concentration camp, they seek out other Christians. In the Gulag archipelago, Christians are not so fussy about creedal precision and liturgical regularities. The stakes are too high. They need prayer, mutual building up in the faith, and a shared smuggled Bible. They would pay whatever they have for a hymnal. Those who remember a few Bible stories tell them. Those who remember a few hymns or psalms teach them. No one screens by rigorous creeds. The stakes are too high. The weakening of the body of Christ through the loss of a member is too costly. They keep the peace with each other.

But Christians do not build a civilization in the Gulag. They survive; they do not build. Once out of the Gulag, it is time to become precise once again. And so it goes: from survival to construction, from unity to diversity.

The Church Is Christ's Body

What we need is institutional trinitarianism: unity with diversity. We need the division of labor with institutional cooperation. What we need is the body of Christ:

> For I say, through the grace given to me, to everyone who is among you, not to think of himself more highly than he ought to think, but to think soberly, as God has dealt to each one a measure of faith. For as we have many members in one body, but all the members do not have the same function, so we, being many, are one body in Christ, and individually members of one another.

Having then gifts differing according to the grace that is given to us, let us use them: if prophecy, let us prophesy in proportion to our faith; or ministry, let us use it in our ministering; he who teaches, in teaching; he who exhorts, in exhortation; he who gives, with liberality; he who leads, with diligence; he who shows mercy, with cheerfulness (Romans 12:3-8).

For as the body is one and has many members, but all the members of that one body, being many, are one body, so also is Christ. For by one Spirit we were all baptized into one body — whether Jews or Greeks, whether slaves or free — and have all been made to drink into one Spirit. For in fact the body is not one member but many. If the foot should say, "Because I am not a hand, I am not of the body," is it therefore not of the body? And if the ear should say, "Because I am not an eye, I am not of the body," is it therefore not of the body? If the whole body were an eye, where would be the hearing? If the whole were hearing, where would be the smelling? But now God has set the members, each one of them, in the body just as He pleased. And if they were all one member, where would the body be? But now indeed there are many members, yet one body. And the eye cannot say to the hand, "I have no need of you"; nor again the head to the feet, "I have no need of you" (1 Corinthians 12:12-21).

Notice that Paul's verbs are all in the present tense. He is not speaking of a future millennial age. He says that the Church of Jesus Christ *is* a body. We *are* members. We may not be strong members, or members marked by dexterity. We may be the equivalent of arthritic members, gnarled and stiff, but we are members.

The Doctrine of Imputation

Christians know that their only hope of eternal life is that Christ's righteousness *has been imputed* to them already. God looks at Christ's perfect righteousness as a human being, and declares, "I declare as the Judge of history that your righteousness belongs to this formerly lost sinner. I declare him 'not guilty' in My court of eternal law." This declaration of "not guilty" comes as a result of Christ's perfect humanity, His perfect walk before God in history.

But if Christ's perfection as a God-incarnate human being is imputed to an individual, then it is also imputed to the Church International. The Church is *Christ's body*; therefore, Paul says, "there should be no schism in the body, but that the members should have the same care for one another" (1 Corinthians 12:25). This body is unified in principle; it is also diverse in principle, just as God the Trinity is both unified and diverse.

What is true *in principle* concerning a person's status as a God-redeemed person is to be manifested *progressively* in his lifetime, and manifested *finally* at the last judgment. He is saved, is being saved, and will be saved, all by the sovereign grace of God.

What is true *in principle* concerning the Church International's status as a God-redeemed institution is to be manifested *progressively* in history, and manifested *finally* at the last judgment. It is unified and diverse, is becoming unified and diverse, and will be revealed as unified and diverse, all by the sovereign grace of God.

The problem for the Church International is that it has over-emphasized diversity at the expense of unity. It has sinned. It has needed creedal precision, but it has not needed schism. Like Solomon, who was born of a marriage established through adultery and murder, so the Church has achieved greater theological precision through schism. The wisdom of Solomon was not a justification for adultery and murder. The increasing theological precision of the Church is no justification for schism.

"Can You Shoot Straight?"

If you were a soldier in the front line, sitting in your trench, and you saw the enemy's troops coming over the ridge 500 yards in front of you, would you ask the man at your left about his theology or his ability to shoot straight?

If you were suffering from a brain tumor, and you heard about a physician who specializes in operating on the brain, would you consult him about his theology or his former patients' rate of survival?

There is such a thing as common grace. Pagans have been given skills by God so that they can serve His people. When we are buying a service, we care about its quality, not the theology of the person who delivers it.

There are exceptions. We do not want to subsidize evil. If a physician practices abortion, Christians should seek out another physician to heal them. But if your spouse were bleeding to death at the side of the road, and a known abortionist offered to save his life, would you refuse his assistance? No, you would take it. And after your spouse recovered, you would again be found marching in the picket line in front of his office.

We need to look at the skills of Christian brothers in the same way. Each Christian group "brings something to the table," as the slang of business says. They bring something to God's table, as the language of the Lord's Supper says. It is our God-assigned task to seek out the positive contributions of every Christian group in order to discover what others possess in abundance that each of us is lacking. Our job is to imitate their strengths without sacrificing any of our own.

The division of labor is institutional and international within the Church International. There are whole denominations that see better than others. (Presbyterians, for example.) There are denominations that walk better than others. (Baptists, for example.) There are denominations that prosper economically more than others. (Episcopalians, for example.) There are denominations that tithe more than others. (Mennonites, for example.) There are denominations that show enthusiasm more than others. (Pentecostals, for example.) There are denominations that have persevered under oppression longer than others. (Eastern Orthodoxy, for example.) There are denominations that have captured pagan cultures better than others. (Roman Catholicism, for example.) They all bring something unique and valuable to God's table.

On the other hand, how many Christians would want to study Christian philosophy at a Pentecostal seminary, study missions at a Presbyterian seminary, study youth work at an Episcopalian seminary, study military strategy at a Mennonite seminary, study church cooperation at a Baptist seminary, study cultural transformation at an Eastern Orthodox seminary, or study Church-State relations at a Roman Catholic seminary? (All this assumes that anyone would want to attend seminary.) Not many, I would guess.

A hermetically sealed container is one that allows nothing to escape because it allows nothing to get in. Christian traditions have been very nearly hermetically sealed from each other. This has been especially true of Protestantism, though Eastern Orthodoxy may be the king of ecclesiastical isolationism. Christians do not know what other church traditions are. American Christians are astoundingly ignorant about Church history. They care nothing about history. They are uninterested in the progress of the Church in history. Why? Because they have no doctrine of the Church in the future. They do not believe that the Church will make a fundamental difference in the transformation of world civilization. They do not believe that the Church International has served, is serving, and will serve as the world's proper model for nationhood. They are Christian isolationists. It is not surprising that they are also nationalistic isolationists.

They do not look into Church history to find examples of successful ventures in Church unity. They do not look across a border — denominational or geographical — to learn how other Christians are dealing with cultural, economic, and political problems. They do not expect to find Biblical solutions to real-world problems. And because they do not expect them, they do not discover them. They do not ask other Christians, "Can you shoot straight? Can you shoot straighter than I can under all circumstances? Can you teach me how to shoot in a new situation?"

Meanwhile, the enemy has now advanced to 300 yards, and is closing in fast.

The Shooting Has Begun

What is happening to Russian Orthodoxy under the Soviets is worse than what is happening to Eastern Orthodoxy under the Turks. What is happening to Christians in South Africa — "necklacing" — is a taste of things to come. (Necklacing is the term for tying a person's hands behind his back, putting a tire soaked in diesel fuel around his neck, and setting it on fire. The Marxist African National Congress revolutionaries are using this technique against Christian blacks in South Africa. In January of 1987, U.S. Secretary of State George Shultz had a much-publicized meeting with ANC president Oliver Tambo. Everything was cordial. Christians might consider sending used tires to George Shultz as a symbolic gesture.)

Christian parents in the United States are being sent to jail for teaching their children at home. Their children are being sent to foster homes.

Christians in Cuba live under the tyrant who was trained in Catholic schools, and who turned against the Church—a familiar pattern among humanists, from Judas to Rousseau to Castro.

No one is safe. The Communist noose is getting tighter. Yet the Church's main stronghold, the United States, is sleepwalking. It thinks of all this as distant. It sits, hypnotized, in front of the flickering colored shadows of the television, watching reruns for half the year—reruns of shows that were not worth watching the first time. The vast majority of their children are in humanist-controlled government schools. (See Robert Thoburn's book in the Biblical Blueprints Series, *The Children Trap*.) They do not exercise the right that millions of Soviet Christians would give what little they own in order to possess: the right to send their children to a Christian school.

Until the churches begin to think of themselves as members of the institutional, international body of Christ, little will be done.

But signs of positive change are taking place. A growing minority of Christians are cooperating in a battle against abortion. They are setting up Christian schools. They are getting involved in politics as Christians. They are beginning to reject the myth of neutrality, which is the first step in returning to Biblical law as the only God-ordained standard of righteous action. All this is tentative. These are the first steps of cultural toddlers. But even these few uncertain steps have frightened the humanists, who correctly suspect that they are on their last legs culturally, doddering rather than toddling.

Crisis, Then Unity

The crisis of the West is almost upon us. When the crisis hits — a combination of disasters, in every area of life — then Christians will at last have to face reality: Jesus Christ and His law are alone sufficient to restore righteous rule. There will be no more humanist alternatives. The humanists will pull the last rabbit out of their high-tax hat: a dead rabbit. The humanists' house of cards is tottering. Get ready for the collapse.

When Christians at last recognize that they can no longer sit under the table of the humanists, surviving on whatever crumbs may fall, they will at last learn that the only bread on any man's table is the Bread of Life. Without Christ's grace in history, there would not be life. Adam would have died in the garden. The humanists live on stolen bread — bread stolen from Christians, stolen ideas, stolen capital, stolen vision, stolen everything. Satan's followers are squatters. Christians are the rightful heirs.

But to claim our inheritance in history, we must outperform the squatters in every area of life. We must work together to overcome organized evil. They are organized only in opposition to Christ. Satan's kingdom is divided in principle; Christ's is united in principle. Only when Christians make use of each other's skills and talents will the Church International become an army on the march.

And then the world will at last have a visible model for the international kingdom of God.

What Can Be Done?

There must be international support of churches that are living under tyranny. Every Christian can appreciate the plight of a person in a concentration camp. When whole societies are inside concentration camps, Christians who are presently outside, but who may be headed inside, had better pay attention to their responsibilities. Prayer and money are needed by Christians under tyranny abroad. Some ministries that are assisting foreign Christians are listed in Chapter Twelve.

There must be more cooperation on the missions field. The present practice of rival U.S.-based parachurch television ministries of bidding competitively against each other to sign up local missionaries with large groups (on paper, anyway) under them is an outrage, yet it goes on. It enables fund-raising television appeals based on the claim that "this year we gained one thousand new converts to Christ," when in fact the ministry simply paid an extra ten dollars a month to recruit a foreign evangelist away from a rival ministry. Donors are unaware of this practice, but it goes on. They respond to the bidding war in "scalps" for their donated funds, so the ministries continue the same bidding war in foreign nations. "Our donors want converts!" What the donors get is statistics of new bodies added to the rolls in groups.

A far more useful statistic is the number of laymen who have entered the ministry as ordained deacons or ministers, and who have been on the rolls as laymen over the previous four or five years. That would tell you if a program of discipleship is going on.

Churches need to develop programs with missionaries for locating and discipling middle-class converts and college students in foreign nations. These converts have to be presented with a vision of world transformation superior to the vision offered by the liberation theologians and outright Communists. Missionaries are wasting precious human talent by feeding educated converts with simplistic gospel tracts. These converts are proverbial sitting ducks for revolutionaries. Churches need to target these men with books, tapes, and evangelical materials that present the total claims of Christianity, rather than just the simple gospel that we give to five-year-olds. The Communists are not content with the equivalent of gospel tracts for Marxism. They have a program of identifying potential leaders and providing them with education and materials. Some of their best recruits have come from the churches. Fidel ("Faithful") Castro, a former Jesuit trainee, is a good example. He had been a youth leader hand-picked by the Roman Church.[1] He became an infidel.

---

1. Tad Szulc, *Fidel: A Critical Portrait* (New York: William Morrow, 1986), ch. 3.

Why shouldn't Christian families pay to bring in a young man for training? He can study, live in a Christian home, and receive a new vision of what Christian fellowship is all about. The Communists put them in dormitories; Christians should put them in homes. Churches located near universities should work with local Christian campus ministries to identify new foreign converts and get them out of campus living quarters. The money the students save in room and board can be put to better purposes, such as supplying the people back home with food and literature.

Churches should put up money to have good Christian literature "de-nationalized" and translated into foreign languages. The cost of getting out 5,000 copies of a cheap paperback book is getting lower and lower: under $5,000. Local churches could pool money until an agreed-upon book is ready. Dominion Press is willing to cooperate with churches by locating translators and handling the production of Biblical Blueprints Books, as well as removing all royalty rights on books translated into Third World foreign languages. (We have already done this with a church that wanted to publish a Spanish-language version of *Liberating Planet Earth*.) Contact:

Translation and Publication
Dominion Press
P.O. Box 8204
Ft. Worth, TX 76124

Christian mission efforts have been limited to saving souls and ignoring cultures. This is understandable; that is how most fundamentalist Christians view the gospel. Missionaries have brought the ABC's of the gospel to foreign pagans, but have not had any vision of the KLM's, let alone the XYZ's of the faith. The result has been that when even significant numbers of converts have been brought into the churches, they have not been given the tools to confront the domestic paganism at home and the paganism imported from Communist nations. They have become cannon fodder for their enemies.

There are many fundamentalist Christians who, if they were to read this chapter, would react negatively. "Our job isn't to seek Church unity. That's ecumenicism. That's liberalism. Jesus doesn't want His people to waste their time seeking the impossible. He will establish Church unity by force when He returns with resurrected, perfect saints after the Rapture to set up His thousand-year kingdom. Until then, we are only supposed to preach the gospel." They would reaffirm this position with respect to the establishment of an international Christian federation of nation-states. They see all efforts by Christians to establish anything international as evil. Their operating principle is "We have to wait for the millennium."

These same fundamentalists would not say, however, that we ought to wait for the millennium to pass laws against heroin sales to children. They would not say that churches need to wait until the millennium to fight liberals in the denominations, the way that conservative, Bible-believing Southern Baptists have done so successfully since 1979. They would not say that it is wrong to try to get our churches out of the National Council of Churches or the World Council of Churches. They would probably say that the United States ought to get out of the United Nations, and that we should also get the United Nations out of the United States. They would agree that we ought to get out now, not in the millennium. Why, then, should we wait for the millennium at least to begin to do what Christ says we should do with regard to Church unity?

It is immoral to tell people that they should not work to do what God requires, even if you do not think the goal can be accomplished in your lifetime. Each Christian should do whatever he can, whenever he can, wherever he can to build up the kingdom of God. But what old fashioned, world-retreating fundamentalists do is to persuade other Christians to abandon Christ-required projects that fundamentalists do not really approve of by saying that the successful completion of such projects is impossible and therefore a waste of time, that only Jesus can force the Church to do the right thing in the millennium. Until then, Jesus does not expect us to obey Him. In fact, *Jesus wants us to disobey*

Him, by doing nothing positive. This is pietism at its worst, a self-conscious retreat from responsibility. They say, as Canadian dispensationalist newsletter writer Peter Lalonde says: "It's a question, 'Do you polish brass on a sinking ship?' And if they're working on setting up new institutions, instead of going out and winning the lost for Christ, then they're wasting the most valuable time on the planet of earth right now. . . ."[2] Lalonde implicitly argues that *obeying Jesus* in the realm of social and political affairs — never clearly defined — is *wasting precious soul-winning time.*

Whatever these retreatists do not personally want to do, whatever they find it personally difficult to do, whatever they find themselves personally incompetent to do, they say publicly should not be done by any Christian, even those who are personally competent. And so, by default, they transfer the social world to the humanists. They become apologists for the idea of the inevitable triumph of evil during the so-called "Church Age" (as though there could be some age after Calvary that is not the Church age).

Summary

The Church International is unified in principle, yet diverse in principle. God is also unified and diverse. Thus, the Church in history is supposed to display both unity and diversity. The division of labor is to mark the Church International of Jesus Christ.

This unity has been sadly lacking. The triumphs of the Church over the last 500 years have been the triumphs of diversity, or precision through division. What is needed is a new unification based on better creedal awareness, yet also based on the comprehensive talents of the members of the Church.

The Church International is the proper model for the nations. Nations must learn about cooperation and the division of labor by watching the Church International. The failure of the Church to display unity has hampered Christians in their quest for interna-

---

2. *Dominion: A Dangerous New Theology,* Tape One of Lalonde's three-tape interview with Dave Hunt: *Dominion: The Word and the New World Order* (1987), published by *Omega-Letter,* Ontario, Canada.

tional peace. The humanists want unity on anti-Christian terms, yet Christians are unable to conceive of internationalism among civil governments because they have been failures in establishing what Jesus Christ set forth as a basic requirement for presenting the gospel successfully: Church unity.

Under crisis, Christians can and must unify. The problem is, after the crisis is over, Christians historically have gone back to squabbling. They then turn over society to humanists, for squabblers cannot successfully build anything. The common "lip" of Christianity has turned into the confused "lips" of Babel. This is the judgment of God against sinful Christians. Meanwhile, the new Babylonians are building an international Tower.

Revival will give Christians another opportunity to build God's temple, so that the world will come to Zion in order to hear God's law and His message of spiritual and cultural healing. The question is: When will this revival come? Before a world crisis? During a world crisis? Or half a millennium after the crisis that has led to a new dark age?

12

WHAT THE INDIVIDUAL CHRISTIAN CAN DO

"Behold, I send you out as sheep in the midst of wolves. Therefore be wise as serpents and harmless as doves" (Matthew 10:16).

Not all serpents are poisonous. But when we see one, our first reaction is to freeze, just in case.

This should be the reaction of humanists to Christians. They should never be quite sure which we are. They should always assume that we are a threat to them, even if this or that Christian may be a harmless garden snake.

There are harmless snakes that look almost identical to deadly ones. This is an advantage for snakes with no fangs. We would not expect snakes without fangs to complain about snakes that have fangs. There is even one breed of harmless snake that puffs up, hisses, and pretends to go on the offensive. It strikes at the enemy, never quite hitting the mark. But how is the enemy sure of what kind of snake it is dealing with?

Many Christians, however, are not as wise as serpents. They prefer to imitate the movements of fangless serpents rather than their wisdom. They slither through life on their bellies, looking for cover, always afraid that some humanist is going to step on them or beat them with a stick. They become outraged when other Christians make a public fuss or even attempt to bite a humanist or two. "You will only get us fangless snakes in needless trouble," they complain. "The humanists will start looking for snakes to step on. And us fangless snakes will be their first targets."

I wish this were true: it would reduce the number of fangless snakes.

Comprehensive Responsibility

Fangless snakes are fangless because they preach a fangless theology of world-retreat and institutional surrender. They refuse to recognize the power of God's law and the power of the Holy Spirit. Lacking confidence in God's covenant, they flee the very idea of Christian responsibility outside the walls of home and the local church. They create a vacuum of responsibility, and humanists gratefully rush in to fill it, usually with tax dollars confiscated by the Christian majority, who dutifully re-elected politicians who use the modern principle of "theft by ballot box."[1]

The issue here is commitment to the gospel — Christ's *comprehensive* gospel.[2] This gospel calls all people to repentance. It then calls them to redeem their time by working to work out the implications of their Christian faith with fear and trembling (Philippians 2:12). This gospel influences every area of life. All the world is in sin; all the world is in darkness. The gospel shines into every area of darkness. It illuminates everything.

"I have come as a light into the world, that whoever believes in Me should not abide in darkness" (John 12:46).

No more darkness — political darkness, economic darkness, educational darkness, or any other form of darkness. This requires comprehensive light. This is why Christian reconstruction of every human institution is mandated by God. Christians dare not flee their comprehensive responsibilities:

"You are the salt of the earth; but if the salt loses its flavor, how shall it be seasoned? It is then good for nothing but to be thrown out and trampled underfoot by men. You are the light of the world. A city that is set on a hill cannot be hidden. Nor do they light a lamp and put it under a basket, but on a lampstand, and it

---

1. Gary North, *Inherit the Earth: Biblical Blueprints for Economics* (Ft. Worth, Texas: Dominion Press, 1987), ch. 3.
2. Gary North, *Is the World Running Down? Crisis in the Christian Worldview* (Tyler, Texas: Institute for Christian Economics, 1987), Appendix C: "Comprehensive Redemption: A Theology for Social Action."

gives light to all who are in the house. Let your light so shine before men, that they may see your good works and glorify your Father in heaven" (Matthew 5:13-16).

This includes political good works, economic good works, educational good works, and all other forms of good works. This requires comprehensive good works. For too long, Christians have tried to escape personal and institutional responsibility for performing these good works. They have foolishly assumed that there is an army of religiously neutral non-Christian experts ready and able to shoulder these vast social responsibilities, leaving Christians free to preach the gospel—a gospel of non-involvement politically. Christians have voted for the same government-financed welfare schemes that pagans have voted for. They have deferred to the decisions of government experts in every branch of government. They have accepted the great myth of this century: that the State alone is sufficiently competent to perform the works of institutional healing that God has assigned to Christians. Nowhere is this defection more obvious than in the field of international relations.

International Relations: A State Monopoly?

We must escape the definition of international relations that most humanists have adopted: inter*governmental* relations. No one has stated this with greater consistency than George Kennan, the most famous and widely read diplomat-scholar-journalist in the history of the State Department. As Solzhenitsyn says, Kennan never got anything straight concerning the intentions of the Soviet Union. Unfortunately, he certainly got into print with his errors for four decades. His errors were fundamental and continual; they began with a false definition of diplomacy:

> It is important to bear in mind that in international affairs it *is* governments, not peoples, with whom we have to deal. Many Americans do not like this. The American mind entertains a yearning for relations from people to people, unmarred by the pernicious interference of governments. Unfortunately, such a thing

is not practicable. There is no way for a people to speak in the counsels of the nations except through that political authority that has control over the inner processes of its life. This is a question of the inevitable association of responsibility with power. To conduct foreign policy means, at bottom, to shape the behavior of a nation wherever that behavior has impacts on its external environment. This is something only a government can do. For that reason, only a government can speak usefully and responsibly in foreign affairs.[3]

In other words, there was no valid American foreign policy until, say, sometime around 1889, the year arbitrarily designated by Richard W. Leopold as the transition year between old fashioned U.S. foreign policy and modern U.S. foreign policy.[4]

This is nonsense, pure but not simple. It is the attempt of State-worshipping humanists to grab international relations away from Christian missions and free market international trade. It is the assertion that civil government is the only proper institution for shaping "the behavior of a nation wherever that behavior has impacts on its external environment." It is faith in the State as savior, which alone possesses the "political authority that has control over the inner processes of its [a nation's] life."

It is imperative that individual citizens and people operating through voluntary associations recapture international diplomacy from the State and the State's self-certified foreign service professionals. If Christians refuse to do this, then we will continue to be burdened by the foreign service monopolists. We cannot expect to fight something with nothing.

Missions at Home and Abroad

Individual Christians must begin to support missionaries, foreign exchange students, the translation of Christian literature into foreign languages, and international charities that send food and

---

3. George Kennan, *Realities of American Foreign Policy* (Princeton, New Jersey: Princeton University Press, 1954), pp. 42-43.

4. Richard W. Leopold, *The Growth of American Foreign Policy: A History* (New York: Knopf, [1962] 1969), p. viii.

tools to the needy. They must also take great pains to make sure that the gospel being preached by the missionaries is not a Marxist version of liberation theology. (See my book in the Biblical Blueprints Series, *Liberating Planet Earth*.)

Christians should not join pressure groups to restrict international trade through tariffs, import quotas, and other State restraints on voluntary transactions.

Christians should not become advocates of closed borders to those who are coming here to work. Obviously, revolutionaries may accompany the immigrants, but trained revolutionaries are going to get into a free nation anyway. The borders are not that tight, and they cannot be made that tight. We are not Communist nations.

Christians should not vote for State-financed welfare programs that will pay immigrants (or anyone else) not to work. Paul's warning is clear: "If anyone will not work, neither shall he eat" (2 Thessalonians 3:10b). By voting for tax-financed welfare schemes, Christians have helped to create a closed-borders mentality. To keep out immigrants who might go on welfare (though few do), voters pressure legislatures to seal off the borders. A century ago, immigrants were welcomed, or at least tolerated, because they came to work, to serve the consumers. Socialism has led to a world of passports, visas, and immigration quotas. Voters are afraid that poor immigrants will vote themselves rich. This is the grim heritage of democratic socialism's version of the eighth commandment: "Thou shalt not steal, except by majority vote."

Christians must financially support churches that serve immigrants. This is the unique division of labor that foreign language churches can offer. Because these will normally be segregated liturgically and linguistically, no denomination will have the funds and trained pastors to meet the needs of every immigrant group. Yet the message of Acts 2 is clear: immigrants are to be taught the gospel in their own tongue until they can master English, which the first generation should not be expected to do. Thus, people of one denomination will have to accept the fact that some other denomination will become the trainer and spokesmen for particular immigrant groups. For instance, Spanish-speaking Latin American immigrants are going to be served by Roman Catholics, Pentecostals, and Baptists. Individuals must pick which church is closest to their views, and then finance that one's missions efforts or its local Spanish-speaking churches.

Foreign pen pals programs are a good idea for children. Foreign children are trying to learn English. English-speaking children can locate foreign students through a missions board and start writing.

Specific Ministries

Several ministries have "shoebox evangelism." Children put together shoeboxes filled with soap, toothpaste, small toys, and similar scarce items, and send them to a foreign missionary group or other charity. Extremely important is the photograph of the child who sends it. This photograph establishes visual contact with the recipient child.

A very good example of such a program is the one operated by Kefa Sempangi, a Ugandan pastor. He was a victim of Idi Amin's dictatorship, and suffered some harrowing experiences. He wrote a remarkable book about his experiences, *A Distant Grief.* He operates an orphanage for 8,000 children. He says that the official government estimate is that there are at least 800,000 orphans in Uganda, and this was before the AIDS epidemic broke out.

He related this story to me. After having received a shipment of shoeboxes from American children, he tried this experiment. He went before the children to tell them of some terrible people who hate Ugandans. "They are called Americans." He said the response was immediate. "No, no!" they shouted. "Americans are our friends. We have pictures of Americans. They are our friends."

I asked him what they needed in Christian literature. "Anything," he said. They have no printing press, almost no Bibles, no tracts, nothing. Uganda had been evangelized in the late-nineteenth century, but no Christian testimony remains. Idi Amin was ruthless and efficient. Now the AIDS epidemic threatens the country's very existence.

A shoebox full of soap and simple toys, a gospel of John or other Bible literature, plus a photograph of a child, can do a great deal to replace the collapsing foreign policy of the West's professional diplomats. What have they done for Uganda lately—or anywhere else? Anyone interested in sending a shoebox to Sempangi's orphanage can address the package to:

> Orphanage
> Box 4100
> Kampala, Uganda

A similar program of shoebox evangelism has been adopted by a Christian organization that sets up refugee camps for the families of the men fighting Communist tyranny in Nicaragua. The poverty of these people is desperate, yet the men risk their lives to return to the battle, something that the other refugee camps will not allow. In the camps operated by the Red Cross and other international ministries, if the husband returns to the fight, the family is evicted. The organization is:

> Friends of the Americas
> 914 N. Foster Dr.
> Baton Rouge, LA 70806

A missions organization that is truly international, and which is staffed by over 20,000 full-time missionaries, is Youth With A Mission. The unique feature of YWAM is that only about 20 percent of them are American citizens. This makes it the largest international missions organization in the world. Its missionaries are not automatically regarded as representatives of any one nation, which avoids some obvious difficulties. It has regional training centers all over the world, and a university aimed at Far Eastern students which is located in Hawaii. For information, write:

> Youth With A Mission
> 75-5851 Kuakini
> Kailua-Kona, HI 96740

Finally, there is my favorite illegal enterprise, Brother Andrew's Bible-smuggling organization. This group smuggles Bibles behind the Iron and Bamboo Curtains. Too bad the State Department doesn't. (Someone ought to start smuggling Bibles into the State Department.)

Open Doors
P.O. Box 27001
Orange, CA 92799

International Business

Christians who have business skills should consider the possibility of working in a foreign country. This usually means working at a sacrifice. Families must be uprooted. But children can learn a new language, and learn the ways of international communications. As time goes on, such skills will become increasingly valuable.

Christians may work for firms that have international operations. They may also belong to trade associations that have international contacts. Sometimes foreign universities will allow businessmen to come and teach, if their wage demands are low enough. This is an ideal opportunity to get established in a foreign nation, and to work with future business leaders. The best of these schools in Latin America is Francisco Marroquín University in Guatemala City, Guatemala, a free market business school built on the economic philosophy of F. A. Hayek.

Such employment abroad need not be permanent. It may be only for a year or two. A period of foreign service abroad should be regarded as part occupational calling and part missionary calling. Someone has to do it. Someone will do it. The Communists are doing it. When will Christians start doing it?

Retired people also have an ideal opportunity to serve abroad. They may not know a foreign language when they leave, but English is common in most countries. It is the international language of business and technology. This is a tremendous advantage for English-speaking Christians at this point in history, comparable to understanding Latin or Greek in Christ's day. But money spent in a high-intensity, one-on-one language course, such as those sold by Berlitz, is money well spent.

Let Them Come to Zion

Foreign students come by the hundreds of thousands to the nations of the West to study in our universities. They are sent home as skilled, indoctrinated humanists. We must establish evangelism programs aimed at foreign students on every campus in America.

Millions of immigrants, legal and illegal, also come to Western nations to learn how to work. The business that employs immigrants is perhaps the greatest potential missions organization in the history of Christianity. Yet little is done by businessmen to turn their businesses into a pulpit for practical Christianity. We do not have enough Christian businessmen. Those who are Christian owners of businesses seldom see themselves as missionaries to the lost, both foreign and domestic, who are employed by their companies. We are missing a great opportunity.

The Bible says over and over that the lost will see the earthly abundance that covenantal obedience to God produces, and that they will "come to Zion," just as the Queen of Sheba came to visit Solomon. But Zion has erected immigration barriers to those who wish to come. Zion's people now fear those who would come to serve as hewers of wood and drawers of water in the land of the free and the home of the brave. This is because freedom is departing and bravery has departed. The power-seeking humanists of the West are no match for the Communists. They have lost their nerve. So have the voters, who think they are no match for the work-oriented pagans who would come to work in our lands.

Yet in 1913, no Western nation had a passport system, and they opened their borders to law-abiding people who would come to work. But there were no socialist nations then, and no government welfare programs that immigrants might enroll in and benefit from the State-confiscated taxes of the more successful. Socialism has made the West tight-fisted, nasty, and hostile to honest people who only want a chance to serve consumers, mostly in low-paying menial jobs. The humanist welfare State has made economic cowards of the workers of the West, just as it has made military cowards of the leaders of the West. The answer is faith in God *and God's law*:

> "Only be strong and very courageous, that you may observe to do according to all the law which Moses My servant commanded you; do not turn from it to the right hand or to the left, that you may prosper wherever you go. This Book of the Law shall not depart from your mouth, but you shall meditate in it day and night, that you may observe to do according to all that is written in it. For then you will make your way prosperous, and then you will have good success" (Joshua 1:7-8).

Summary

There will be terror and consternation when economic disruptions, Communist terrorism, AIDS, and political extremism hit the United States and other Western nations. People will not know where to turn. At that point, Christians had better be ready with answers, both theoretical and practical. If they are unprepared, as they are today, then those who take responsibility will inherit the power, and they will not be Christians.

Christians should prepare themselves mentally for the crisis to come. They must discipline themselves today to take minimal action, so that they will have more experience later on.

International relations begins with contacts between people, not governments. It is our job to establish personal contacts now, before the crisis hits. We must do small things now to get ready to do larger things later. We start with first steps. We cannot win the whole world in one generation. But we must begin.

And we must never forget: winning the world to Christ means winning it back from the clutches of the professional diplomats. International relations begins with people, not diplomats.

12

WHAT THE STATE CAN DO

Why do the nations rage, and the people plot a vain thing? The kings of the earth set themselves, and the rulers take counsel together, against the LORD and against His Anointed, saying, "Let us break Their bonds in pieces and cast away Their cords from us." He who sits in the heavens shall laugh; the LORD shall hold them in derision (Psalm 2:1-3).

We are in a war that has been going on for a long time. The theological issues have not changed. The issue is the sovereignty of man vs. the sovereignty of God, man's covenant vs. God's covenant.

This does not mean that nothing has changed. A great deal has changed. Faces and tactics have changed; capital and technology have changed; and most important of all, time has changed. Satan is closer to the end, as are his followers. The shift from rationalism to irrationalism that the West has seen since 1965, paralleling the shift from science to occultism, indicates that we are close to the end of an era. Humanists are reverting to older, occult forms of humanism, indicating that Satan is just about out of new diversions and new visions. His followers are returning to the "old time religion"—the second-oldest religion. Such is the fate of the power religion. Its underlying faith in occultism rather than rational science has begun to manifest itself, just as C. S. Lewis said it would in his great novel, *That Hideous Strength* (1945).

Unfortunately, Christianity also slipped backward theologically and culturally at the beginning of this century.[1] American

---

1. George Marsden, *Fundamentalism and American Culture: The Shaping of Twentieth-Century Evangelicalism, 1870-1925* (New York: Oxford University Press, 1980).

Christians began a steady retreat from positions of cultural and political leadership.[2] They have returned like dogs, again and again, to the vomit of eighteenth-century natural law theory and the myth of neutrality, long after the humanists have abandoned these doctrines except as deceptive intellectual tools for confusing Christians and paralyzing them politically. They have sought political peace with their theological mortal enemies. They have preached the doctrines of permanent political pluralism, especially the academic Christians in college classrooms.[3] They have not departed from their impotence-producing ecclesiastical separatism, and in order to regain lost unity, they have adopted the humanists' late-nineteenth century doctrine of the neutral State. Christians have not yet pulled together as an explicitly, self-consciously Christian cultural, educational, economic, educational, and political force—an international force. They have sought peaceful coexistence, not through the Church, but through the leftover dregs of humanism's dying theory of permanent political pluralism. And they have done it all in the name of Jesus.

The secular world of the West has imitated the weakness of the Christians. They have not united to oppose Communism, just as the International Church has remained divided. The leaders of the West have sought peaceful coexistence with the West's mortal enemies, just as Christians have sought peaceful coexistence with their theological mortal enemies. The West has retreated from confrontations, just as Christians have retreated from confrontations. The West has shortened its time perspective, just as Christians have shortened their time perspectives. What we see, then, is that the Western humanists who fill the corridors of power have reflected the condition of the Church in their midst. As the testimony of the Church International has faded, so has the will to resist among the West's humanists.

These observations return us to the underlying theme of this

---

2. Douglas W. Frank, *Less Than Conquerors: How Evangelicals Entered the Twentieth Century* (Grand Rapids, Michigan: Eerdmans, 1986).

3. James Davison Hunter, *Evangelicalism: The Coming Generation* (Chicago: University of Chicago Press, 1987), pp. 165-80.

book: what the Church International does or fails to do will set the pattern for the West, for good or evil. We must seek reform first in the Church, not in the State. The focus on the State as the primary institution of life is the humanist myth of the age. It must not become the myth of Christian reconstruction. Thus, Christians should not expect to be able to reform the foreign policy of any nation, let alone the nations of the non-Communist West, before they reform the churches. Any proposed program of reform must recognize that the humanist world reflects the Christian world. If the Church remains blinded and impotent because of its lack of self-confidence in the power of the gospel and the Holy Spirit to transform the world for good, then the humanist West will remain weak, and initiative will pass (as it passed three generations ago) to the Communist empires, which *are* self-confident in the religion of power, even if they have lost faith in the Marxist creed.

The proposals I sketch in this chapter cannot work and will not work unless accompanied by a revival on a scale not experienced in human history. They will not work until Christians become self-conscious defenders of the crown rights of King Jesus in every area of life. We cannot seriously expect to see a Christian reconstruction of international relations in the realm of civil government until we have seen it in Church government. The underlying basis of unity must be the same in both Church and State: the death, resurrection, and ascension of Jesus Christ, the Word of God, the sacraments, and the power of the Holy Spirit. If Christians continue to de-emphasis the work of Christ, the authority of the Bible as the basis of reconstruction, and the power of the Holy Spirit in history, then they will remain for generations to come what they have been in this century: a huge joke, a laughing stock, doormats for covenant-breakers.

To put it as bluntly as possible, if Christians are too stupid to pull their children out of the government-funded, humanist school system, then they are too stupid to avoid the Gulag Archipelago. (See Robert Thoburn's book in the Biblical Blueprints Series, *The Children Trap*.)

If Christians are too gutless, spineless, and thoughtless to picket abortion clinics, then they might as well pack their bags for a one-way trip to the concentration camp, or the firing squad. The Communists are not playing around; they are playing for keeps.

Until Christians begin to take seriously Church unity, all talk about reforming foreign relations will remain speculative and hypothetical to a fault.

Until Christians recognize that the humanist leaders of humanist nations are at war with the God of the Bible, they will continue to be unsuccessful politically. They will not believe that they have been anointed by God to come before this civilization and confront it with God's covenant lawsuit, just as Jonah confronted Nineveh. They will not have the courage to do this, nor will they know how to prosecute it.

Covenant and Social Order

The Biblical covenant is the basis of social order.[4] When men break this covenant, they should expect the judgment of God. This is what Christians should expect. God's judgment has two aspects: blessing and cursing.[5] Thus, if Christians do their work faithfully, the judgments of God in history will transfer the inheritance, including capital and political power, to Christians as the lawful heirs (Proverbs 13:22b),[6] and do so relatively rapidly, perhaps within a few generations. On the other hand, if Christians continue to drift along with contemporary humanist culture, refusing to challenge it in every area of life, allowing humanists to speak in the name of all people in terms of the doctrine of permanent political pluralism, then they will find themselves under the general or common cursings that God is about to bring on humanist civilization. In such a case, it may take ten generations before the transfer of the inheritance approaches completion.

This is why Christians need to prepare themselves for the

---

4. Ray R. Sutton, *That You May Prosper: Dominion By Covenant* (Tyler, Texas: Institute for Christian Economics, 1987).

5. *Ibid.*, ch. 4.

6. *Ibid.*, ch. 5.

transfer of the inheritance. As they build up their skills, capital, and influence, they must be ready to take the reigns of power in a crisis, not through an activist *coup d'état*, but through a massive political default, such as the Roman Empire experienced in the early fourth century, A.D. Such a transfer must be like the one experienced by the Hebrews as they walked out of Egypt: their former taskmasters will load them down with spoils voluntarily (Exodus 12:35-36). This transfer is God's doing, not man's. The premature grab for power is what characterized Adam's rebellion. He was not willing to declare God's judgment against Satan and wait for God's return to bring final judgment.

Our job is to think through the fundamental Biblical principles of every area of personal responsibility, and then to begin to obey God whenever and wherever our personal talents bring us lawful responsibility. Christians will not run for Congress until they have served for a while as dogcatcher. They will work from the bottom up. Like the Israelites who were to be preceded into the land by hornets, so the Israelites could drive out their enemies year by year, and not overnight (Exodus 23:27-30), so should we plan for the transition. We must not pursue the false dream of the overnight *coup d'état*. That would merely substitute new scoundrels for old, and worse, scoundrels wrapped in the rhetoric of Biblical faith.

The visible sign of a premature "grab for the robes" would be a call for political transformation in advance of Church reformation. Christians must get first things first this time. The lure of political salvation is still very great in the minds of Christians, for they are products of the government schools, and salvation by politics and confiscated taxes is the religion of the government schools.[7]

How Bad Is the U.S. State Department?

First, there is the important question of security risks. The holes that Alger Hiss represented[8] in the late 1940's were never

---

7. R. J. Rushdoony, *The Messianic Character of American Education* (Phillipsburg, New Jersey: Presbyterian & Reformed, [1963]).

8. Allen Weinstein, *Perjury: The Hiss-Chambers Case* (New York: Knopf, 1978).

plugged. There was an attempt to do so by W. Scott McLeod, a State Department security officer in the mid-1950's. His investigations created a collapse of morale inside the Department. It was in 1954 that Henry Wriston, President of Brown University and also President of the Council of Foreign Relations, was put in charge of a committee to propose remedies for this low morale. Buried in a footnote in Prof. Pratt's textbook on U.S. foreign policy is this revealing fact: the Wriston committee recommended that McLeod be relieved of his responsibilities.[9] Here is a summary of what happened:

> During the mid-1950s, a State Department security specialist named Otto Otepka reviewed the files of all department personnel and found some kind of derogatory information on 1,943 persons, almost 20 percent of the total payroll. He told the Senate Internal Security Subcommittee years later that of the 1,943 employees, 722 "left the department for various reasons, but mostly by transfer to other agencies, before a final security determination was made." Otepka trimmed the remaining number on the list to 858 and in December 1955 sent their names to his boss, Scott McLeod, as persons to be watched because of Communist associations, homosexuality, habitual drunkenness, or mental illness.
>
> McLeod's staff reviewed the Otepka list and narrowed it down to 258 persons who were judged to be "serious" security risks. "Approximately 150 were in high-level posts where they could in one way or another influence the formulation of United States foreign policy," said William J. Gill, author of *The Ordeal of Otto Otepka*. "And fully half of these 258 serious cases were officials in either crucial Intelligence assignments or serving on top-secret committees reaching all the way up and into the National Security Council." As many as 175 of the 258 were still in important policy posts as of the mid-1960s, but Otto Otepka had been ousted from the State Department by that time and we are not aware of anyone like Otepka keeping track of security risks since then—and that was more than 20 years ago.[10]

---

9. Julius W. Pratt, *A History of United States Foreign Policy* (New York: Prentice-Hall, 1955), p. 13n.

10. *The New American* (May 11, 1987), p. 29.

Writes Richard A. Johnson, who served for a time as the executive director of the State Department's Board of Examiners for the Foreign Service: "The Wriston Committee expressed deep concern about the effects of the security program on morale and efficiency. Its first audit report of October 12, 1954, recommended that 'the security program be completed as promptly as possible.' "[11] Eventually, the program was scrapped.

Are things better today? Consider the following pair of news reports. They give a clear picture of the incomparable incompetence (or malevolence) of those who operate the professional diplomatic corps of the United States. They appeared on the same day, December 4, 1986, in the *Dallas Morning News*. The first headline reads: "New U.S. Embassy in Moscow riddled with spy devices." Here are the details:

> The new U.S. Embassy being built in Moscow is riddled with Soviet listening devices planted in its main structural components, according to several members of Congress who received secret briefings about its problems.
>
> They said an elaborate and far-reaching network of spying equipment was concealed inside precast concrete construction units, including beams, walls and floor slabs, and that the devices may be impossible to remove without wrecking the building.
>
> Construction has been stopped on the nine-story building, already three years behind schedule and more than $20 million over its projected cost, while U.S. officials decide what to do. The building is not occupied.

The building was begun in 1979. It is expected to cost anywhere from $30 million to $40 million to remove the spy devices.

Who put in the devices? The Soviets, of course. But how? Simple: a 1977 agreement allows them to supply the construction workers. Only nine U.S. government inspectors were even permitted on the job. In August of 1985, the devices were discovered, and Soviet workers were locked out of the site.

---

11. Richard A. Johnson, *The Administration of United States Foreign Policy* (Austin: University of Texas Press, 1971), p. 112. This appears in Chapter 5: " 'Wristonization,' 1954-1960."

The Embassy was supposed to be part of a multi-building complex. The original cost estimate for everything was $89 million. By late 1986, the bill had reached $192 million. But the building was needed, officials believed. The present U.S. Embassy is vulnerable to spying devices, too, because it abuts another building. In 1985, officials even found microphones in Embassy typewriters.

Who put them there? Soviet workers, of course. They staff the U.S. Embassy. No one connected with this fiasco suggests the obvious: destroy the building and start over. Obviously, no one in high places suggests what should be even more obvious: the wisdom of our breaking diplomatic relations with the government of the Soviet Union, tyrants who are the international grand masters of human rights violations, and our sworn mortal enemies. No one even suggests firing the Russian employees of the State Department. Which leads me to the second headline: "U.S. Diplomats say lack of Soviet staff hurts their work." Here are the details:

> The work of the U.S. Embassy has been more seriously impaired by the withdrawal of Soviet employees than expected, according to American diplomats.
> Five weeks after the loss of the Soviet support staff of 200, morale has plummeted, unfinished business has piled up, officers are having their tours cut short and normal strains have been exacerbated, the diplomats said.

Well, you may be saying to yourself, at least we threw the Commies out. So it took a year and a half after the microphones were discovered, but at least we threw them out. Wrong. The Soviet government pulled them out in retaliation for the U.S. government's cuts in Soviet personnel in the United States.

Do the Soviets hire U.S. workers to staff their Embassy? You've got to be joking. But they *do* put every conceivable telephone monitoring device on their Embassy and Consulate roofs, to monitor all of our unscrambled satellite-carried calls. They buy the building that is on the highest ground in the particular cities.

In March of 1987, Congressmen Richard Armey of Texas introduced legislation to get the Soviet Embassy off Mt. Alto—Mt. "High"—in Washington, D.C., the highest point in the city. The bill was so uncompromising—"Get them off, now!"—that the House Foreign Affairs Committee, under pressure from the Administration and the Speaker of the House, substituted a compromise amendment to get them off Mt. Alto within a year, but which would grant the President authority to allow the Soviets to keep their Embassy if this was seen by the President as being in the national interest . . . of the United States, that is.

The U.S. Embassy staff was outraged at the increased work load, for they had to wash cars and take out garbage. "It's just so difficult," one American said. Another complained: "We are operating on a wing and a prayer."

A wing, maybe. No prayer. That is the heart of the problem with this nation's foreign policy: no prayers.

Yet it gets worse. The man who served as U.S. ambassador to Moscow, Arthur Hartman, in 1984 sent a cable to the State Department. It attacked "right wing" Reagan extremists for using anti-spy programs to subvert U.S.-Soviet Relations. Hartman accused U.S. officials of "wrapping themselves in the mantle" of counterintelligence in order to ruin U.S.-Soviet relations through counterespionage efforts. Under the proposed plan, Hartman claimed, the Soviet embassy would have had to hire U.S. workers, which would have forced the Soviets to shut down their embassy. It would be tantamount to breaking diplomatic relations, he argued.[12]

A Clean Slate

The bugging of the U.S. embassy is an old, old story. A letter to the editor from Leonard Saffir published in the *New York Times* (April 4, 1987) is choice. It was titled: "How Porky and Bugs Outwitted the Russians."

---

12. *Washington Times*, April 13.

Listening devices in the United States embassy in Moscow are nothing new. In 1973, I traveled to the Soviet Union as chief of staff and press secretary of Senator James L. Buckley of New York. On advice from a Soviet watcher, we carried two children's writing slates, the kind where the writing disappears the moment the plastic sheet is raised.

I assigned the Bugs Bunny pad to Jim Buckley and kept the Porky Pig. On our first night at the Rossiya Hotel in Moscow, the two of us sat in our suite, sipping vodka, conversing via the kid slates. We gloated over having beaten the Soviet system.

Sure, it seems strange—two grown men, one a United States Senator—communicating in this fashion, but it was the only way.

It wasn't any better in Leningrad. When I asked one of the American officials in our consulate for a typewriter, I was told all typewriters were bugged. To beat the K.G.B., I was ushered into a safe room in the consulate's attic. Only then, as I pecked away at my Smith Corona, was I satisfied with my privacy.

What's surprising to me today is that we have gone through four administrations since my days with Jim Buckley and nothing has been done to improve the situation. Where have all the intelligence specialists been?

I still have my Porky Pig slate if Secretary Shultz wants to borrow it for his coming talks.

DISPATCH FROM MOSCOW.

This has been going on from the day that President Roosevelt recognized the Soviet Union in 1933. George Kennan notes in his memoirs that during his assignment in Moscow in the late 1930's, he and an associate hid in separate rooms all night "to see whether we could catch the individuals who, only too obviously, were installing primitive listening devices. . . ."[13] It will always go on. They do their best to place their U.S. embassy and consulate buildings on the highest point of a city in order to monitor the telephone calls of U.S. officials. They bug us in the Soviet Union, and in retaliation, we allow them to bug us in the United States.

Yet the faces seldom change. The architects of past disasters survive. Robert Rothstein is correct: ". . . the problem is not simply government by experts; it is also that the same experts, with the same perceptions, have remained constantly 'on tap' (and too frequently 'on top')."[14]

What In Principle Needs to Be Done

First and foremost, Christians in every nation must do whatever they can to get their nation out of the United Nations. This humanist internationalist organization is, as Rushdoony has called it, a religious dream—the religion of humanism. No nation that expects the blessings of Jesus Christ should be a part of this pseudo-covenant nation of nations. To take communion symbolically inside this one-world humanist organization is an abomination. While the UN is not a major threat, given its impotence, membership in it is symbolically evil. It is an organization dedicated to the proposition that the God of the Bible is irrelevant in history. It preaches the existence of universal human rights irrespective of religion. It establishes these goals in Article 1:

> 3. To achieve institutional cooperation in solving international problems of an economic, social, or humanitarian character, and in promoting and encouraging respect for human rights and for

---

13. George Kennan, *Memoirs, 1925-1950* (Boston: Little, Brown, 1967), p. 189.
14. Robert L. Rothstein, *Planning, Prediction, and Policymaking in Foreign Affairs: Theory and Practice* (Boston: Little, Brown, 1972), p. 197.

fundamental freedoms for all without distinction as to race, sex, language, or religion; and

4. To be a center for harmonizing the actions of nations in the attainment of these common ends.[15]

It asserts sovereignty over the whole world. Article 2 states:

6. The Organization shall ensure that states which are not Members of the United Nations act in accordance with these Principles so far as may be necessary for the maintenance of international peace and security.[16]

Article 2 begins with this principle: "The Organization is based on the principle of the sovereign equality of all its Members." Yet at the Yalta Conference of 1945, Roosevelt and Churchill agreed to allow the Soviet Union to have three votes in the General Assembly: the two extra votes are for the Ukrainian SSR and the Byelorussian SSR.[17] The United States pays one-third of the total UN budget, the maximum required for any nation.[18] So much for "sovereign equality."

It even requires an oath from its staff members that places the UN above all other civil government loyalties:

I solemnly swear . . . to exercise in all loyalty, discretion, and conscience the functions entrusted to me as an international civil servant of the United Nations, to discharge these functions and regulate my conduct with the interests of the United Nations only in view, and not seek or accept instructions in regard to the performance of my duties from any Government or other authority external to the Organization.[19]

---

15. Charter of the United Nations (June 26, 1945), Chapter 1, Article 1 (emphasis added). Leland M. Goodrich and Evard Hambro, *Charter of the United Nations: Commentary and Documents* (rev. ed.; Boston: World Peace Foundation, 1949), p. 584.

16. *Idem.*

17. G. Edward Griffin, *The Fearful Master: A Second Look at the United Nations* (Boston: Western Islands, 1964), p. 88.

18. *Charter*, p. 185.

19. Cited by Arkady N. Shevchenko, *Breaking With Moscow* (New York: Knopf, 1985), p. 220.

The United Nations has always served as a major spy center for the Soviet Union, for its accredited representatives possess diplomatic immunity. The highest-level Soviet spy ever to defect to the U.S. was the Under Secretary General of the UN. When he first was sent to the UN in 1966 as chief of the Security Council and Political Affairs Division of the Mission, he reports, "I had a staff of more than twenty diplomats. I soon discovered that in fact only seven were real diplomats; the remainder were KGB or GRU [military intelligence — G.N.] professionals under diplomatic cover."[20] Of course, a lot of their time was spent spying on the real Soviet diplomats.

Shevchenko says of the required loyalty oath to the UN: "Every Soviet national who takes the organization's oath must commit perjury. Before an individual's candidature is submitted by the Soviet Union to the Secretariat's Office of Personnel, that individual undertakes an obligation to do his or her best in the interests of the Soviet Union and to use his or her prospective job to achieve this purpose."[21]

It is time to get out of the UN.

The Structure of Authority

Every foreign policy official in every nation must serve solely at the pleasure of the person or agency that is constitutionally empowered with responsibility for national foreign affairs. There must be no legal restraints on hiring or firing by the head of State. In the United States, this means the President. If he wishes to retain the services of specialists, then this is his decision. National policy must be conducted by the authorized agent, with constitutionally authorized consent of the elected representatives in certain specified areas. The conduct of foreign policy, like the conduct of military affairs, must be lodged in one person. The kings of Israel and Judah conducted foreign policy as monopoly prerogatives, and the same centralization has existed ever since.

---

20. *Ibid.*, p. 131.
21. *Ibid.*, p. 221.

That such military centralization is dangerous to civil liberties in wartime is obvious, but divided command is far more dangerous. This is always recognized by everyone when the shooting begins. In peacetime, there are dangers of such foreign policy centralization, but there is no escape from this centralization. The legislatures are too diverse, their concerns too fragmented, for them to operate national foreign policy. The U.S. Constitution recognizes this, and grants to the President the authority to make treaties (with a two-thirds vote of Senators present) and to nominate ambassadors, with the majority consent of the Senate (Article II, Section 2).

The great danger here is that treaties can be regarded as equal to the U.S. Constitution, although the Constitution does not say this explicitly, and the Supreme Court has not said it. Certainly, it is widely believed by American intellectuals that treaties possess this degree of authority. This authority of treaties would place in the President's hand, if supported by two-thirds of a quorum for the Senate, the right to amend the Constitution. This would be potentially disastrous, especially when there is no requirement that the government publish all treaties in one place. It would establish rule by an elite.

A Constitutional amendment is therefore needed that will distinguish between international covenants and international alliances. A *covenant treaty* would have to be ratified as a Constitutional amendment, for it would become equal in force to the Constitution. An *alliance treaty* would be no different from any other national law: both the House and Senate would have to approve it by majority vote, and it would be subject to reversal by future legislation, and also subject to constitutional review by the highest judicial body. The President would retain the initiative in signing treaties, but always under advice and consent of both houses of Congress. The two-thirds vote of the Senate would disappear.

The inherent dangers of centralization would also be reduced by reducing the importance of national political foreign affairs. By removing restraints on trade and immigration, and by transferring authority to the private sectors—church missions, business, private charity, and private education—international relations would become the concern of the people, not the self-appointed elite. The "old boy network" that dominates Anglo-American foreign policy would have its monopolistic teeth pulled.

The legislature must be given authority to bind the President in any specific area of foreign policy. If the Congress wants the U.S. to cease a particular activity conducted by the President, it can and should do so. It can pass legislation to this effect, and then override the President's predictable veto. This has been done in the past. Presidents usually claim that such hampering legislation is unconstitutional. Even conservative constitutional scholars have argued that the President is immune to such restraints.[22] If he is, then a Constitutional amendment overturning this authority is in order. While the President should have the authority to initiate foreign policy, he must never be regarded as absolutely sovereign in this regard. The Congress, as representatives of the voters, must be able to block foreign policy moves that they do not approve. In fact, Congress *does* possess this vetoing authority under the Constitution.

This does not mean that Presidents cannot initiate moves to defend the nation. But Congress can veto these moves, simply by *refusing to authorize further funding*. This has long been recognized. "The matter arose initially in 1796 in connection with the Jay Treaty, certain provisions of which required appropriations to carry them into effect. In view of the third clause of Article I, Sect. 9, which says that 'no money shall be drawn from the Treasury, but in Consequence of Appropriations made by law . . .', it seems to have been universally conceded that Congress must be applied to if the treaty provisions were to be executed."[23] Congressman James Madison led the fight against this "automatic appropriations" argument of the Jay Treaty's supporters, despite the

---

22. Robert F. Turner, *The War Powers Resolution: Its Implementation in Theory and Practice* (Philadelphia: Foreign Policy Research Institute, 1983).

23. *The Constitution of the United States of America: Analysis and Interpretation*, Congressional Research Service, Library of Congress (Washington, D.C.: Government Printing Office, 1973), p. 487.

treaty's ratification by the Senate. The House offered Madison's resolution when it voted the money required by the treaty:

> . . . when a treaty stipulates regulations on any of the subjects submitted by the Constitution to the power of Congress, it must depend for its execution as to such stipulations on a law or laws to be passed by Congress, and it is the constitutional right and duty of the House of Representatives in all such cases to deliberate on the expediency or inexpediency of carrying such treaty into effect, and to determine and act thereon as in their judgment may be most conducive to the public good.[24]

The study goes on to say that "This early precedent with regard to appropriations has apparently been uniformly adhered to."[25] However, because Congress has found itself incapable of controlling spending in this century, it has lost control of the national government. It has therefore lost its ability to restrict Presidential power. Centralization has continued as a result. Centralization is the inevitable result of big spending by the nation-state.

What is desperately needed is a Constitutional provision to distinguish between a state of war and defensive operations against a formally undeclared war against the nation. Peace must not be defined as a condition of undeclared hostilities. The military encirclement of the United States by the Soviet Union is an act of war, declared by Lenin and all his successors. But because the Soviets have not launched a nuclear first strike against the U.S., the government pretends that we are not in fact losing a comprehensive war, including a military war. Trading with the enemy goes on. The President should have the authority to suspend diplomatic relations, including trade relations, with any nation that he deems as a military threat to the U.S., subject to the approval of Congress, meaning a two-thirds vote of both houses of Congress— what it would take to override his veto. In fact, he probably possesses this authority now, and it should be exercised against the USSR and Nicaragua, just as it has been exercised against Cuba.

---

24. *Ibid.*, p. 488. A similar resolution was adopted by the House in 1871.
25. *Idem.*

I am not calling for wholesale revisions of the Constitution today. These changes must be implemented only after a full-scale revival and the clear-cut political triumph of Christians as self-conscious Christian voters. Attempting to amend the Constitution before you have the votes is suicidal; this would play into the hands of the humanist left wing. Just as internationalism prior to international revival is extremely dangerous, so is attempting any Constitutional amendment nationally before national revival. This would be a top-down political transformation, something quite foreign to Christian social theory.[26] It puts the cart before the horse. The religious transformation must precede the political transformation; the political transformation must precede the Constitutional transformation.

We must therefore content ourselves for the present with small steps.

First Steps

The fundamental principle of the covenant is the transcendence of God. He is in control of the nations. Thus, there is no cause for alarm. If the foreign policy elite were all to resign tomorrow, the nation could still carry on.

Our strategy as Christians must initially be personal, as outlined in Chapter Eleven. We cannot beat something with nothing. If we maintain that international relations means personal relations, and economic relations, and missions, then we must build these up as we do our best to tear down the statist monopoly of modern diplomacy. This will take time, skill, patience, and a lot of money. If Christians are not faithful in this regard, then we can expect a God-imposed crisis to speed up the process of transition.

---

26. On this point, I am in complete disagreement with James Jordan's recommended program of self-conscious elitism in social and political transformation, which he calls a top-down system, despite its tendency toward "impersonal bureaucracies" and the obvious anti-evangelism attitude fostered by such an elitist outlook, which he admits has been the result historically. "Elites seldom feel any need to evangelize." Precisely! See Jordan, *The Sociology of the Church* (Tyler, Texas: Geneva Ministries, 1987), pp. 17-22.

Publishing the Files

If Christians should begin to capture political power, they will have to call the State Department to full accountability. All treaties should be published in one set of documents with comprehensive documentation. They should be put on laser disk, with a computer program to search that disk. The State Department has always resisted the perfectly reasonable demand that a complete published set of international covenants be made available to Congress, let alone the general public. What Bryton Barron complained about a generation ago is still a problem: "With respect to the first category of treaty information, it is unfortunate that there is no convenient collection of United States treaty texts which is complete. The Department of State has never provided the country with such a collection. Only by piecing together the thousands of separate prints of treaties and agreements that have been brought into force through the years, many now out of print, scattered in several series, and confusingly numbered, can you hope to have anything like a complete collection. Probably not more than a dozen individuals or libraries in the country have attempted so difficult a task."[27]

There should be no significant time lapse between the signing of any agreement and its publication. The *Congressional Record* is typeset, printed, and delivered to each Congressman's office overnight. Yet it takes decades to get treaties and other State Department documents into print.

The State Department should have no top secret status for any document older than two years old, unless initialed by the President of the United States or the Secretary of State. This means that no top secret document older than two years would remain inside the State Department unless initialed by the President or the Secretary of State. If such clearance is sought by an official in the Department for any other document, then the document would be transferred to an appropriate military service or to the

---

27. Bryton Barron, *Inside the State Department: A Candid Appraisal of the Bureaucracy* (New York: Reflection Book, Comet Press, 1956), pp. 112-13.

FBI. The other agency would be responsible for classifying it or not. There should be a tracer on every such document. Some general or admiral would become responsible for improper withholding of data, should it be shown to be improper. His career for improper classification of documents would be on the line. This way, he would not be tempted to classify a document as top secret just because some bureaucrat in the State Department wants to cover his own flanks. A military officer is directly under the President and other officers. If a piece of paper is vital to the nation's security, let the military or the FBI be its protector. The crucial requirement is that no bureaucrat within the State Department should be allowed to cover up the secret deals made by the State Department.

It takes 25 years for many documents to be published. Some never are published. Some are published in edited versions. The Yalta Conference papers are the best example. This quest for secrecy is a bureaucratic religion. It is the breeding ground of conspiracy, and international conspiracy at that. Teams of editors from outside the Department should be given access to most files immediately, with classified files to be made public or transferred to another agency within six months. Any Foreign Service Officer who balks at opening the files is demoted or fired. He can become a third-level clerk in the embassy in Chad.

There is no doubt that there is an available pressure group that would back such a move: historians. Conservative, libertarian, and Marxist historians all would like to get their hands on these files. Let them. Come one, come all: hurry, hurry, hurry, get on board every historian's dream of a lifetime, namely, access to documents never before seen, and which will make lifetime reputations for those fortunate historians who get access to them first. Offer access to foreign historians, too.

One requirement would be made: a photocopy of every cited document would have to be made, and the author would be required to pay for a microfiche of these documents. This would cost a couple of hundred dollars. The microfiche cards would be placed on file in the State Department and the Library of Congress, so that critics could come in and check out the context of every citation. This will increase the level of controversy, and therefore increase the likelihood that even more State Department errors and skulduggery will come to light.

Let the journalists in on this bonanza. Then any attempt to block access will get a proper roasting. "Bureaucratic intransigence!" "Don't deny freedom of the press!"

Naturally, photocopy machines will be placed in every square inch of available space. Charge enough to make a profit. The money raised in this fashion would be used to put documents on microfiche and laser disks.

And then the final blow. Offer a reward to any State Department employee who can offer evidence proving that a division chief or someone acting in his name has tampered with the files or has deliberately delayed publication. Offer the whistle-blower a reward of up to $100,000, with none under $10,000, plus a bonus of one percent of the transgressing division's budget for this year. Then dock the offending division the award money and the one percent bonus payment. This way, the easiest way for some Civil Service employee to make a bundle of needed extra money will be to snoop around.

A market for whistles to blow will develop as soon as the first $100,000 reward is paid to an employee. An employee in one division will seek out opportunities to exchange evidence of tampering in his division for evidence of tampering in another department. Both employees get rewarded this way.

Where will they spend all their extra time, plus a lot of time that is not extra time? They will spend it snooping in the secret affairs of other divisions. Instead of spying for the Russians, they will spy on each other. No one will trust anyone.

This will destroy morale, destroy careers, create envy, and introduce well-deserved paranoia into everyone's working environment. In other words, this is just what the State Department has needed since at least 1941, and probably a decade earlier.

Budget Cuts and Retirement

The budget for the State Department must be cut. Only the historical records division will avoid the cuts, and only as long as it stays on schedule in the release of documents to scholars, Congressmen, and the Government Printing Office. The staff, including the Foreign Service Officers, must be cut by at least 50 percent within two years. This may be too slow. Everyone over the age of 55 would be allowed to retire early—what the liberals did to the FBI to weed out agents who came up through the ranks during the J. Edgar Hoover era. Anyone who balks gets that coveted assignment in Chad.

There is no legitimate excuse for employing 24,000 people. It is bureaucracy run wild.

All Civil Service protection or other protection from firing would be removed. Some protection against arbitrary firing could be established, such as severance payments of half the annual salary for anyone with over three years of continuous service. But there would be no assured, lifetime employment. It would be run like a business.

Let them go to the Civil Service Commission to complain. Let them form a union. Pray that they strike. Nothing would serve the interests of this nation better than a successful strike of all State Department employees.

Shut it down. Wait. Then go out and hire the replacement staff from the business community. Forget about a Foreign Service examination. Just make sure every person hired is fluent in the foreign language of his choice. (It is interesting that the Wriston Committee recommended in 1954 that the foreign language examination requirement be dropped for Foreign Service applicants, which the State Department did in 1955.)[28] Require applicants to take an exam in the culture of the nation in question, with the selection of textbooks and the responsibility for writing and grading the exams placed entirely in the hands of retired businessmen and missionaries who have come back from the nation in question, plus suggested readings from the diplomats of that nation.

Finally, we need at least two separate and competing offices to check the security risk status of Department employees. By hav-

---

28. Johnson, *Administration of U.S. Foreign Policy*, p. 105.

ing two competing offices, there will be less likelihood of successful "stonewalling" by bureaucrats. The two security check programs will be in competition.

The Foreign Service Examinations

In order to reduce the power of the primary screening tool in the selection of the foreign policy bureaucracy—the Foreign Service examinations, written and oral—the President must unilaterally establish a new rule by Executive Order: any required written examination would have to be taken every five years by all existing senior Foreign Service personnel. Thus, the ability of those who have already passed the exam to reduce the number of competitors by making future exams more difficult would disappear. If passing the exam really is vital for effective Foreign Service, then any Foreign Service expert who cannot pass the same exam given to applicants must be regarded as incompetent, and would have to be fired until he can pass the exam. (He would also lose his seniority in the interim.) Under this rule, we would learn, much to our "amazement," that Foreign Service experts now on the government payroll would discover almost overnight that the written exam really is not that important, and can safely be dropped.

Counter-Attack

A whole series of steps is absolutely necessary. First, we must break diplomatic relations with every Communist country. This symbolically announces that we regard them as declared enemies of the West, and not fit to place their buildings on our soil. An embassy building is legally foreign territory in a nation; they should not have access to any such sanctuary.

This will serve notice to captive peoples that the United States has had enough. It will also indicate to Communist leaders that we have at last begun to take seriously their declarations of perpetual war against the West.

Broadcasting

The next step would be to begin a coordinated counter-propaganda effort. Propaganda is a pejorative word used to describe our enemies' public announcements. Every nation uses it. The question is: Is it true? The Soviet Union uses lies—disinformation[29]—as no other nation in history has used them. It is a nation based on lies. The West must counter lies with truth, and then tell the truth daily about the Soviet Union.

Broadcast more shows into the Soviet Union. Forget about jazz broadcasts, except as lures to increase the propaganda ratings. Play suppressed classical Russian music. News broadcasts, yes. Even news unfavorable to the West. True news, in other words. We can afford to tell the truth. The Soviets cannot deal with truth.

News on Soviet deaths in Afghanistan should be daily offerings —or whatever other up-to-the-minute embarrassment that would create resentment of the Soviet people against their leaders.

Offer history lessons on the Russian past. Read literature from the pre-Bolshevik era. Read Solzhenitsyn's novels. Read all three volumes of *The Gulag Archipelago*. Read *samizdat* literature: the underground typewritten literature written by Russians.

Then focus on the Soviet Union's suppressed nationalities. Read their suppressed national literature, stressing religious history and any heroes who fought for liberty against Soviet tyranny. Let representatives of the various emigré groups select the literature and supply the announcers.

Let Russian Orthodox Church services be broadcast around the clock, or close to it. Let Bible readings be beamed in around the clock.

Let radio broadcasts into Islamic nations give the death totals in Afghanistan day by day. "The Soviets are killing Muslims" should be the full-time refrain of U.S. broadcasts into the Middle East, day after day. Have interviews with the victims of Soviet aggression.

---

29. Richard H. Shultz and Roy Godson, *Dezinformatsia: Active Measures in Soviet Strategy* (New York: Pergamon-Brassey's, 1984).

Crucial to this operation is a complete housecleaning of every present official in charge of broadcasting news into the Soviet Union. Fire them, transfer them, retire them, or even keep them on the payroll as consultants—and never, ever consult them. Keep the foreign language announcers, if they are known to have a good audience. Everyone else must be removed from any area of responsibility, for they are the appointees of today's liberal humanist elite. They will torpedo the shift to offensive broadcasting. Get them out.

New technologies exist for beaming radio broadcasts into Communist nations. These should be financed and used.

Democratic humanism suffers from a major propaganda problem: there is no universal consensus of the voters concerning what is most positive about the West. To broadcast positive features of Western religious life is anathema to humanists. Yet you can't fight something with nothing. You can't successfully fight hardcore humanism with soft-core humanism.

This is why Christians must pioneer the propaganda effort privately until the West returns to the covenantal faith that made the West possible in the first place. Let the President go on television and call for tax-deductible donations to Christian-oriented radio broadcasting beamed into the Soviet Union. Let him promote Brother Andrew's Open Doors program of smuggling in Bibles.

By all means, he should focus on all aspects of religious persecution. He should publicly call attention to the desire of Jews to emigrate.

The Soviet Union must be embarrassed at every point.

Creating Internal Disruptions

No more trading with the enemy, unless approved by the military high command, and unless they allow missionaries to enter the country and hand out Bibles and literature. No more taxpayer-guaranteed loans at below-market interest rates. No private loans to Communist nations. A war is in progress.

No more summit conferences between the President and

Communist leaders. No more publicized meetings between high Western officials and high Soviet officials. Would Churchill have posed with Hitler for photographs in 1942? "Don't you know there's a war on?"

Sanctuary should be given to defectors. The Chinese government on Taiwan offers a fortune in gold to any pilot who defects by flying his jet to Taiwan. So should Korea. So should Japan.

Summary

George Washington ran the Department of State with six people. All of them were loyal to the U.S. That was a long time ago.

Modern foreign policy has become humanistic, bureaucratic, secretive, and elitist. It has also become internationalist. It seeks to accommodate the growth of the Soviet Union, and most important, to confuse Americans about why the diplomats are so accommodating.

The goal of Christian international relations should be to transfer most of these activities to realms outside the direct authority of the State. It is to substitute missions and business for diplomacy in the vast majority of cases.

The way to achieve this goal is to transform the State Department. This can be done through a program of systematic budget cuts, the enforced publishing of documents, rewards and bounties for those who will expose Department cover-ups, transfers, salary cuts, early retirement, the establishment of new hiring standards — linguistic fluency rather than bureaucratic examinations — and the introduction of careful security checks.

The goal is to shrink the State Department back to its pre-1933 size, though perhaps with some minimal elasticity because of the greater number of nations in the world today. Those Foreign Service Officers needing better information abroad could ask local businessmen and missionaries.

BIBLIOGRAPHY

Abraham, Larry. *Call It Conspiracy*. Seattle, Washington: Double A Publications, 1985.

Allen, Gary. *Say "No!" to the New World Order*. Seal Beach, California: Concord Press, 1987.

Barron, Bryton. *Inside the State Department: A Candid Appraisal of the Bureaucracy*. New York: Reflection Book, Comet Press, 1956.

Brown, Anthony Cave and MacDonald, Charles B. *On a Field of Red: The Communist International and the Coming of World War II*. New York: Putnam's, 1981.

Bouscaren, Anthony Trawick. *Soviet Foreign Policy: A Pattern of Persistence*. New York: Fordham University Press, 1962.

Burnham, James. *The Suicide of the West: An Essay on the Meaning and Destiny of Liberalism*. New York: John Day, 1964.

Cohen, Warren. *The American Revisionists: The Lessons of Intervention in World War I*. Chicago: University of Chicago Press, 1967.

Dawson, Christopher. *The Judgment of the Nations*. New York: Sheed and Ward, 1942.

Department of State. *Freedom From War: The United States Program for General and Complete Disarmament in a Peaceful World*. Department of State Publication 7277, Disarmament Series 5, Office of Public Services, Bureau of Public Affairs (Sept. 1961).

Doenecke, Justus D. *The Literature of Isolationism: A Guide to Non-Interventionist Scholarship, 1930-1972*. Colorado Springs, Colorado: Ralph Myles, Publisher, 1972.

311

_____. *Not to the Swift: The Old Isolationists in the Cold War Era*. Lewisburg, Pennsylvania: Bucknell University Press, 1979.

Finder, Joseph. *Red Carpet*. Ft. Worth, Texas: American Bureau of Economic Research, (1983) 1987.

Gaddis, John Lewis. *The United States and the Origins of the Cold War*. New York: Columbia University Press, 1972.

Halberstam, David. *The Best and the Brightest*. New York: Random House, 1972.

Huddleson, Sisley. *Popular Diplomacy and War*. Rindge, New Hampshire: Richard R. Smith Publisher, 1954.

Isaacson, Walter and Thomas, Evan. *The Wise Men: Six Friends and the World They Made*. New York: Simon & Schuster, 1986.

Kubek, Anthony. *How the Far East Was Lost: American Policy and the Creation of Communist China, 1941-1949*. Chicago: Regnery, 1963.

Levinson, Charles. *Vodka Cola*. London: Gordon & Cremonesi, 1978.

Liggio, Leonard P. and Martin, James J. *Watershed of Empire: Essays on New Deal Foreign Policy*. Colorado Springs, Colorado: Ralph Myles, Publisher, 1976.

Manly, Chesly. *The UN Record: Ten Fateful Years for America*. Chicago: Regnery, 1955.

Martin, James J. *American Liberalism and World Politics, 1931-1941: Liberalism's Press and Spokesmen on the Road Back to War Between Mukden and Pearl Harbor*. 2 vols. New York: Devin-Adair, 1964.

Molnar, Thomas. *The Two Faces of American Foreign Policy*. Indianapolis, Indiana: Bobbs-Merrill, 1962.

North, Gary. *Conspiracy: A Biblical View*. Ft. Worth, Texas: Dominion Press, 1986.

_____. "World War II Revisionism & Vietnam." *Reason* (Feb. 1976), pp. 34-39.

Osgood, Robert E. *Ideals and Self-Interest in American Foreign Relations: The Great Transformation of the Twentieth Century*. Chicago: University of Chicago Press, 1953.

Pipes, Richard. *Survival Is Not Enough: Soviet Realities and America's Future*. New York: Simon & Schuster, 1985.

Quigley, Carroll. *The Anglo-American Establishment*. New York: Books in Focus, 1981.

_____. *Tragedy and Hope: A History of the World in Our Time*. New York: Macmillan, 1966.

Radosh, Ronald. *Prophets on the Right: Profiles of Conservative Critics of American Globalism*. New York: Simon & Schuster, 1975.

Revel, Jean François. *How Democracies Perish*. Garden City, New York: Doubleday, 1984.

Rockefeller Panel Reports. *Prospect for America*. Garden City, New York: Doubleday, 1961.

Rushdoony, Rousas J. *The Biblical Philosophy of History*. Phillipsburg, New Jersey: Presbyterian & Reformed, (1969) 1979.

_____. *The One and the Many: Studies in the Philosophy of Order and Ultimacy*. Fairfax, Virginia: Thoburn Press, (1971) 1978.

_____. *The Nature of the American System*. Fairfax, Virginia: Thoburn Press, (1965) 1978.

Scott, Otto. *The Other End of the Lifeboat*. Part 1. Chicago: Regnery, 1985.

Smoot, Dan. *The Invisible Government*. Boston: Western Islands, (1962) 1977.

Solzhenitsyn, Aleksandr. "Misconceptions about Russia Are a Threat to America." *Foreign Affairs*, Vol. 58 (Spring 1980), pp. 797-834.

_____. *Solzhenitsyn at Harvard*. Washington, D.C.: Ethics and Public Policy Center, 1980.

_____. *Solzhenitsyn: The Voice of Freedom*. Washington, D.C.: American Federation of Labor and Congress of Industrial Organizations, 1975.

Sutton, Antony. *The Best Enemy Money Can Buy*. Billings, Montana: Liberty House, 1986.

_____. *Wall Street and the Bolshevik Revolution.* New Rochelle, New York: Arlington House, 1974.

_____. *Western Technology and Soviet Economic Development, 1917-1965.* 3 vols. Stanford, California: Hoover Institution Press, 1968-73.

SCRIPTURE INDEX

OLD TESTAMENT

315

NEW TESTAMENT

SUBJECT INDEX

Abel, 45
abortion, xii, 268
Abram, 197, 209
acid rain, 50
accountability, 131
Acheson, Dean, 239
Adam
  covenant &, 83, 93
  fall of, 83
  God's claims on, 24
  heirs of, 45
  judge, 136
  king, 47
  tested God, 200-1
Adams, John Quincy, 187
adoption, 45, 49, 146, 230
African National Congress, 268
AIDS, 235, 242, 249, 284
Afghanistan, 66, 104, 241
Alcoholics Anonymous, 7-8
alliances
  peace, 159
  confusing, 111
  covenants and, 197-216
  entangling, 11
  temporary, 14, 208
ambassadors
  allegiance of, 131
  Christ's, 164-67, 233
  Christians as, 46, 233
  one-third, two-thirds, 134
  model, 158
  official, 170-71
  Christians as reconcilers, 233
  witnesses, 157-59
  see also missionaries

American Legion, 57
American Revolution, 54
anarchy, 74, 169
antinomianism, 86
appeals, 61
appeasement, 246
ark of covenant, 159
Armey, Richard, 293
arms control, 127-29
Assyria, 28, 218
Assyrians, 237
Atlantic community, 168
Aurelius, 89

banking crisis, 223-27
baptism, 159-64
Barron, Bryton, 16, 302
battlefield, 141
Bauer, P. T., 192, 220-21
Beelzebub, 91, 209
Benjamin (tribe), 58-59
Bible
  authoritative, 6
  answers to life, 7
  complex, 262
  legal standard, 35
  nation-state &, 34
  oath in court, 163
  standard of God's judgment, 6
  Western Civilization, 108
Biblical law
  covenant &, 93
  creation, 176
  jurisdiction, 82
  kingdom, 81

319

WHAT ARE BIBLICAL BLUEPRINTS?
by Gary North

How many times have you heard this one?

"The Bible isn't a textbook of . . ."

You've heard it about as many times as you've heard this one:

"The Bible doesn't provide blueprints for . . ."

The odd fact is that some of the people who assure you of this are Christians. Nevertheless, if you ask them, "Does the Bible have answers for the problems of life?" you'll get an unqualified "yes" for an answer.

Question: If the Bible isn't a textbook, and if it doesn't provide blueprints, then just how, specifically and concretely, does it provide answers for life's problems? Either it answers real-life problems, or it doesn't.

In short: *Does the Bible make a difference?*

Let's put it another way. If a mass revival at last hits this nation, and if millions of people are regenerated by God's grace through faith in the saving work of Jesus Christ at Calvary, will this change be visible in the way the new converts run their lives? Will their politics change, their business dealings change, their families change, their family budgets change, and their church membership change?

In short: Will conversion make a visible difference in our personal lives? If not, why not?

Second, two or three years later, will Congress be voting for a different kind of defense policy, foreign relations policy, environmental policy, immigration policy, monetary policy, and so forth?

335

Will the Federal budget change? If not, why not?

In short: Will conversion to Christ make a visible difference in our civilization? If not, why not?

The Great Commission

What the Biblical Blueprints Series is attempting to do is to outline what some of that visible difference in our culture ought to be. The authors are attempting to set forth, in clear language, *fundamental Biblical principles* in numerous specific areas of life. The authors are not content to speak in vague generalities. These books not only set forth explicit principles that are found in the Bible and derived from the Bible, they also offer specific practical suggestions about what things need to be changed, and how Christians can begin programs that will produce these many changes.

The authors see the task of American Christians just as the Puritans who came to North America in the 1630's saw their task: *to establish a city on a hill* (Matthew 5:14). The authors want to see a Biblical reconstruction of the United States, so that it can serve as an example to be followed all over the world. They believe that God's principles are tools of evangelism, to bring the nations to Christ. The Bible promises us that these principles will produce such good fruit that the whole world will marvel (Deuteronomy 4:5-8). When nations begin to marvel, they will begin to soften to the message of the gospel. What the authors are calling for is *comprehensive revival* — a revival that will transform everything on earth.

In other words, the authors are calling Christians to obey God and take up the Great Commission: to *disciple* (discipline) all the nations of the earth (Matthew 28:19).

What each author argues is that there are God-required principles of thought and practice in areas that some people today believe to be outside the area of "religion." What Christians should know by now is that *nothing* lies outside religion. God is judging all of our thoughts and acts, judging our institutions, and working through human history to bring this world to a final judgment.

We present the case that God offers *comprehensive salvation* — regeneration, healing, restoration, and the obligation of total social reconstruction — because the world is in *comprehensive sin*.

To judge the world it is obvious that God has to have standards. If there were no absolute standards, there could be no earthly judgment, and no final judgment because men could not be held accountable.

(Warning: these next few paragraphs are very important. They are the base of the entire Blueprints series. It is important that you understand my reasoning. I really believe that if you understand it, you will agree with it.)

To argue that God's standards don't apply to everything is to argue that sin hasn't affected and infected everything. To argue that God's Word doesn't give us a revelation of God's requirements for us is to argue that we are flying blind as Christians. It is to argue that there are *zones of moral neutrality* that God will not judge, either today or at the day of judgment, because these zones somehow are *outside His jurisdiction*. In short, "no law-no jurisdiction."

But if God *does* have jurisdiction over the whole universe, which is what every Christian believes, then there must be universal standards by which God executes judgment. The authors of this series argue for God's *comprehensive judgment*, and we declare His *comprehensive salvation*. We therefore are presenting a few of His *comprehensive blueprints*.

The Concept of Blueprints

An architectural blueprint gives us the structural requirements of a building. A blueprint isn't intended to tell the owner where to put the furniture or what color to paint the rooms. A blueprint does place limits on where the furniture and appliances should be put — laundry here, kitchen there, etc. — but it doesn't take away our personal options based on personal taste. A blueprint just specifies what must be done during construction for the building to do its job and to survive the test of time. It gives direction to the contractor. Nobody wants to be on the twelfth floor of a building that collapses.

Today, we are unquestionably on the twelfth floor, and maybe even the fiftieth. Most of today's "buildings" (institutions) were designed by humanists, for use by humanists, but paid for mostly by Christians (investments, donations, and taxes). These "buildings" aren't safe. Christians (and a lot of non-Christians) now are hearing the creaking and groaning of these tottering buildings. Millions of people have now concluded that it's time to: (1) call in a totally new team of foundation and structural specialists to begin a complete renovation, or (2) hire the original contractors to make at least temporary structural modifications until we can all move to safer quarters, or (3) call for an emergency helicopter team because time has just about run out, and the elevators aren't safe either.

The writers of this series believe that the first option is the wise one: Christians need to rebuild the foundations, using the Bible as their guide. This view is ignored by those who still hope and pray for the third approach: God's helicopter escape. Finally, those who have faith in minor structural repairs don't tell us what or where these hoped-for safe quarters are, or how humanist contractors are going to build them any safer next time.

Why is it that some Christians say that God hasn't drawn up any blueprints? If God doesn't give us blueprints, then who does? If God doesn't set the permanent standards, then who does? If God hasn't any standards to judge men by, then who judges man?

The humanists' answer is inescapable: *man* does — autonomous, design-it-yourself, do-it-yourself man. Christians call this man-glorifying religion the religion of humanism. It is amazing how many Christians until quite recently have believed humanism's first doctrinal point, namely, that God has not established permanent blueprints for man and man's institutions. Christians who hold such a view of God's law serve as *humanism's chaplains*.

Men are God's appointed "contractors." We were never supposed to draw up the blueprints, but we *are* supposed to execute them, in history and then after the resurrection. Men have been given dominion on the earth to subdue it for God's glory. "So God created man in His own image; in the image of God He created him; male and female He created them. Then God blessed them, and God said to them, 'Be fruitful and multiply; fill the earth and subdue it; have dominion over the fish of the sea, over the birds of the air, and over every living thing that moves on the earth'" (Genesis 1:27-28).

Christians about a century ago decided that God never gave them the responsibility to do any building (except for churches). That was just what the humanists had been waiting for. They immediately stepped in, took over the job of contractor ("Someone has to do it!"), and then announced that they would also be in charge of drawing up the blueprints. We can see the results of a similar assertion in Genesis, chapter 11: the tower of Babel. Do you remember God's response to that particular humanistic public works project?

Never Be Embarrassed By the Bible

This sounds simple enough. Why should Christians be embarrassed by the Bible? But they *are* embarrassed . . . millions of them. The humanists have probably done more to slow down the spread of the gospel by convincing Christians to be embarrassed by the Bible than by any other strategy they have adopted.

Test your own thinking. Answer this question: "Is God mostly a God of love or mostly a God of wrath?" Think about it before you answer.

It's a trick question. The Biblical answer is: "God is equally a God of love and a God of wrath." But Christians these days will generally answer almost automatically, "God is mostly a God of love, not wrath."

Now in their hearts, they know this answer can't be true. God sent His Son to the cross to die. His own Son! That's how much God hates sin. That's wrath with a capital "W."

But why did He do it? Because He loves His Son, and those who follow His Son. So, you just can't talk about the wrath of God without talking about the love of God, and vice versa. The cross is the best proof we have: God is both wrathful and loving. Without the fires of hell as the reason for the cross, the agony of Jesus Christ on the cross was a mistake, a case of drastic overkill.

What about heaven and hell? We know from John's vision of the day of judgment, "Death and Hades [hell] were cast into the lake of fire. This is the second death. And anyone not found written in the Book of Life was cast into the lake of fire" (Revelation 20:14-15).

Those whose names are in the Book of Life spend eternity with God in their perfect, sin-free, resurrected bodies. The Bible calls this the New Heaven and the New Earth.

Now, which is more eternal, the lake of fire, or the New Heaven and the New Earth? Obviously, they are both eternal. So, God's wrath is equally ultimate with His love throughout eternity. *Christians all admit this*, but sometimes only under extreme pressure. And that is precisely the problem.

For over a hundred years, theological liberals have blathered on and on about the love of God. But when you ask them, "What about hell?" they start dancing verbally. If you press them, they eventually deny the existence of eternal judgment. We *must* understand: they have no doctrine of the total love of God because they have no doctrine of the total wrath of God. They can't really understand what it is that God in His grace offers us in Christ because they refuse to admit what eternal judgment tells us about the character of God.

The doctrine of eternal fiery judgment is by far the most unacceptable doctrine in the Bible, as far as hell-bound humanists are concerned. They can't believe that Christians can believe in such a horror. But we do. We must. This belief is the foundation of Christian evangelism. It is the motivation for Christian foreign missions. We shouldn't be surprised that the God-haters would like us to drop this doctrine. When Christians believe it, they make too much trouble for God's enemies.

So if we believe in this doctrine, the doctrine above all others that ought to embarrass us before humanists, then why do we start to squirm when God-hating people ask us: "Well, what kind of God would require the death penalty? What kind of God would send a plague (or other physical judgment) on people, the way He sent one on the Israelites, killing 70,000 of them, even though they had done nothing wrong, just because David had conducted a military census in peacetime (2 Samuel 24:10-16)? What kind of God sends AIDS?" The proper answer: "The God of the Bible, *my* God."

Compared to the doctrine of eternal punishment, what is some two-bit judgment like a plague? Compared to eternal screaming agony in the lake of fire, without hope of escape, what is the death penalty? The liberals try to embarrass us about these earthly "down payments" on God's final judgment because they want to rid the world of the idea of final judgment. So they insult the character of God, and also the character of Christians, by sneering at the Bible's account of who God is, what He has done in history, and what He requires from men.

Are you tired of their sneering? I know I am.

Nothing in the Bible should be an embarrassment to any Christian. We may not know for certain precisely how some Biblical truth or historic event should be properly applied in our day, but every historic record, law, announcement, prophecy, judgment, and warning in the Bible is the very Word of God, and is not to be flinched at by anyone who calls himself by Christ's name.

We must never doubt that whatever God did in the Old Testament era, the Second Person of the Trinity also did. God's counsel and judgments are not divided. We must be careful not to regard Jesus Christ as a sort of "unindicted co-conspirator" when we read the Old Testament. "For whoever is ashamed of Me and My words in this adulterous and sinful generation, of him the Son of Man also will be ashamed when He comes in the glory of His Father with the holy angels" (Mark 8:38).

My point here is simple. If we as Christians can accept what is a very hard principle of the Bible, that Christ was a blood sacrifice for our individual sins, then we shouldn't flinch at accepting any of the rest of God's principles. As we joyfully accepted His salvation, so we must joyfully embrace all of His principles that affect any and every area of our lives.

The Whole Bible

When, in a court of law, the witness puts his hand on the Bible and swears to tell the truth, the whole truth, and nothing but the truth, so help him God, he thereby swears on the Word of God — the *whole* Word of God, and *nothing but* the Word of God. The Bible is a unit. It's a "package deal." The New Testament doesn't overturn the Old Testament; it's a *commentary* on the Old Testament. It tells us how to use the Old Testament properly in the period after the death and resurrection of Israel's messiah, God's Son.

Jesus said: "Do not think that I came to destroy the Law or the Prophets. I did not come to destroy but to fulfill. For assuredly, I say to you, till heaven and earth pass away, one jot or one tittle will by no means pass from the law till all is fulfilled. Whoever therefore breaks one of the least of these commandments, and teaches men to do so, shall be called least in the kingdom of heaven; but whoever does and teaches them, he shall be called great in the kingdom of heaven" (Matthew 5:17-19). The Old Testament isn't a discarded first draft of God's Word. It isn't "God's Word emeritus."

Dominion Christianity teaches that there are four covenants under God, meaning four kinds of *vows* under God: personal (individual), and the three institutional covenants: ecclesiastical (the church), civil (governments), and family. All other human institutions (business, educational, charitable, etc.) are to one degree or other under the jurisdiction of these four covenants. No single covenant is absolute; therefore, no single institution is all-powerful. Thus, Christian liberty is *liberty under God and God's law.*

Christianity therefore teaches pluralism, but a very special kind of pluralism: plural institutions under God's comprehensive law. It does not teach a pluralism of law structures, or a pluralism of moralities, for as we will see shortly, this sort of ultimate pluralism (as distinguished from *institutional* pluralism) is always either polytheistic or humanistic. Christian people are required to take dominion over the earth by means of all these God-ordained institutions, not just the church, or just the state, or just the family.

The kingdom of God includes every human institution, and every aspect of life, for all of life is under God and is governed by His unchanging principles. All of life is under God and God's principles because God intends to *judge* all of life *in terms of* His principles.

In this structure of *plural governments*, the institutional churches serve as *advisors* to the other institutions (the Levitical function), but the churches can only pressure individual leaders through the threat of excommunication. As a restraining factor on unwarranted church authority, an unlawful excommunication by one local church or denomination is always subject to review by the others if and when the excommunicated person seeks membership elsewhere. Thus, each of the three covenantal institutions is to be run under God, as interpreted by its lawfully elected or ordained leaders, with the advice of the churches, not the compulsion.

Majority Rule

Just for the record, the authors aren't in favor of imposing some sort of top-down bureaucratic tyranny in the name of Christ. The kingdom of God requires a bottom-up society. The bottom-up Christian society rests ultimately on the doctrine of *self*-government under God. It's the humanist view of society that promotes top-down bureaucratic power.

The authors are in favor of evangelism and missions leading to a widespread Christian revival, so that the great mass of earth's inhabitants will place themselves under Christ's protection, and voluntarily use His covenantal principles for self-government. Christian reconstruction begins with personal conversion to Christ and self-government under God's principles, then spreads to others through revival, and only later brings comprehensive changes in civil law, when the vast majority of voters voluntarily agree to live under Biblical blueprints.

Let's get this straight: Christian reconstruction depends on majority rule. Of course, the leaders of the Christian reconstructionist movement expect a majority eventually to accept Christ as savior. If this doesn't happen, then Christians must be content with only partial reconstruction, and only partial blessings from

God. It isn't possible to ramrod God's blessings from the top down, unless you're God. Only humanists think that man is God. All we're trying to do is get the ramrod away from them, and melt it down. The melted ramrod could then be used to make a great grave marker for humanism: "The God That Failed."

The Continuing Heresy of Dualism

Many (of course, not all!) of the objections to the material in this book series will come from people who have a worldview that is very close to an ancient church problem: dualism. A lot of well-meaning Christian people are dualists, although they don't even know what it is.

Dualism teaches that the world is inherently divided: spirit vs. matter, or law vs. mercy, or mind vs. matter, or nature vs. grace. What the Bible teaches is that this world is divided *ethically* and *personally*: Satan vs. God, right vs. wrong. The conflict between God and Satan will end at the final judgment. Whenever Christians substitute some other form of dualism for ethical dualism, they fall into heresy and suffer the consequences. That's what has happened today. We are suffering from revived versions of ancient heresies.

Marcion's Dualism

The Old Testament was written by the same God who wrote the New Testament. There were not two Gods in history, meaning there was no dualism or radical split between the two testamental periods. There is only one God, in time and eternity.

This idea has had opposition throughout church history. An ancient two-Gods heresy was first promoted in the church about a century after Christ's crucifixion, and the church has always regarded it as just that, a heresy. It was proposed by a man named Marcion. Basically, this heresy teaches that there are two completely different law systems in the Bible: Old Testament law and New Testament law (or non-law). But Marcion took the logic of his position all the way. He argued that two law systems means two Gods. The God of wrath wrote the Old Testament, and the God of mercy wrote the New Testament. In short: "two laws-two Gods."

Many Christians still believe something dangerously close to Marcionism: not a two-Gods view, exactly, but a God-who-changed-all-His-rules sort of view. They begin with the accurate teaching that the ceremonial laws of the Old Testament were fulfilled by Christ, and therefore that the *unchanging principles* of Biblical worship are *applied differently* in the New Testament. But then they erroneously conclude that the whole Old Testament system of civil law was dropped by God, and *nothing Biblical was put in its place*. In other words, God created a sort of vacuum for state law.

This idea turns civil law-making over to Satan. In our day, this means that civil law-making is turned over to humanists. *Christians have unwittingly become the philosophical allies of the humanists with respect to civil law.* With respect to their doctrine of the state, therefore, most Christians hold what is in effect a two-Gods view of the Bible.

Gnosticism's Dualism

Another ancient heresy that is still with us is gnosticism. It became a major threat to the early church almost from the beginning. It was also a form of dualism, a theory of a radical split. The gnostics taught that the split is between evil matter and good spirit. Thus, their goal was to escape this material world through other-worldly exercises that punish the body. They believed in *retreat from the world of human conflicts and responsibility*. Some of these ideas got into the church, and people started doing ridiculous things. One "saint" sat on a platform on top of a pole for several decades. This was considered very spiritual. (Who fed him? Who cleaned up after him?)

Thus, many Christians came to view "the world" as something permanently outside the kingdom of God. They believed that this hostile, forever-evil world cannot be redeemed, reformed, and reconstructed. Jesus didn't really die for it, and it can't be healed. At best, it can be subdued by power (maybe). This dualistic view of the world vs. God's kingdom narrowly restricted any earthly manifestation of God's kingdom. Christians who were influenced by gnosticism concluded that God's kingdom refers only to the institutional church. They argued that the institutional church is the *only* manifestation of God's kingdom.

This led to two opposite and equally evil conclusions. *First*, power religionists ("salvation through political power") who accepted this definition of God's kingdom tried to put the institutional church in charge of everything, since it is supposedly "the only manifestation of God's kingdom on earth." To subdue the supposedly unredeemable world, which is forever outside the kingdom, the institutional church has to rule with the sword. A single, monolithic institutional church then gives orders to the state, and the state must without question enforce these orders with the sword. The hierarchy of the institutional church concentrates political and economic power. *What then becomes of liberty?*

Second, escape religionists ("salvation is exclusively internal") who also accepted this narrow definition of the kingdom sought refuge from the evil world of matter and politics by fleeing to hide inside the institutional church, an exclusively "spiritual kingdom," now narrowly defined. They abandoned the world to evil tyrants. *What then becomes of liberty?* What becomes of the idea of God's progressive restoration of all things under Jesus Christ? What, finally, becomes of the idea of Biblical dominion?

When Christians improperly narrow their definition of the kingdom of God, the visible influence of this comprehensive kingdom (both spiritual and institutional at the same time) begins to shrivel up. The first heresy leads to tyranny *by* the church, and the second heresy leads to tyranny *over* the church. Both of these narrow definitions of God's kingdom destroy the liberty of the responsible Christian man, self-governed under God and God's law.

Zoroaster's Dualism

The last ancient pagan idea that still lives on is also a variant of dualism: matter vs. spirit. It teaches that God and Satan, good and evil, are forever locked in combat, and that good never triumphs over evil. The Persian religion of Zoroastrianism has held such a view for over 2,500 years. The incredibly popular "Star Wars" movies were based on this view of the world: the "dark" side of "the force" against its "light" side. In modern versions of this ancient dualism, the "force" is usually seen as itself impersonal: individuals personalize either the dark side or the light side by "plugging into" its power.

There are millions of Christians who have adopted a very pessimistic version of this dualism, though not in an impersonal form. God's kingdom is battling Satan's, and God's is losing. History isn't going to get better. In fact, things are going to get a lot worse externally. Evil will visibly push good into the shadows. The church is like a band of soldiers who are surrounded by a huge army of Indians. "We can't win boys, so hold the fort until Jesus comes to rescue us!"

That doesn't sound like Abraham, Moses, Joshua, Gideon, and David, does it? Christians read to their children one of the children's favorite stories, David and Goliath, yet in their own lives, millions of Christian parents really think that the Goliaths of this world are the unbeatable earthly winners. Christians haven't even picked up a stone.

Until very recently.

An Agenda for Victory

The change has come since 1980. Many Christians' thinking has shifted. Dualism, gnosticism, and "God changed His program midstream" ideas have begun to be challenged. The politicians have already begun to reckon with the consequences. Politicians are the people we pay to raise their wet index fingers in the wind to sense a shift, and they have sensed it. It scares them, too. It should.

A new vision has captured the imaginations of a growing army of registered voters. This new vision is simple: it's the old vision of Genesis 1:27-28 and Matthew 28:19-20. It's called *dominion*.

Four distinct ideas must be present in any ideology that expects to overturn the existing view of the world and the existing social order:

> A doctrine of ultimate truth (permanence)
> A doctrine of providence (confidence)
> Optimism toward the future (motivation)
> Binding comprehensive law (reconstruction)

The Marxists have had such a vision, or at least those Marxists who don't live inside the bureaucratic giants called the Soviet Union and Red China. The radical (please, not "fundamentalist") Muslims of Iran also have such a view.

Now, for the first time in over 300 years, Bible-believing Christians have rediscovered these four points in the theology of Christianity. For the first time in over 300 years, a growing number of Christians are starting to view themselves as an army on the move. This army will grow. This series is designed to help it grow. And grow tougher.

The authors of this series are determined to set the agenda in world affairs for the next few centuries. We know where the permanent answers are found: in the Bible, and *only* in the Bible. We believe that we have begun to discover at least preliminary answers to the key questions. There may be better answers, clearer answers, and more orthodox answers, but they must be found in the Bible, not at Harvard University or on the CBS Evening News.

We are self-consciously firing the opening shot. We are calling the whole Christian community to join with us in a very serious debate, just as Luther called them to debate him when he nailed the 95 theses to the church door, over four and a half centuries ago.

It is through such an exchange of ideas by those who take the Bible seriously that a nation and a civilization can be saved. There are now 5 billion people in the world. If we are to win our world (and these billions of souls) for Christ we must lift up the message of Christ by becoming the city on the hill. When the world sees the blessings by God upon a nation run by His principles, the mass conversion of whole nations to the Kingdom of our Lord will be the most incredible in of all history.

If we're correct about the God-required nature of our agenda, it will attract a dedicated following. It will produce a social transformation that could dwarf the Reformation. This time, we're not limiting our call for reformation to the institutional church.

This time, we mean business.

Dr. Gary North
Institute for Christian Economics
P.O. Box 8000
Tyler, TX 75711

Dear Dr. North:

I read about your organization in your book, *Healer of the Nations*. I understand that you publish several newsletters that are sent out for six months free of charge. I would be interested in receiving them:

☐ *Biblical Economics Today*
  Christian Reconstruction
  and *Covenant Renewal*

Please send any other information you have concerning your program.

_____
name

_____
address

_____
city, state, zip

_____
area code and phone number

☐ Enclosed is a tax-deductible donation to help meet expenses.

Jesus said to "Occupy till I come." But if Christians don't control the territory, they can't occupy it. They get tossed out into cultural "outer darkness," which is just exactly what the secular humanists have done to Christians in the 20th century: in education, in the arts, in entertainment, in politics, and certainly in the mainline churches and seminaries. Today, the humanists are "occupying." But they won't be for long. *Backward, Christian Soldiers?* shows you why. This is must reading for all Christians as a supplement to the *Biblical Blueprints Series*. You can obtain a copy by sending $1.00 (a $5.95 value) to:

Institute for Christian Economics
P.O. Box 8000
Tyler, TX 75711

_____
name

_____
address

_____
city, state, zip

_____
area code and phone number

The *Biblical Blueprints Series* is a multi-volume book series that gives Biblical solutions for the problems facing our culture today. Each book deals with a specific topic in a simple, easy to read style such as economics, government, law, crime and punishment, welfare and poverty, taxes, money and banking, politics, the environment, retirement, and much more.

Each book can be read in one evening and will give you the basic Biblical principles on each topic. Each book concludes with three chapters on how to apply the principles in your life, the church and the nation. Every chapter is summarized so that the entire book can be absorbed in just a few minutes.

As you read these books, you will discover hundreds of new ways to serve God. Each book will show you ways that you can start to implement God's plan in your own life. As hundreds of thousands join you, and millions more begin to follow the example set, a civilization can be changed.

Why will people change their lives? Because they will see God's blessings on those who live by His Word (Deuteronomy 4:6-8).

Each title in the *Biblical Blueprints Series* is available in a deluxe paperback edition for $7.95, or a classic leatherbound edition for $15.95.

The following titles are scheduled for publication:

- Liberating Planet Earth: An Introduction to Biblical Blueprints
- Ruler of the Nations: Biblical Blueprints for Governments
- Who Owns the Family?: Biblical Blueprints for Family/State Relations
- In the Shadow of Plenty: Biblical Blueprints for Welfare and Poverty
- Honest Money: Biblical Blueprints for Money and Banking
- The Children Trap: Biblical Blueprints for Education
- Inherit the Earth: Biblical Blueprints for Economics
- The Changing of the Guard: Biblical Blueprints for Political Action
- Healer of the Nations: Biblical Blueprints for International Relations
- Second Chance: Biblical Blueprints for Divorce and Remarriage

Please send more information concerning this program.

_____

name

_____

address

_____

city, state, zip

Dominion Press • P.O. Box 8204 • Ft. Worth, TX 76124